Acts of Compassion

Acts of Compassion

CARING FOR OTHERS
AND HELPING OURSELVES

Robert Wuthnow

PRINCETON UNIVERSITY PRESS

PRINCETON, NEW JERSEY

Copyright © 1991 by Princeton University Press
Published by Princeton University Press, 41 William Street,
Princeton, New Jersey 08540
In the United Kingdom: Princeton University Press, Oxford

Library of Congress Cataloging-in-Publication Data

Wuthnow, Robert
Acts of compassion : caring for others and helping ourselves /
Robert Wuthnow
p.   cm.
Includes index.
1. Volunteerism—United States.   2. Helping behavior.   3. Caring
4. Individualism—United States.   I. Title.
HN90.V6488 1991
ISBN 0-691-07390-2
302'.14—dc20   91-2128   CIP

This book has been composed in Linotron Palatino

Princeton University Press books are
printed on acid-free paper, and meet the guidelines
for permanence and durability of the Committee
on Production Guidelines for Book Longevity
of the Council on Library Resources

Printed in the United States of America

3   5   7   9   10   8   6   4   2

Contents

Acknowledgments

I am deeply grateful for the support I have received from so many people during the course of writing this book. Its inception can be traced to a conversation I had several years ago with Robert Lynn, then Vice President for Religion at the Lilly Endowment, which led to a sizable research grant from that foundation. With that support I was able to involve a number of people in the project from which this book evolved. I organized several symposiums on the topic at Princeton University, plagued my students with questions and hypotheses, culled stacks of sermons and popular stories about caring, collected pictures, conducted dozens of personal interviews, and hired a polling firm to carry out a major national survey. I want to thank especially my research associates, Wende Elliott, Suzannah Wilson, Lisa Frodsham, Helen Hunter, and Elaine Friedman, for their assistance in conducting interviews. Kevin Hartzell and David Jacobson helped comb through the scholarly literature. Harry Cotugno assisted in refining the survey instrument, which more than two thousand randomly selected people generously gave of their time to respond to, and Timothy Clydesdale did much of the computer work necessary in analyzing the survey results. Those whose participation in symposiums contributed to the shaping of the project include John F. Wilson, Julian Wolpert, James Douglas, Paul Starr, Jeffrey Alexander, Randall Collins, Paul DiMaggio, Jane Mansbridge, John Meyer, John Sutton, Robert Liebman, Edward Freeland, and Richard Rogers. Later in the project the participants in my faculty discussion group at Princeton—Susan Harding, Michèle Lamont, Steven Warner, George Thomas, Wilfrid Spohn, Frank Dobbin, and Gene Burns—provided a valuable sounding board. Robert Payton read the entire manuscript and offered a number of helpful suggestions. Craig Dykstra, Robert Lynn's successor at the Lilly Endowment, has given enormous assistance and encouragement. Cindy Gibson did yeoman service in keeping the finances of the project straight. Blanche Anderson and Natalie Everett did much of the typing and transcribing. I am also grateful for the support and encouragement of Walter

Lippincott and Gail Ullman at Princeton University Press. The deepest personal caring and encouragement has come from Sally, my wife, and from Robyn, Brooke, and Joel, my children. As so many of the voices that speak in the following pages point out, we are all in it together in everything we do. And yet our individuality matters too. I have tried to retain the individual integrity of those whose reflections I present. I am sure my own biases, for better or for worse, will be evident as well.

PART I

THE PROBLEM OF INDIVIDUALISM

CHAPTER ONE

An American Paradox

In 1896 JANE ADDAMS journeyed to Russia to visit Tolstoy. He was the famous writer. She was the internationally renowned founder of Hull House in Chicago. Their meeting was destined to be a clash of titans.

Years earlier Jane Addams had begun reading Tolstoy's books. Moved by his message of compassion, she decided to devote her life to helping the needy. Despite shyness, homesickness, and poor health, she gave up the comfortable life she had known as a child. She moved from the splendor of a country estate to the squalor of an urban slum. She gave up everything to help the poor.

Now she was arriving at Tolstoy's country estate, the faithful disciple on a pilgrimage to the master. Among the many thousands of his followers, she had been true to the calling. She had put emotion into practice. She had followed Tolstoy's call to identify totally with the suffering of the poor. And she had done it successfully. Her efforts had put her at the head of the settlement-house movement in America. She was known far and wide as a woman of compassion.

Tolstoy was not impressed. The great man approached her clad in humble working clothes, dirty from the hayfields where he had been toiling shoulder to shoulder with the peasants. Why was she dressed in such finery, he wanted to know, glancing distrustfully at the monstrous sleeves of her traveling gown. A whole dress for a peasant girl could be made from the cloth in those sleeves. He was horrified that she did not eat porridge, horrified that she was the absentee landlord of a farm in Illinois, horrified that she had a servant to prepare her meals.

Jane Addams was mortified. She went away deeply troubled by the barriers she had erected between herself and those she was trying to serve. Tolstoy was right. She cared for them, but she had not made herself their equal. She had tried to help, but had not truly identified with their suffering. Tolstoy and his daughter worked all day in the hot sun alongside the peasants. She sat in her parlor and planned cultural events for the neighbors. He baked his own bread and ate porridge. She had her meals brought to her. She must change. On her way home she resolved that she too would bake her own bread, that she would spend two hours every morning at it, that she would learn the lesson of the poor, as she said, that griefs are always lighter with bread.

But when she arrived back in Chicago the whole scheme seemed utterly preposterous to her. Bread labor became her shibboleth. She could not do it. She could not care the way Tolstoy did. Her life was too busy, too demanding. Compassion was different—it had to be different—in Chicago, in America.[1]

· 2 ·

Several miles from where I live stands a large manor house that bears the name of Tolstoy's beloved estate. I invent nothing in reporting this. The name is emblazoned in large white letters, twice—once on either side of the iron gates that stand guard in front of the villa. It was put there by the third wife of the owner in memory of the great writer from her homeland. A visit to this estate was also about to reveal something of the character of compassion in America.

At exactly 10:13 P.M. on a cold evening in late November the iron gates swung open, letting an orange and white emergency vehicle speed through. At the bottom of the hill that sloped gradually away from the highway, nearly shielded from view by a thicket of oaks stretching dark limbs to the night sky, stood the manor house. Those lucky enough to have been inside said it was one of the finest mansions in all the world. There were ninety-six rooms spread out symmetrically across three floors, and in back was a large doghouse with its own air-conditioning system and a brass staircase. The owner, everyone knew, was the founder of one of the largest companies in the world. His profits were said to be among the highest in the world. He had had the good sense to find a way to make money by marketing comfort to the suffering. Cynics said he made a nickel every time a schoolboy scraped his knee, a quar-

4

ter every time a woman had her period. But now, as the emergency vehicle wound its way down the long driveway, the owner lay bent in agony, clutching his chest with the desperate intensity of a man near death.

The driver of the emergency vehicle brought it to a screeching halt under the large portico at the front of the house. From the passenger side a lanky young paramedic jumped out, barked an order to the driver, and bounded up the steps toward the door. On the way, he muttered another quick command to his companion, who caught his eye and grinned widely; then both disappeared inside.

In less than a minute and a half Jack Casey and his assistant had sized up the situation, loaded the ailing gentleman into the emergency vehicle, taken vital signs, radioed the local hospital, and begun their ascent back up the driveway to the main road. The mission had been accomplished with the smooth efficiency of trained professionals.

For Jack Casey, tonight's call was simply part of a familiar routine. Within the past twenty-four months he had responded to more than five hundred such calls. He had also dragged people from burning buildings, helped his teammates cut through the twisted wreckage of automobiles to reach trapped drivers, and risked his personal safety responding to cases where victims were stabbed by their own family members. Once, not long before this, he had swum through icy water fully clothed without a life jacket, dragged an unconscious woman back through the water to shore, and administered cardiopulmonary resuscitation just in time to save her life.

But Jack had done none of these things as a paid professional. Like millions of Americans, he was an unpaid helper who gave his time freely because he cared for others.

· 3 ·

According to recent estimates provided by a national survey conducted for Independent Sector, eighty million Americans are engaged in some kind of voluntary caring activity. They bake cookies for the local elementary school, take meals to the elderly, visit the sick, and donate time to nursing homes and hospitals. They staff hotlines and crisis intervention centers, teach Sunday school classes, organize fund-raising drives, and serve on the boards of nonprofit organizations. In one capacity or another, approximately 45 percent of all Americans age eighteen or over are involved in these activities.[2]

On the average, each volunteer in the United States gives about five hours of his or her time every week. Collectively, this means that volunteers donate approximately twenty billion hours of service to their communities each year. Of this amount, approximately five billion hours are devoted to informal volunteering, such as visiting a friend in the hospital or helping a neighbor who needs assistance. The other fifteen billion hours consist of specific time commitments to organizations such as churches, hospitals, shelters for the homeless, fraternal associations, civic groups, foundations, rescue squads, and volunteer fire departments. If these activities were not provided by unpaid volunteers, they would cost our society an estimated $150 billion annually.[3]

The cold statistics on volunteering are hugely impressive, in one respect, and yet they are neither so telling nor so powerful as the warmhearted individuals who make up these statistics. Jack Casey's story shows what a volunteer can do—the difference he makes to those around him—and the ways in which a caring attitude is sometimes shaped and nurtured by other volunteers.

As we sit together sipping coffee in the firehouse where he is on duty, Jack Casey talks about how he became a volunteer for the rescue squad. "It was all a natural progression," he recalls. He had started attending Boy Scout meetings as a young child, and through scouting developed an interest in helping people. Each month the popular scouting magazine *Boys' Life* supplied him with vivid stories about rescuing people from danger. Scouting also encouraged him to do things for needy people in the community to earn merit badges.[4]

Jack remembers one particular scout leader he loved and admired when he was in the fifth grade. From him Jack learned rudimentary first-aid techniques. "I was very lucky," he says. "That guy had had some real experiences and taught us really well." At about the same time, a health class in school was adding to his budding interest in first aid. "It got me interested in all the body parts and bones and things."

Over the next few years Jack continued with scouting, eventually achieving the distinction of Eagle Scout in high school. When he was fifteen he got a summer job as a lifeguard that required him to gain further skills in first-aid and rescue operations. After graduation he joined the local volunteer fire company, and when he went away to college he continued serving as a fire fighter. Periodically he taught Red Cross and water-safety classes free of charge. Still finding time left over, he decided to help freshmen become oriented by starting an outdoor action program. He also began teaching evening classes in first aid as a volunteer, took more advanced classes himself in emergency medicine, and soon gained the credentials necessary to volunteer for the rescue squad.

At this point Jack's narrative is broken by an incoming call on the loudspeaker. I am fascinated by the dedication he seems to have to the people in his community. I am curious about the reasons underlying this dedication. I also sense there is another side to him that he has not yet revealed.

· 4 ·

Volunteering is one of the ways Americans show care and compassion. Not many have the opportunity or the training to show it as dramatically as does Jack Casey: of all the volunteer jobs people listed in the Independent Sector survey, less than 1 percent were related to fire or rescue-squad work.[5] But volunteering is a way to reach out, to do what one can, to use one's skills, often in quiet ways, to make the community a better place. In fact, many of our community organizations depend largely on volunteers for their very existence. Approximately 31 million people do volunteer work each year for their churches or synagogues. Twenty million provide free services to schools, tutoring programs, and other educational organizations. Sixteen million donate time to some kind of hospital, nursing home, clinic, or health agency.[6]

Formal volunteering is only one of the ways in which Americans show care and compassion. In small ways, millions of Americans also extend a helping hand informally to their neighbors, relatives, and friends. They visit them in the hospital, help them through personal crises, lend money, provide a sympathetic ear when one is needed, and encourage those they care about to give up addictive behaviors. According to a national survey I conducted for this volume, six people in ten visited someone in the hospital during the past year. Three in four had at one time or another helped a relative or friend through a personal crisis, and half of these had helped someone through a crisis during the past year. Six persons in ten had lent more than one hundred dollars to a relative or friend—half within the past year. Slightly more than half the population had tried to get someone to stop using alcohol or drugs—29 percent in the past year.[7]

The level of caring shown toward strangers is understandably lower than that shown toward relatives and friends. But the numbers of people who have done something to show kindness toward some stranger in need are considerable. Six people in ten report having stopped to help someone with car trouble; three in ten say they did this within the past year. One person in two has given money to a beggar—23 percent in the past year.

Many of these activities, whether for friends and relatives or for strangers, require rather small investments of energy. They take only a few minutes of one's time. But other acts of caring require much time and energy. Large numbers of people are also involved in these activities. More than half the respondents in my survey, for example, reported having cared for someone who was very sick—one person in four had done this in the past year. Sometimes these acts of compassion, though limited in time and effort, are also enormously consequential, like Jack Casey's heroic swim across an icy lake. A striking 16 percent of the population—one person in six—claim to have saved someone's life, and four percent say they did this in the past year.

· 5 ·

A century and a half ago on his visit to the United States, Alexis de Tocqueville observed that voluntary cooperation—a spirit of generosity and helpfulness toward one's neighbors—was deeply ingrained in the American heart. "If an accident happens on the highway," he wrote, "everybody hastens to help the sufferer." And, he observed, "if some great and sudden calamity befalls a family, the purses of a thousand strangers are at once willingly opened and small but numerous donations pour in to relieve their distress."[8]

What Tocqueville observed in the early nineteenth century was already a well-established tradition. Two centuries earlier, when the first colonists appeared on North American soil, caring for the needs of one another had been a matter of both physical necessity and religious devotion. While still aboard the ship *Arbella*, John Winthrop, the first governor of the new Puritan colony in Massachusetts, admonished his flock to bear one another's burdens, practicing the Christian duty of love, rather than looking only to their own concerns. "We must delight in each other," he told them, "make other's conditions our own, rejoice together, mourn together, labor and suffer together: always having before our eyes our commission and community in the work, our community as members of the same body."[9] If they adhered to these principles, he promised, God would truly dwell among them and bless them in all their endeavors.

As the colonies—and then the nation—grew in population and prosperity, other voices continued to articulate Winthrop's vision of Christian charity. Primers taught children the importance of caring by telling such stories as that of "Generous George," the soldier who helped his injured companion, and by negative example, Aesop's familiar fable of the dog in the manger. Preachers reminded their followers of biblical injunctions to feed the hungry, clothe the naked, and give to the poor. Educators placed compassion high on the list of virtues they wanted young men of privilege to cultivate. As John Witherspoon, the Scottish educator who was to be among the signers of the Declaration of Independence, reminded his class of Princeton seniors in 1768, the whole of our duty toward one another can be summarized in one straightforward principle: "Love to others, sincere and active."[10]

By the time Tocqueville visited America in the 1830s it was evident that the spirit of caring had become tempered by other passions and interests, if it had not always been so. Tocqueville expressed doubt that Americans helped their neighbors because of altruistic principles alone. Yet he was impressed that even in this land where traditional European notions of honor were so lacking, people showed an extraordinary propensity to be helpful when the need arose. Americans, he observed, "are always cold and often coarse in their manners." They do not provide services to their neighbors eagerly; nevertheless, "they do not refuse to render them." He had often seen help given, he acknowledged, "spontaneously and with great goodwill."[11]

During the century following Tocqueville's visit, thousands of charitable institutions were founded. Christian benevolent societies grew, as did the number of missionaries sent out and the number of hospitals and orphanages founded. Tens of millions of children learned the story of the Good Samaritan—not only at their churches, but in the public schools, where they found the story printed in their McGuffey Readers. Secular leaders like Jane Addams emerged with visions of how to put charitable principles into practice. Robber barons sometimes became magnanimous philanthropists. Neighborliness, service, cooperation, and even heroic deeds of self-sacrifice continued to be extolled in popular literature and the press.[12]

There are many indications that the spirit of caring and giving is still a prominent theme in the public pronouncements that shape American culture. Preachers continue to expound on the story of the Good Samaritan and admonish their congregations to become involved in helping the needy. Politicians scramble to have their pictures taken among the homeless, voice concern for the victims of natural disasters, and award medals to ordinary men and women for brave acts of heroism and service. Newspapers carry story after story of individual volunteers who have made some small difference for good in their local communities.[13]

In addition to the evidence I have already cited on volunteering and helping, data on values also suggest the extent to which the American population is committed to the importance of caring. When asked how important "helping people in need" was to them, three-fourths (73 percent) of the public in my survey said it was absolutely essential or very important; another 24 percent said it was fairly important; only 2 percent said it was not very important. To another question in the same survey, nearly two-thirds (63 percent) said "giving your time to help others" was absolutely essential or very important to them, 32 percent said this was fairly important, and only 4 percent said it was not very important.

· 6 ·

If this were the whole story we might well raise our collective chins, stick out our chests, and tell our detractors that the picture of America is brighter than they had supposed. The level of volunteering and caring in our society suggests an image of wholesomeness, health, nurturing, and goodness. But this Wonder Bread image of American society is only half the loaf, still preposterously different from Tolstoy's bread labor. There is another side to our character.

Although millions of hours are donated to volunteer activities each year, this effort falls far short of what is needed. I mentioned earlier that two-thirds of the American people have visited someone in the hospital in the past year and a quarter have taken care of someone seriously ill in their homes. But thousands of people have no one to care for them. Substantial numbers in our society fear they could not count on anyone for help if they or a member of their family became seriously ill. Nearly four in ten (37 percent) feel they could not count on their immediate neighbors. Almost as many (36 percent) think they could not depend on church or synagogue members for help. One person in three doubts it would be possible to count on relatives outside the immediate family. And when it comes to volunteer and government agencies, the proportions who express doubt are even higher. Half the population think volunteers in their communities could not be counted on for help; two people in three think this about social welfare agencies.

As a society we pay lip service to altruistic values, but these values must be seen in the context of our other pursuits, the majority of which focus on ourselves rather than others. From the variety of breakfast cereals in our supermarkets to the vast efforts we make to spend quiet evenings and weekends alone, our behavior demonstrates that we cherish individual freedom almost as deeply as life itself. If we talk incessantly about "community," we live our lives in a way that says individual freedom is better. Ours is a society that places equally high value on the dogged determination and long hours of hard work it takes to achieve individual success. We are also a society in which self-interest, whether in money, physical health, self-expression, or matters of the heart, assumes a dominant role in our thinking.

Freedom to do what we want is perhaps the most prized of all our national possessions. It distinguishes the United States from totalitarian societies. At the political level it means we—individually and collectively—have a voice in choosing our laws and our representatives. At the personal level it often means much more than this. It constitutes a basic right to individual autonomy. It means not having anyone tell us what to do, not having to listen if they do, not having to conform. It means having the capacity to make our own decisions, rather than simply living up to the expectations of the community or fulfilling obligations to someone else. It means the independence to be different, to strike out on our own, to look out for ourselves, instead of getting tied down. Freedom says, "I need space; don't bother me now."

Our culture has also taught us to value the struggle for individual success. It makes us feel good when our teams win at sports. It makes us feel good individually when we achieve some goal we have set for ourselves, whether it be gaining admission to a prestigious university, graduating from college with honors, landing good jobs, getting raises, or keeping our lawns looking better than the neighbors' lawns. We believe in hard work, in developing our skills, in achieving our potential. "Be all that you can be" is a slogan that resounds far beyond the sleek canyons of Madison Avenue. We enjoy competition—or at least we let ourselves be seduced by the prospect of winning in nearly everything we do. We also believe that hard work will be rewarded. Spending an extra hour at the office, bringing the briefcase home on weekends, taking a night class, pushing our kids to sign up for summer school and honors courses, we tell ourselves, will all pay off sooner or later in getting us what we want. Part of the freedom we enjoy means there is nothing to hold us back but ourselves. Thus, anyone who sets his or her mind to the task and works diligently is likely to succeed.

Self-interest is the third cultural pillar undergirding our way of life. In economic terms this means looking out for ourselves: getting the most for our money, making wise investments, driving the hardest bargains we can. But throughout our nation's history self-interest has also had broader connotations. It has generally encompassed a wide range of bodily pleasures and material comforts. As Tocqueville observed in his time, "the effort to satisfy even the least wants of the body and to provide the little conveniences of life is uppermost in every mind."[14] It has often conjured up images of health and physical fitness. Eating right, getting enough exercise, and seeing the doctor regularly are all said to be in our self-interest. It is to our benefit, as well as being part of our responsibility, to look after our self-interest in these ways. Increasingly, self-interest also means taking care of ourselves psychologically and emotionally. Thus, we not only emphasize physical health; we also attach special importance to learning how to relax, giving ourselves positive messages, knowing what we need at any particular moment, and learning how to get what we need. Self-interest means knowing the inner recesses of our selves, finding ways to express our selves, and making sure nobody else tells us what our selves want and need.

Collectively, these values make up what is popularly referred to as American individualism. They are among our most widely shared values. They are deeply embedded in the mythic legacy we have all inherited. The American frontier, with its cowboys and pioneers, symbolizes freedom and the rewards of hard work. Heroes like Abraham Lincoln and Davy Crockett conjure up images of nonconformity, being true to one's own convictions, and the ability to succeed. In the twentieth century, these heroes of the past live on while a new generation of rugged individualists takes its place alongside them: the astronaut who finds glory in hard work and freedom in the vast frontiers of outer space, the movieland adventurer (Indiana Jones, Han Solo, Rambo) who strikes out on his own and defies everyone's expectations, the figure of a Jonathan Livingston Seagull who finds strength deep within and rises to miraculous heights, and the real estate magnate who plays his or her hand more skillfully than everyone else and trumps them all in the deal's cleverness.

We saw earlier that three-quarters of the American people say helping people in need is very important to them and nearly two-thirds say giving time to help others is very important. These figures represent a high level of agreement about the importance of being concerned for others. But an equally large share of the population, according to my survey, attaches high value to the various aspects of individualism we have just considered. The extent to which personal freedom is valued is evident in the fact that seven persons in ten (71 percent) say it is either absolutely essential or very important to them to "be able to do what you want." Our collective love affair with the success ethic is revealed by the vast majority of the public (78 percent and 77 percent respectively) who say it is very important to them to be successful in their work and to live comfortable lives. An even higher proportion—88 percent—say taking care of themselves (one way of expressing our attachment to self-interest) is very important.

These values are also reinforced by the assumptions we make about reality itself. Freedom, success, and self-interest are goals to be pursued, but the pursuit of these goals depends on certain understandings of the constraints and opportunities confronting us. If I value success, it is also likely that my culture will have taught me to believe success is within my grasp as long as I apply myself diligently. By implication, I may also believe that failure comes about through some fault of the individual. Both these assumptions, judging from my survey, are widely shared in American culture. For instance, four persons in five say they agree with the statement "I can do anything I want to, if I just try hard enough." A majority (54 percent) agree with the statement "People generally bring suffering on themselves."

· 7 ·

After dispatching a mobile intensive unit to an address on Maple Avenue, Jack Casey continues his story. On the average, he says, he responds to at least one call a day for the rescue squad. He figures he probably goes to at least six general-alarm fires over the course of a year as a volunteer fire fighter. He still spends three hours a week teaching a Red Cross course in first aid. In recent weeks he has also been doing volunteer work as an instructor for a course on the heart as part of the outdoor-safety program he initiated several years ago.

He admits his experiences as a volunteer have been mixed. Some have been so much fun he probably would have done them even if they had not benefited anyone else. He cites the outdoor program as an example. He enjoys backpacking anyway, so by leading a group of students, he is merely doing what he wants to without having to pay a fee: "Congratulations! You've saved yourself $45." The first-aid course, in contrast, he describes as "an amazingly thankless job." "All we get is grief from the Red Cross because they think we should be doing it differently."

What strikes me most about Jack Casey, in addition to the volunteer activities he describes, is the fact that even his choice of language consistently puts others first. He gives much of the credit for his own interest in first aid to the scout leader he had been "lucky" enough to have in the fifth grade. He describes his involvement with water safety in high school as merely a "rare opportunity." He says he could not take credit for the outdoor-action program because "the kids do all the work."

Nor are his efforts to help others limited to these volunteer activities. In daily life he finds himself trying to be helpful just by meeting the little needs of those around him, such as providing transportation. "Somebody'll call me up at midnight and ask me to drive them to the airport, so I will; or somebody'll call me at three in the morning and ask me to pick up their friend at the train station. So I'll say, sure I'll pick them up." Pausing to reflect for a moment, he adds, "I'm inclined whenever someone asks for help to try and help them. That's just the way I am. I guess it's part of my self-image to picture myself as someone who other people can rely on."

In all these ways Jack Casey epitomizes caring and compassion. His desire to help others has taken him well beyond the bounds of most people's commitments to their communities. If the typical volunteer donates five hours a week, Jack donates at least fifteen. If the average American has visited someone in the hospital, Jack has made sure the sick and injured have gotten there in the first place. But there is another side to Jack Casey.

He also prides himself on being a rugged individualist: someone who not only thinks for himself and does what he wants to but also refuses to burden his friends or let himself be dependent on anyone. "I'm the kind of person who likes to be relatively independent of other people," he says. That means not having—and not needing—any "specific reference point," such as a group of friends who support one another or a stable community with which to identify.

Jack's individualism also involves taking care of himself emotionally, even if this means denying some of his feelings. His brand of individualism shows little patience for the touchy-feely kind of person who focuses on his or her emotions. He speaks disparagingly of his sister ("a person with a huge heart who can't take care of herself") and his friends who are constantly "stressed out" about little things. Jack's brand of individualism is more that of the rugged stoic. "I always have too much to do to get stressed out about it all the time." He says he has discovered that "after a while you just have to develop an iceman personality."

Individualism in Jack's case also means being free to do whatever he likes, and no matter what it is, letting it boost his ego. When asked to think of someone he most admired, he describes a woman a few years older than he whom he had met in college. What he most respects about her is that "she could take care of herself anywhere." She exemplifies self-sufficiency: "Drop her off in the woods, drop her off in a big city, and she wouldn't have any trouble." Indeed, she had demonstrated her independence after graduation by going to teach in Appalachia. It is the free spirit in her that seems to attract Jack above all: "She's wonderful, somebody you just couldn't help liking. She's a genuine free spirit."

In speaking about himself, Jack expresses the same philosophy. Uppermost in his thinking is the fact, as he puts it, that "I really want to do what I want to do." Translated: "It isn't justified to make any permanent sacrifices of myself." Even when he is out on a run for the rescue squad, his philosophy is always "I'm number one, my crew is number two, and the patient is number three." Further translated, this means he does not have to be a "total egomaniac" or go around all the time saying how wonderful he is, but it does mean "valuing yourself."

· 8 ·

How is it that Jack Casey is able to be such a rugged individualist and so deeply compassionate at the same time? How is it that he manages to risk his life in the service of others and yet hold firmly the conviction that he is Number One? How does he manage to devote himself so selflessly to the community and still claim to be the iceman who depends on no one?

How is it that we as a people are able to devote billions of hours to volunteer activities, to show care and compassion in so many ways to those around us, and still be a nation of individualists who pride ourselves on personal freedom, individual success, and the pursuit of self-interest? How do we reconcile these paradoxical elements in our tradition?

Caring and/for Our Selves

A CHORUS of criticism about the level of self-centeredness in our society has risen to a crescendo in recent years. First it was the "me generation" of the 1970s. In contrast to the social and political awareness of the sixties, the seventies seem to have been a decade of turning inward, of finding one's self. Trying to make a difference in one's community—or even finding a community—was out of vogue. Suddenly the whole society seemed to be caught up in a quest for self-identity, inner peace, security. Then it was the "decade of greed," as some writers dubbed the 1980s. In the words of one, "greed was in and success was defined less by accomplishment than by acquisition. Whoever dies with the most toys wins."[1] And after that, as some commentators termed the 1990s, it was the "decade of freedom." To American eyes, the upheavals in Eastern Europe constituted a great ideological victory. People were rising up, shucking off the shackles of communism, yes, in the name of freedom. But to American eyes freedom meant far more than the mere political freedom associated with democratic elections. Certainly it did not mean democratic socialism. It meant new markets, free trade, the freedom to buy and sell. It meant that capitalism, the American way of life, was vindicated. Our individualism, our freedom to make our own choices and do whatever we wanted to, was after all pretty good. It was what people really wanted in their heart of hearts.

Serious observers of American culture have targeted both the resurgence of traditional individualistic values and a redefinition of these values as dominant trends in the last quarter of the twentieth century. Although such values as freedom, success, and self-interest have long been a part of our culture, critics now argue that these pursuits are eroding our capacity to care genuinely for one another. Being a free spirit, they argue, makes it difficult to empathize with the needs of others, especially those who may be suffering. Freedom becomes a problem when it ceases to mean liberty in civil society and becomes a fetish for more varieties of breakfast food. Maybe we do help out at the neighborhood bazaar, but is that really helping? For whom do we care most when the chips are down: our neighbors or ourselves? Hard work in the pursuit of individual success was once fine when it meant tilling your own garden or starting your own business. But in a society of bureaucratic and urban sprawl, of international trade and corporate mergers, a focus on personal success is likely to deaden one to the ways in which one's behavior affects those less fortunate than oneself. We may give at the office, as the expression goes, but we can do that without ever leaving the sheltered world of the bureaucracy in which we work. Self-interest has also grown to dangerous proportions, say the critics, when it no longer involves an understanding of give-and-take, when it involves only self-absorption, when it means helping yourself instead of caring for others.

Public perceptions of our society largely agree with these criticisms. Only a minority of the American public cling to the belief that we are a people of compassion; the majority believe instead that we are driven by self-interest. In response to the question, "On the whole, do you think people in our country are genuinely concerned about helping the needy, or are they mostly concerned about their own activities and interests?" only 24 percent of the people in my survey expressed confidence that there was genuine concern for the needy; in comparison, 67 percent said people are concerned with their own activities and interests. Another question asked if "people only looking out for their own selfish interests" was a problem in the United States. Eight people in ten said it was a serious problem, and three of these eight (32 percent in all) thought it was an extremely serious problem.

Other polls indicate that cynicism about the self-interestedness of our society has been spreading in recent years, reversing an earlier trend toward wider perceptions of helpfulness. One question used repeatedly in national surveys asks: "Would you say that most of the time people try to be helpful, or that they are mostly just looking out for themselves?" In 1972 the proportion who thought people try to be helpful was 47 percent. This proportion rose to 56 percent in 1975 and reached a high of 60 percent in 1978. After that it declined, back down to 52 percent by 1984, and then to 44 percent in 1987. Over the same period the proportion who thought people mostly look out for themselves declined from 47 percent in 1972 to 35 percent in 1978, and then increased to 52 percent in 1987.[2]

When asked to project their perceptions into the future, most Americans also envision the society becoming more self-interested rather than more altruistic. Thus, by a margin of 63 percent to 28 percent in my survey, the public thinks people in our society are becoming less interested in helping one another, rather than more interested.

While these perceptions of what may happen in the future may well be mistaken, there is at least some evidence that they are accurate appraisals of what is currently taking place. The question that has been used most consistently in national polls as an indicator of caring behavior asks, "Do you, yourself, happen to be involved in any charity or social-service activities, such as helping the poor, the sick, or the elderly?" Until recently the proportions answering "yes" appeared to be on the rise: from 27 percent in 1977 to 31 percent in 1984, and then reaching a high point of 39 percent in 1987. More recent (1989) figures, though, register a decline: back down to 31 percent.

In short, recent criticisms of American society suggest that the delicate balance between individualism and altruism that has been part of our history may now be tipping in a direction that spells trouble for the well-being of our nation. Self-interest and a fascination with our own individual needs and wants may be undermining the ethic of caring that has so long been a feature of our culture. Some observers fear the balance may have already been tipped; others suggest only that this is a possibility; still others see signs of a more caring society on the horizon. The common assumption in all these scenarios, though, is that individualism and altruism are antagonistic to each other. An intense commitment to personal freedom makes it difficult for people to attach themselves to others or be concerned about the needs of others. An ambition to succeed in one's career, with all the hard work and long hours that entails, necessarily conflicts with volunteering one's evenings and weekends to help the homeless and visit the sick. Self-interest runs counter to group interest because taking care of my needs and pursuing my own comforts inevitably puts me ahead of you. The "me society" stands in opposition to the "we society." Looking out for myself gets in the way of putting others first.

· 2 ·

If these assumptions are valid, it should be the case that the most altruistic among us are the least individualistic, and the most individualistic are the least altruistic. But the evidence we have seen in Jack Casey's remarks about himself seems to contradict this expectation. Jack Casey can scarcely be faulted for his compassion: not only does he value helping people in need, he spends a great deal of his time doing just that, sometimes at great risk to himself. Yet by his own admission he is intensely individualistic in all the ways that have been assumed to diminish the charitable impulse. In his case at least, as I have already suggested, individualism and altruism appear to be combined in complex ways.

How typical is Jack Casey? Is he like the Lone Ranger, a fictional anomaly who somehow helps the townspeople whenever they are in danger and then disappears to be by himself? Or are there features of his character that reflect more common patterns in American culture? Stated differently, is the question of how individualism and altruism can coexist in American culture really a nonissue because we are talking about two groups of people: the individualists in one camp and the altruists in a different camp? Or are we a complex people who, like Jack Casey, somehow try to combine individualism and altruism within the same personality?

The evidence we have already considered from various national studies makes it possible to answer this question. Those who deeply value caring and who are engaged in helping behavior can be compared with those who do not manifest these traits. They can be compared to see if the one type of person is less likely than the other to be oriented toward self-interest, personal freedom, material success, and the like.

The Independent Sector study I referred to in the last chapter also included several questions about values of other kinds. Some of these questions provide indicators of self-oriented values, such as realizing one's talents, having a good home and other nice things, and traveling for pleasure. A comparison of the people who said these self-oriented values were absolutely essential to them with the sample as a whole did not show any significant differences in their propensity to do volunteer work. Being intensely committed to self-realization and material pleasure did not seem to be incompatible with doing volunteer work.[3] My analysis of these data also revealed a slight *positive* relationship between these self-oriented values and placing importance on charitable activities.[4] In other words, people who were the most individualistic were also the most likely to value doing things to help others.

Greater detail on the relations between individualistic and altruistic values is available from my own survey. Perhaps the most intensely individualistic value in this study was expressed by the phrase "being able to do what you want." Among those who completely rejected this value (said it was not very important to them), 79 percent said helping people in need was personally very important. But among those who placed the highest importance on this kind of individualism (said it was absolutely essential to them), an even higher proportion (83 percent) said helping people in need was very important to them.

Adhering to individualism of this kind also did not seem to be associated with any less actual involvement in caring activities. Among those who valued being able to do what they wanted, and among those who did not share this value, virtually the same proportions were currently involved in charitable or social-service activities, had donated time to a volunteer organization during the past year, had cared for someone who was sick, had given money to a beggar, and had stopped to help someone having car trouble.[5]

Holding the belief that one can do anything if one just tries hard enough did not appear to be inconsistent with caring values either. Among those who held this view, 75 percent said helping others was very important, compared with only 66 percent of those who did not share it. The former were also somewhat more likely than the latter to say they valued giving time to help the needy.[6] Even when individualism provides an explanation for suffering that blames the victim, it does not seem to dampen the importance people place on caring. The majority who agreed with the statement "people generally bring suffering on themselves" were neither more nor less likely than the minority who disagreed with this statement to say they valued helping others or giving time to help the needy.[7]

Turning the question around—are the caring any less individualistic than the noncaring?—yields the same conclusion. Among those who were currently involved in volunteer charitable or social-service activities, and among those who were not, virtually the same proportions responded that doing what they wanted to do was absolutely essential (20 and 22 percent respectively), that taking care of themselves was absolutely essential (43 and 38 percent respectively), that being successful in their work was absolutely essential (30 and 23 percent respectively), and that living a comfortable life was absolutely essential (22 and 23 percent respectively).[8]

In the American population as a whole, therefore, it appears that individualism does not necessarily contradict holding altruistic values and engaging in a wide variety of caring and community-service activities. In this respect, Jack Casey is not at all an exception to the rule. The most compassionate in our midst, it appears, have not become caring individuals by giving up their individualism. Like the vast cross section of Americans, they also value their personal freedom, believe in the efficacy of self-determination, strive hard to succeed, take care of themselves, and pursue the comfortable life. And those who believe most intensely in the importance of pursuing their own self-interest in these ways seem not to be any less oriented toward caring for others than those who attach less importance to their self-interest.

How is this possible? How is it that we have been able to cling so tenaciously to our self-interest as individuals and yet show compassion to our neighbors? Have we found some happy way to have our cake and eat it too—to be selfish and altruistic at the same time? Have we developed a style of charitable individualism that works in reality? Or do these contradictory impulses live together in a fragile and precarious tension?

· 3 ·

Reconciling the altruistic side of his life with his deeply individualistic orientation has been a struggle for Jack Casey. At times he warms to the idea that maybe his efforts to be compassionate spring mainly from the gratifications he receives. Speaking with animation, he describes the excitement associated with volunteering for the fire company. "I love being a fireman, putting on my gear, and driving down Main Street, sirens blazing." Elaborating the same point, he explains, "Going to a fire is an adrenaline rush. It's exciting. Putting on your mask and running into a burning building is a raw, stupendous thrill!"

He also revels in the glory. Common to both the fire company and the rescue squad, he says, are jokes about how they are "protecting the town." "It's an ego trip."

Jack also speaks candidly about some of the other selfish reasons that may underlie his seemingly self-sacrificial activities. There are a fair number of "perks," he acknowledges. Two of the benefits that come from rescue-squad work are being able to "drive as fast as I want to on the highways" and being able to "park wherever I want to."

Another thing he likes about doing volunteer work is the sense of "being on the inside." People in the community know him and he in turn knows a great deal about what is going on in the community. Sometimes he even reaps tangible rewards, such as special dispensations from the police and local businessmen. "Like one of the cops will come along and say I won't ticket your car, I know what you do. Well, that's just a payback for what you do. Or, there's a guy here in town who gives me breakfast because he knows I'm on the squad."

These are all gratifications that come from being altruistic, but Jack carefully brackets them from playing too large a role in his account of himself. To focus only on the more selfish or individualistic side of his behavior does a disservice to the extensive caring activity in which he is involved. Consequently, he hastens to point out that some people "start out for the thrill," but excitement alone is unable to sustain them. And he identifies the more tangible benefits he receives as "paybacks" rather than "motivations." They are "just the nice things people do for you."

Reflecting for a moment on these paybacks, he also comes to the conclusion that "there's gotta be more than that." The gratification alone fails to be enough. "That can't get you very far, not with all the shit you have to put up with. You do an awful lot and seldom get much thanks for it at all." Thus he is only partially successful in reconciling his individualism with his compassionate behavior through the language of rewards and benefits. He recognizes that he cannot explain away his altruism by saying it is simply in his own interest to care for others.

A secondary narrative Jack resorts to in trying to understand his life draws on the language of therapy. Recognizing that he sometimes really does not enjoy helping people, he wonders why he is so driven to serve. His behavior seems to him to be compulsive, rooted in some unconscious need that he does not fully understand. Perhaps it is a "savior complex," he speculates. "You know, I like to be a hero, saving beautiful maidens from burning buildings."

In less mythic language he implies that his caring may stem from some kind of personal insecurity or need for self-justification. "I don't feel I have self-worth unless I'm helping people, so I'm really justifying my existence by helping somebody else." As if to convince himself, he mentions that he had been having some emotional problems about the time he joined the rescue squad and his joining helped resolve these problems. "It gave me a focus, a centering point, something I could dedicate myself to."

Something in him, he feels, drives him to help people even when he does not want to. "I've always wondered, why do I do these things; I don't always enjoy them. But somehow I invite them, I do them." But Jack admits this line of reasoning leaves him with more questions than answers. Sometimes his compulsion to help has even led him to do dangerous things, such as the time he rescued the woman from the lake. "I shouldn't have gone out without a life jacket; it was a stupid thing to do." But still he somehow cannot deny his impulse to help; he sacrifices himself even when it is not necessary. "So I wonder why," he ponders. "I don't know."

Judging by the tone of his voice and the manner of his expression, Jack is best able to make sense of his charitable activities in a way that does not deny his strong individuality when he frames his discourse as a personal narrative. He seems hesitant in his use of the more generalized languages of gratification and therapy, but an account of a significant experience in his life gives him the opportunity to say why he is altruistic in a way that still focuses much of the explanation on himself.

The narrative begins with a realization Jack became aware of in high school. "I realized at some point, probably in high school, that I had a fear (still do I guess) that I would see somebody hurt, and God forbid it would be someone I knew and cared for, and I would know there's something that could be done for this person to save them, but I wouldn't know what it was. I'd just be helpless and watch them die."

This realization terrified him; he began to make efforts to overcome the terror by learning whatever he would need to know to prevent such a situation from occurring. At first he was able to resolve his fear by learning water safety. "I knew that watching someone drown would kill me, so I learned to be a lifeguard." Soon after, he added first aid to his skills. "Watching someone bleed to death—so I learned how to treat them. Then I took advanced first aid, and it was a great class." Just knowing the skills helped him overcome his fear. But knowledge alone was not enough. He was still terrified thinking about having to use his knowledge for the first time. And then a critical event occurred.

"Near the end of that course I had this amazing experience of seeing probably the worst motor vehicle accident I've ever seen. I was going out to buy groceries one evening, and I was with some people in a van from the class who were involved in rescue-squad work. We pulled up to an intersection, and a guy who had been intoxicated and driving fifty miles per hour through town had plowed into another car that was trying to turn left; and that car went straight back into the car behind it, and bounced off two other cars; five critical patients, two fatalities. We were the first ones there. We just happened to drive up within fifteen seconds of when the accident happened. It was really eerie because it was totally quiet.

"We were right there, and my two companions were both members of the rescue squad. Immediately they pulled over and jumped out and went to work. I just felt helpless because I'd learned in the first-aid class that motor vehicle accidents are no place for amateurs. I was also in awe of how much these guys were able to do. They just jumped out and went to work.

"I wound up playing a very small part—a *very small* part. One person had been thrown free and wasn't injured, so I just went over and stayed with her. And in less than a minute and a half the police and the ambulances were all there. She was standing there in the cold and I just went over and talked to her, found out what was going on, put her in the police car, and let her get warm. It was really something.

"And I realized I'd been taking all these classes, but they weren't enough. I wanted to know that if there was somebody in front of me who needed it I could help them. And the only way I could know that was to do it. So, for the sake of wanting to find out how good I was, not really that, but knowing that I could really do it, knowing that I could really save people, I joined the squad."

Making sense of why we do things is never easy. When it involves complex motives and several alternative languages for describing these motives, it becomes even more difficult. The various stories Jack Casey tells about his behavior illustrate these difficulties. He is an exceptionally thoughtful, caring, and articulate young man, and yet he develops several narratives about himself that are neither internally consistent nor entirely compatible with one another. He can talk fluently about some of the self-interested reasons why he gives of himself to help others; at the same time, he recognizes the limitations of these reasons. He recognizes that he continues to show care and compassion even when such gratifications cannot account for his actions, but he admits that his behavior remains puzzling to him. His story about the terror of seeing someone die and not being able to help provides an explanation for his entry into rescue-squad work. But his inability to articulate a meaningful story of his present activities, including his apparent lack of language to explain his sense of altruism and to express the emotional qualities of compassion, raises serious doubts about the durability of his commitments.

Once he graduates from college he expects to attend medical school, where he can devote himself to learning more about emergency medicine. At this point in his life, he exhibits little sympathy for physicians who make huge salaries. But he also

27

admits he would not mind being paid for what he does. He will undoubtedly succeed in channeling into his profession his desire to help people. How well he will be able to balance his compassion for others against his rugged individualism is less predictable. He acknowledges that everyone must find the appropriate balance for himself or herself, but remains unclear about how best to accomplish that task.

· 4 ·

Jack Casey is not alone. I believe the concerns he expresses are ones with which many of us can identify. For all the talk about a "me generation" and who can accumulate the most toys before we die, most of us recognize the importance of caring for others and many of us put that value into practice. At the same time, few of us want to be Mother Teresa, few of us are attracted to the stifling small-town images of community we find championed in social-science textbooks, few of us are willing to give up any of the intense individualism we have inherited from our culture. And so we struggle like Jack Casey to figure out a story for ourselves that allows us to be at once caring and individualistic.

The problem with Jack Casey is that he does indeed, as he says, have a savior complex that sets him apart from most of the crowd. Although he is quite human, quite vulnerable, quite endearing in much of what he says, the very nature of his caring activities makes it hard to identify very closely with him. He is, after all, an Eagle Scout, a rescue-squad worker, a fire fighter. He has lived out every rugged individualist's dream of following his own star, working hard, and succeeding. He has simply happened to pursue success in a way that also allows him to be caring.

In this respect Jack Casey is not what the critics of our society have in mind when they suggest we need to reform. Their ideal of the kind of person who will make our society a better place is a person whose individualism has been more deeply chastened by the needs of other people. They have in mind someone with genuine attachments to the community rather than the Lone Ranger who rides through town in an orange-and-white van with the siren blaring. They would want to know

whether a truly caring person could be as intensely individualistic as Jack Casey or whether he or she would have to temper
that individualism in order to form secure and supportive
attachments.

· 5 ·

Marge Detweiler is nothing at all like Jack Casey. At age forty-
eight she is old enough to be his mother. She has four children
of her own, all of whom are grown and away from home. She
lives in a different part of the country thousands of miles away.
Having gotten a divorce several years ago, she now runs a
small printing business to earn a living. About the only thing
she and Jack Casey have in common is that they both do volunteer work.

But Marge Detweiler's volunteer work is of a very different
kind. A recovering alcoholic, Marge gives generously of her
time to Alcoholics Anonymous (AA). She sponsors several
people in the program, which means being available to them
whenever they call for help, going to lunch or having coffee
with each one at least once a week, and just being their friend.
She also leads an AA meeting each week and from time to time
does work for the organization at the state level.

As she has grown accustomed to doing in AA, Marge intro-
duces herself by briefly telling her story. "My story," she says,
"happens to involve going to an alcoholic treatment center
three times. That's when they introduced me to AA. All three
times I came out and started drinking again. So the fourth time,
it was a case of two things. Number one, I kind of thought I
hadn't given AA a real shot to get at me. And number two, I
was going to commit suicide within two or three days. I knew
that. So the fourth time I went, it worked—for whatever reason. AA got me sober and has changed my life around. I went
there only to learn how not to drink, and what they handed me
was a program of living."

In this very literal sense, AA is Marge's life. Her closest
friends are part of the AA community. One of the women she
sponsored became her business partner. Another is now
Marge's sponsor. Marge recognizes not only that the program
is what keeps her alive, but also that it animates her entire life.

At the meetings she attends twice weekly, she sees herself in other people. In the newcomers she sees what life would be like if she started drinking again. She also shares their joys. "I see those same people's victories, as they ease up, and it gets better, and their life gets simpler, and they find that they can handle being a human being without having to run away from it. I get to share that."

The community has taught Marge how to relate to other people, how to trust, and how to be loved. "It was a kindergarten for me about how to be a human being and how to deal with people. One of the things I did was to hide behind all these masks. And when I quit drinking I found I couldn't do that anymore. AA showed me who I am and how to act with people, how to share, how to talk, and they did it in a very loving atmosphere. I had never found that anywhere else. All the other relationships I'd ever had were very critical and very judgmental. And AA wasn't that way at all."

By becoming a member of the AA community, Marge has come to realize how much she needs other people. "I don't need them because they'll make me happy or because they can fulfill me in my life. But I need them—hmm, I wonder why I do? I need them because they add to my life. Before, I always used to think I needed people or things to make me happy. Because of AA I know I don't anymore. But I do need people in my life. They're what fill it up."

Marge's giving of herself for others is thus interwoven with her attachment to—her dependence on—a caring community. The people she knows there sustain her, love her, teach her, fill her. The community, she admits, creates a very protective environment that she needs and likes. The time she spends leading meetings and sponsoring other women is merely a way to pay back the community for saving her life. She does not think of herself as the Lone Ranger, the way Jack Casey does; the Lone Ranger, in her view, is perverse.

But Marge Detweiler does think of herself as an individualist. She says she has actually worked very hard to become an individualist. She has spent a great deal of time and expended a lot of energy finding out who she is, stripping away the masks, discovering what she wants in life. To her, being an individualist means "finding out what I'm good at and then doing the best I can with it, because this country gives me the choice." It also means *"only* being concerned about being the best I can be; not being concerned about what you can be, not gouging you with prices, and if I'm the best person I can be at whatever I do, I get showered with blessings."

· 6 ·

Marge Detweiler is nothing at all like Jack Casey. But because she too tries to combine caring and individualism, she struggles with finding the proper combination. One of the hardest struggles she has is deciding how much to follow her own dictates, being true only to herself, and how much to depend on other people. As the remark she made about happiness indicates, she has decided that happiness must come from within; she cannot expect other people to make her happy. Yet she also realizes she needs people and is not quite sure how to understand this need. Her candid question to herself—"hmm, I wonder why I do"—echoes through all the chambers of her life.

Marge's effort to be her own person and yet show compassion toward others has forced her to set some strict limits on her caring relationships. "I have sponsored people," she admits, "and what they do is just take, take, take." When this happens, she feels exploited and drained. She becomes frustrated and angry; indeed, she sometimes feels like starting to drink again. At this point, she has learned the necessity of letting cold realism take over. "A beautiful part about the whole sponsorship relationship is that I then end it." She says she just tells the person she has been sponsoring: "I know what I have to give and you don't want it. If you want it a week from now or a month from now, I'll be here for you. But I don't have anything to give you now."

Getting what she wants from the people in her community has been another challenge for Marge. Without her fully realizing it, AA has given her a very sophisticated language for describing the relationship between herself and others. She says there are always three or four people she can turn to for help. "They are always there for me. It doesn't matter what's going on, they will drop anything if they know I need them." Marge claims they actually give her unconditional love. They define the meaning of compassion for her. They give her the accep-

tance she never received anywhere else. They never criticize
her, never judge her, never fail her. They identify totally with
her. They live out Tolstoy's ideal of bread labor.

Frankly, they do the impossible. How do they accomplish it?
Language is the key. Marge has learned a language that makes
the essential distinctions, that provides a way of defining total
compassion and still makes compassion humanly possible in
an individualistic world. Although her friends never judge her,
for example, "what they give me is their honest opinion"—
something that can only exist when individuals have a strong
sense of ownership of what they think. And those who care for
her "give me unconditional love no matter what I do." But:
"They will make fun of it when I act like a three-year-old. They
will let me laugh. They always say they understand. They always tell me that it makes perfect sense that I would feel that
way. And then they show me ways to take the three-year-old
and grow her up a bit."

Despite all the differences, then, Marge is a lot like Jack
Casey. Compassion is something each has had to define. It has
had to be defined within the context of what was possible for
them as individuals. They have had to set limits around it.
They have also had to figure out how to talk about it without
demeaning it or diminishing its importance, and yet talk about
it in a way that is true to their personal goals, ambitions, and
self-interests. Being part of a warm, supportive community has
helped Marge find the right words to use in describing herself
and her compassion. But it has not solved the problem of how
to reconcile her individual needs with those of the community;
if anything, it has made the problem more intense.

· 7 ·

Marge Detweiler and Jack Casey both give of themselves to a
far greater extent than many of us do. In sheer numbers of
hours, they spend far more time doing volunteer work each
week than the average person does. Indeed, according to national statistics, only one person in eight devotes more than
five hours a week to volunteer work.[9]

Jack and Marge are clearly in the minority. Helping people is
a very important part of their lives. What of the majority? Per-

haps the tensions I have been describing between self-oriented and other-oriented values exist only for those who have become heavily involved in caring activities. Perhaps, as the surveys show, most Americans hold both individualistic and caring values, but their caring is so minimal or sporadic that they experience little conflict between these values. Perhaps self-interest is really all that matters for most people most of the time: even though they may be involved in some kind of caring activity, they can easily justify it in self-oriented terms.

Janet Russo provides a useful contrast to Jack Casey and Marge Detweiler. She is an attractive woman in her late thirties who speaks confidently about herself and her interests. For several years she did some volunteer work on Friday afternoons at the elementary school her two children attended. Before that she had been active from time to time on parent-teacher committees and association boards in her community. At present, though, the only caring activity she is involved with outside her family is a center for abused women called US. The center provides shelter, clothing, and child care, offers short-term support, and puts abused women in touch with other social-service agencies. Janet donates an hour or two to the center every Wednesday as a peer counselor.

When asked why she started volunteering at the center, she explains: "It was purely selfish. I moved here in July, two years ago, and I was really lonely. In the neighborhood, there was never anyone around; I felt like I lived in the country and had no neighbors."

Janet had "had it up to here" with school committees, so she vowed she was not going to do volunteer work just to overcome her loneliness. "I wanted to just be an ordinary parent and mind my own business." But one day, while she was doing some gardening in her backyard, a neighbor came over to talk. "I was saying how September was coming and I needed to find something; and she said, 'I know where you belong.' She told me about US and about Women's Week, which is a week in September when they celebrate women, or US actually."

So Janet decided to attend Women's Week. "When I walked in I felt very comfortable and everybody welcomed me, and there were sign-up sheets, and my girlfriend next door had said sign everything because it doesn't bind you, they'll just call and talk to you about it, and you can pick out what you're interested in. So that's how I got started."

Now that she has become involved with US she regards it as a home away from home, a warm place, a friendly place. She also admits she donates her time for less than altruistic reasons: "I guess I'm just selfish. I enjoy it because it's different every time I walk in the door." Jobs for pay had always bored her because she had to do the same thing every day. Working at the center gives her the variety she likes. Her husband earns enough money for the family, so she is able to do things without pay simply for the enjoyment. "It's also enabled me to feel good about myself," she observes. "I've become a catch-all here anytime somebody needs something, and that makes me feel real good about myself. I guess that affects my attitude. I feel I don't really need anyone anymore. I'm just who I am, and they need me."

They need me. I don't need anyone anymore. Janet Russo seems to typify the kind of volunteer who is involved strictly for herself. She gives of her time because she has no need to work, because she would be lonely otherwise, because it gives her a change of pace, and because it makes her feel good. She also places strict limits on the caring she does. When asked if she ever helped any of the women she meets at US outside the center, or ever tried to befriend them, she shies away from the question, suggesting it would be awkward to do that.

Although Janet is a devoted mother and wife, it is also hard to find evidence in the rest of her life of a deep sense of caring toward anyone outside her immediate family. When asked to think of some special time when she had shown compassion to someone, she recounts a story of a dead man. "It was when I was still working and had no children, probably fifteen years ago. I was working in a nursing home. I had a very kindly old man die, and he was just a wonderful patient. They were going to bury him in potter's field, which is for paupers; it's mass graves, unmarked graves. It upset me tremendously. There was something about this man that he should not be buried that way, some sense of dignity, and I decided that something had to be done. I didn't know exactly what, so I contacted a funeral home, and spoke to a friend I had who was learning the funeral business, and he spoke to his boss and one thing led to another. I found out that there are ways to keep people who don't have money from being buried in potter's field, and so we had to put a stop on the body being given to the city and all. So we went to the Veterans Administration and ran around and did all this stuff. What came of it was a group of volunteer funeral-home directors who were willing to be listed in local nursing homes to help people not be buried in potter's field. I felt real good about that. We went out and buried him in the cemetery for veterans. I felt great."

As she says this she seems to relish again the feeling of having done something good. But I am struck by the fact that it is the feeling that matters to her more than anything else, by the number of times she uses "I" in her account, and by the fact that she has chosen to tell about caring for a corpse rather than for someone who was alive.

As she talks on, I gain an even stronger impression that Janet is someone whose name would be counted among the eighty million Americans who volunteer, but who finds it very difficult to care for anyone other than herself. She admits she dropped out of nursing because it was too stressful for her physically and mentally (she did not say emotionally). She also admits that her own mother regarded her as "a cold-hearted bitch" who would never succeed in nursing.

This assessment of herself is one she does not share. Janet Russo does not think of herself as a shameless, ruthless egotist. But like millions of her fellow citizens she does think it crucial to speak up for herself, to make sure she gets what she deserves, to be independent, and to expect others to be independent as well. She holds people who have not learned to say "no" in disdain. They seem loving and caring, she says, but really they just get dumped on. She sums up her view of herself in these words: "I'm really very independent basically, so I don't look to other people to help me through things. If I was seriously ill or something, I'd just deal with it myself."

· 8 ·

Despite the volunteer work she does, Janet Russo seems to be a Gold Card member of the "me generation." Self-interest colors her language like the sequins on an heiress's evening gown. It is difficult to dismiss Janet Russo as a mere narcissist, though. She also finds it important to make a place for caring in her life. One way she tries to do this is to define individualism in such a way that it does not necessarily conflict with compassion. "I hold onto my own ideas, and I think that makes me an individualist," she says. "I do things the way I do them, and no one else does it quite the same way. So that makes me what I am." She focuses on the kind of individualism that means nonconformity, not the kind she displays elsewhere in her narrative when she describes herself as totally self-sufficient. As a nonconformist, as someone true to her own values, she believes she can be compassionate. "I can still care about other people. I don't think being an individualist means just keeping to yourself; you have to share."

Another part of her thinking that helps her make a place for caring in an otherwise individualistic worldview came to the surface when she was asked whether some people are just basically selfish. Not willing to see any fundamental conflict between selfishness and caring, she suggests that nobody is purely selfish. Everybody has some selfishness in him or her, and some level of concern for others. The reason they appear to be different, she believes, is that some people "have just never been approached." She explains: "I think everybody is willing to volunteer. When we tried to set up a new PTA committee, we had a list of names, and everyone said how are we going to get them to do it, and I said try calling them on the phone and asking, and they all looked at me like it was a new and different idea, and I said just give me the list and a phone and I'll call, and they gave me a phone, and there were very few people who said no to me. I think that's what it takes, and don't expect more of them than what they're willing to give, like if someone says I don't have a whole lot of time, fine, whatever you can give is great, and praise them, that always gets everybody, just say you've been highly recommended, and we have this position, and we think you could do it, and I don't have time to wait for you to think about it, so just give me a quick yes or no. Nine times out of ten it's going to be yes. So probably some people just don't think about it. If approached, they probably would do it."

By attributing individual differences to the accidents of specific situations, she in effect denies the importance of motivation. Thus it becomes easier in a way for her to admit that she does caring things for selfish reasons. She cannot be categorized as a selfish person or as a caring person because nobody can. Some people care a lot but seem selfish because they have never been asked to give of themselves. Others actually do give of themselves, but may not "come across" as compassionate people. Janet points to her mother-in-law as an example: "She doesn't appear to be a warm individual, but I think she's loving. She does all sorts of volunteer work, and yet to talk to her you would not pick her out as a compassionate person. She comes across as very stern and hard. There's probably a lot of people like that. They have a kind of facade, but deep down they're compassionate."

Janet is reluctant to judge whether anyone is genuinely selfish or genuinely compassionate. This reluctance is contingent on her ability to draw a number of fine distinctions about motivations and behavior. As the example of her mother-in-law reveals, Janet insists on an inner/outer distinction—a separation between what one feels internally and how one shows those feelings externally. She also resorts to a means/ends distinction in reconciling selfishness and altruism. "I guess there are some people out there," she ventures, "who are basically selfish, but out of that selfishness, you can get some good things. It may be that someone is volunteering for purely selfish motives, and yet you get some good man-hours, even if the motives aren't exactly what you'd like them to be."

These distinctions work for her up to a point. Where she has trouble is that she does, as her last remark suggests, still worry about having the kind of motives "you'd like them to be." This is especially important, she says, when she is trying to be an example for her children. "It's nice to be able to tell your kids you helped someone; it's even nicer if they know WHY you did something and don't need to ask." The character of people's motives also becomes important when she wants to distinguish her kind of caring with examples of caring she does not respect. Although one part of her wants to let anyone be selfish as long as he or she still does some good for others, another part of her lashes out against certain kinds of selfish behavior.

After suggesting that it is acceptable to help others in order to "feel good about yourself," she cites one of her neighbors as an example of the wrong kind of selfishness in caring. "One of my neighbors is a very cheerleader type of person. The first time my husband met her he said something to the effect that she must have been an ex-cheerleader. She belongs to the country club and this organization and that organization. I just don't picture her doing it for what I consider the right reasons. She belongs to an awful lot of things, and I don't think she does a good job for any one of them. She's there for what it might do for her and what it might do for her husband's career. She's not doing it just to help someone in the community."

But then checking herself, as if suddenly realizing how judgmental the story was becoming, she remarked, "I guess everybody's different. I'm just not a believer in doing something because it's going to get you ahead in the world. I don't care if I'm recognized for it. It's just fun to do it."

So she struggles to find an appropriate way of making herself clear, of reconciling the side of her that wants to believe in compassion in some unsullied form with the side that wants to make room for selfish motives, and not only make room for them but also make them compatible with caring. She tries one more time to offer a generalization, but quickly retreats into a statement referring only to herself. "I think everyone has some selfish motives, including myself. Like I said, it helps me to help other people, so that's selfish, even though the outcome is good. But if it's *purely* for selfish reasons, and you don't even look to what you're doing, I think that's unfortunate." Unfortunate, but in what sense? Unfortunate in a self-interested sense: "If it just happens to benefit you too, then it's like getting two for the price of one, it's a good bargain."

· 9 ·

In their own unique ways Jack Casey, Marge Detweiler, and Janet Russo all reflect the dilemmas our culture imposes on those who would be compassionate. They try hard to care deeply about others, but they are also intensely individualistic, and so they struggle as they talk about themselves to find a language that allows them to be both. Were Tolstoy their interlocutor he would probably not be impressed, any more than he was with Jane Addams. Total identification with the suffering, to the point of sharing their entire life situation, he would point out, is lacking in all three. Were Jane Addams their interlocutor she would probably feel much more at home with their style of caring. They do what they can and try to do it effectively. What good is it, she would ask, if someone becomes so obsessed with sharing the pain that he or she is unable to help those experiencing it?

But new interlocutors have arisen since Jane Addams and Tolstoy. They would recognize the voluntarism typified by Jack Casey, Marge Detweiler, and Janet Russo as familiar patterns of behavior in American culture. They would not, however, see anything particularly problematic about the fact that voluntarism and individualism coexist in our society. In one way or another each interlocutor has found a way to wish away the problem, to think it out of existence so that it simply vanishes from sight rather than being an issue with which any thoughtful person actually has to struggle.

The first interlocutor wishes the relation between caring and individualism out of existence by focusing on rationality. Imagine the following situation, this interlocutor would suggest. Two prisoners are being held in separate cells and are incommunicado. Each has been accused of committing a major crime. But there is insufficient evidence. Without a confession from at least one it will be impossible to convict either of them. A surprising thing happens. Both confess! Apparently they are genuine altruists. Each seems to have cared so much for the other that he confessed rather than protecting himself by keeping his mouth shut.

But wait, this interlocutor would caution. What you did not realize was that the sheriff is an extraordinarily clever person. With each prisoner he made a separate deal. If you confess and the other guy does not, you will go free and he will receive a sentence of ten years in jail. If he confesses and you do not, you will get the ten-year sentence and he will go free. If you both confess, you will each receive a five-year sentence. And if you both refuse to confess, you will each be convicted on a minor charge and have to spend only a year in jail.

Both prisoners were actually concerned only about themselves. But they were smart. Each made a rational choice. That is, each one figured out that the best way to minimize his time in jail, in the absence of being able to find out what the other guy was going to do, was to confess. Had he not confessed, he would have gotten either a ten-year or a one-year sentence (averaging the two, a probability of 5.5 years). By confessing, he knew he would either get off scot-free or at most receive a five-year sentence (averaging the two, a probability of 2.5 years). What looked like altruism was really self-interest.[10]

According to this interlocutor's logic, people always act in their self-interest. What sometimes makes it seem as if they are altruistic is that the rules of the game have been orchestrated to make that option the most rational (rationally self-interested) choice. To promote altruism, one simply needs to set up the situation in the right way. If pursuing my own interests happens to benefit you too, then so be it. It is, as Janet Russo suggests, like getting two for the price of one.

Many years before the invention of rational-choice theory, and long before probability theory showed certain choices to be the most rational, Tocqueville managed to reconcile the two opposing tendencies he observed in American society with a similar argument. Individualism, he argued, actually made Americans more dependent on one another. If they acted rationally, they would not only pursue their own interests, but would help one another because this helping would be in their interest as well. This attitude he called "self-interest rightly understood."[11]

Confronted with Jack Casey, Marge Detweiler, or Janet Russo, our rational-choice theorist would argue that each is merely pursuing a strategy of self-interest rightly understood. Jack Casey wants to be a doctor some day. Until he has his medical degree he cannot actually practice medicine. But he needs experience, both to gain admission to medical school and to do well once he is admitted. So he finds volunteer work that gives him this experience. Rescue-squad work happens to benefit others, but he does it basically because it is in his self-interest. Marge Detweiler gives time to people in AA because it is also in her interest to do so. They keep her sober and give her enough emotional support that she can run a business and make a living. Janet Russo is no different. The time she spends at the abused women's center on Wednesday afternoons may help others, but she basically does it because she is lonely and bored. It is in her interest to have something to do. It is only logical in all their cases to be both intensely individualistic and also caring.

The other interlocutor who has found a way to wish the tension between individualism and caring out of existence would address our three cases therapeutically. Whether or not it is in your interest to be caring is not the real issue. Even if you happen to be genuinely moved by some altruistic impulse, you cannot be very effective at it unless you also take care of yourself. Loving your neighbor as yourself means that you must truly, and above all, love yourself.

Suppose you want to devote your life to working with mentally retarded children, the therapist would say. That in the abstract is a laudable goal. But before losing yourself in this pursuit you must ask yourself "Why am I attracted to it? Is it perhaps because I have not faced some insecurity of my own?" If so, you must work through this weakness. You must make yourself strong in order to help others. Once you find yourself working with mentally retarded children, you must also learn how to fulfill your needs on a daily basis. You must get enough fulfillment, enough affirmation, enough support, enough time to yourself. Otherwise you will burn out. If you do not take care of yourself first, you will very quickly become of no use to anyone else.

This interlocutor would seize immediately on the psychological aspects of Jack Casey's testimony. Yes, indeed, he is working out his emotional insecurities. Probably he was not loved enough as a child and thus came to fear intensely that someone close to him would die. He pushed himself to be an amateur doctor. But he is unable to empathize genuinely with those he helps. His iceman view of himself is symptomatic of unfulfilled needs. If he does not find a way to take care of himself, he will probably burn out.

Much the same line of argument would be applied by this interlocutor to Marge Detweiler and Janet Russo. Marge's alcoholism is perhaps also symptomatic of a codependent personality, of someone who always cared too much, and therefore found herself with a self-destructive addiction. It is a positive sign that she has learned through AA how to set limits, how to take better care of herself. Janet Russo has farther to go. She still cuts herself off. She tries to touch others in a caring way. But her insecurity forces her to be too self-sufficient. She needs to learn how to depend more on others, to open up and let them fulfill her needs. Both women will be able to care for others more effectively only when they learn how better to care for themselves.

Both these interlocutors have important points to make. They have diagnosed important features of our society that must be dealt with in order to understand and advance caring behavior. There is indeed a large dose of self-interest in much that we think of as altruism. There is also an important therapeutic dimension in caring—a dimension of self-knowing that is essential to anyone's ability to reach out in love toward others. But both interlocutors also reveal something deeper. They are themselves symptomatic of how important it is in our culture to reconcile our individualistic and our altruistic tendencies. They provide an interpretation of how altruism works in our culture, but this interpretation itself needs to be relativized; that is, to be seen as a feature of the individualistic culture in which we live, rather than being taken simply as timeless scientific fact. Its assumptions need to be examined in light of how compassionate individuals actually construct their experiences.

The rational-choice theorist makes three crucial assumptions: one, that individuals always and knowingly pursue self-interest; two, that they often do so (as in the prisoner game) without direct social interaction or communication; and three, that some omniscient being has set up simple, easy-to-calculate payoffs. None of these assumptions is valid in most ordinary caring behavior. As the three cases we have considered illustrate, people who care are seldom sure that they are or should be simply pursuing self-interest. Social interaction rather than social isolation—and thus, the necessity of communication—is generally an important part of their behavior. And the payoffs seldom consist of simple quantifiable rewards or punishments.

The therapeutic perspective is truer to the actual life experiences of caring individuals. But it also makes some very strong assumptions: one, that there are more-healthy and less-healthy ways to care; two, that caring is likely to necessitate a high level of direct emotional work, if not actual emotional involvement;

and three, that this emotional work is risky and must be done properly in order to keep yourself and others healthy.

In the three cases we have examined, these assumptions seem largely to be justified. All three individuals struggle with questions about how best to care, how much emotional involvement to sustain, and whether there are personal risks associated with becoming too involved. These may be universal to care givers in all times and places. But they at least reflect the value we place on the individual. They reflect the fact that we view the individual as a complex of emotions, as a reservoir of needs to be filled up, as a precarious being who is deeply sensitive to the influences of intimate interaction. All these are culturally contingent assumptions. The therapeutic interlocutor has not so much wished away the problem of how individualism relates to caring in our society, as he or she has described it.

What the therapeutic interlocutor would admit, if pressed, is that the only thing simple about the therapeutic approach is its emphasis on achieving a healthy balance between one's own needs and the needs of those one loves. How this balance is actually achieved must be worked out in practice. Each person must find the balance that seems best to him or her. But that itself is a matter of negotiation, a matter of self-interpretation and discussion, a matter of finding a culturally suitable language. In each of our three cases we have seen a great deal of self-examination. We have seen the complexity with which motives are described. We have seen the importance of language about emotions, about feelings, about the self and its limits. How people come to grips with these aspects of their caring seems to be terribly important to them. Their efforts to resolve these questions lie at the heart of the relationship between their compassion and their individualism. They illustrate the cultural work that goes into making sense of this relationship.

· 10 ·

For me the essential question in all this is: "Is compassion really possible in our society?" I do not mean voluntarism, care giving, helping behavior, prosocial activity, or similar words that have been invented to give compassion a more contemporary ring. I mean compassion in the old-fashioned sense (for it is an old-fashioned word)—what in most languages means "to suffer with" and in other languages means simply "to feel with," what the Good Samaritan was moved with when he came across the injured man on the Jericho road.

Is compassion possible? Of course, one might say. Look at the statistics on giving time to charitable and social-service organizations. Of course it is possible. And there would be even more of it if people had more free time and were encouraged to give. What we need are more effective appeals, better advertising, more attention to the incentives that make people willing to give, more consideration of the situations in which it becomes possible to give. Or, one might say, look at the feelings of which compassion consists. Of course compassion is possible, at least for most people. A mother catches her hand in the bathroom door; on seeing her grasp it, wincing with pain, her infant daughter does the same. Compassion is natural unless some abnormal experiences cause it to be lost.

None of this is what I have in mind. When I ask whether compassion is possible, I mean, is it *culturally* possible? Are we able to interpret our behavior—to ourselves and to others—in a way that makes sense, in a way that makes sense of it as compassion? Is it possible for us to think of ourselves as persons who have shown compassion, as persons who are capable of showing compassion, as persons who are (at some level) compassionate? Moreover, is it possible for us to think of ourselves collectively in this way? Are we a compassionate people? Or, perhaps more realistically, does compassion play an important role in our society? And, if so, what is that role?

Let me illustrate. Suppose I visit one of my students who is in the hospital. That is an act, a concrete behavior, maybe even a helping behavior (I take him his homework). Suppose he is in some pain and feeling rather depressed. I may leave sharing some of his depression as well, in which case my act has had both a physical and an emotional dimension. But whether it is an act of compassion depends on how I am able to interpret it—to him, to myself, or to anyone who might ask for an account. I might dismiss the importance of my behavior entirely, telling myself that it was simply part of my job, or even that my dean had asked me to make the visit. I might say to myself, this is a chance to further my career, especially if I can ask the student to put in a good word for me next time I am up for a promotion. I might then beat up on myself, pointing out to my conscience that I am too conniving to have any self-respect at all, or that I am so compulsive about such things that I am driving myself crazy. I might also recognize that some part of me wanted to be kind, genuinely cared about this student, and wanted to help. Somewhere in all these interpretations lies the language needed in our culture to make a visit to the hospital an act of compassion. How that language is constituted is the central question with which I am concerned.

When I talk about "acts of compassion," then, I do not mean a particular set of behaviors, taken simply at face value, such as a visit to the hospital or an afternoon of volunteering at a center for abused women. I mean the cultural framework as well: the languages we use to make sense of such behaviors, the cultural understandings that transform them from physical motions into human action. The discourse in which such behavior is inscribed is no less a part of the act than is the behavior itself. The possibility of compassion depends as much on having an appropriate discourse to interpret it as it does on having a free afternoon to do it. To ask whether compassion is possible, therefore, is to ask about the languages on which its very conceivability depends.

But to ask about language inevitably moves us from the level of the individual to the level of society. Each of us must use language to make sense of our individual experiences; this is why the words of individuals like Jack Casey and Marge Detweiler and Janet Russo are so important to understand. We all use the words our language gives us. But they are not words of our own invention. They are the languages we find available in our culture. They reflect broader themes about what it means to be American.

Like Jane Addams, we all must struggle to find out what it means to be compassionate in the unique context of American society. I believe deeply that we all struggle with that issue, whether we are volunteers or people who help our neighbors informally or just individuals who find ourselves needing community. We have to discover how to reconcile our caring for others with the pervasive individualism that so often fragments our society and our lives. I believe we succeed for the most part in doing this—better, at least, than many of our society's critics suggest.

But we also pay a price. We begin with ourselves. We worry a lot about our motives. We pay great heed to the language of good feelings. We struggle even to adapt our religious values and our sense of ethical responsibility to the fragmented society in which we live. These pursuits are all issues that deserve our attention, for they structure much of our thinking about the possibility of being compassionate in a self-interested world. But in the end, we must return to the question of society itself. We must ask, does caring for others primarily help "our selves," as individuals, or can it also help "ourselves," as a society?

PART II

LANGUAGES OF COMPASSION

CHAPTER THREE

Talking about Motives

Not long ago a local newspaper carried the story of an elderly woman who made quilts. For more than half a century she had sewn quilts, donating the proceeds to various causes, such as a hospital, a senior citizens' center, a school for autistic children. Most of the story was no different from hundreds of others printed in local newspapers each day. Such is the fare of human-interest reportage. What made this story distinctive was that it did *not* ask: why did she do it?

Questions about motives go hand in hand with discussions of charitable behavior. Jack Casey, Marge Detweiler, and Janet Russo all talked extensively about their motives. They did so because they were asked. But this was not the first time they had confronted the question. All three mentioned times when they had asked themselves why they did volunteer work. Questions about motives also came up in their public lives. Individuals wanting to join the rescue squad, Jack pointed out, had to appear before a review board. And one of the questions the board always asked was why they wanted to sign up. Marge's story was a well-rehearsed public performance she had given at AA meetings and heard modeled in others' stories at these meetings. Janet mentioned discussing her cheerleader friend's motives with her husband and trying to communicate more laudable motives for caring to her children.

According to one guide to the literature, some seven hundred books and articles on the motives for giving and volunteering have been published in the past few years.[1] We study motivation because we want to encourage more charitable activity. Sometimes motives make us curious because the deeds involve great heroism or sacrifice. We also worry about motives because we believe some may be better than others. How we think about motives, in short, reflects how we understand ourselves and our values.

Having a language to describe our motives for caring is one of the ways in which we make compassion possible in the individualistic society in which we live. It is not enough simply to "be motivated," as we say; not enough to find ourselves in some situation that prompts us to engage in an act of kindness. We must also have a way to talk about our motivations. We must have a language that allows us to explain to ourselves and others why we are doing what we do. And in an individualistic society, where caring is sometimes seen as an abnormality, it becomes all the more important to be able to give an account of ourselves. An adequate language of motivation is thus one of the critical junctures at which the individual and the society intersect: being able to explain why is as important to our identity as a culture as it is to our sense of selfhood as individuals.

· 2 ·

Our culture supplies a number of repertoires to draw from whenever we want to construct an account of our motives for caring. These repertoires are reproduced in sermons and speeches. They can be found in books and articles discussing the motives of public figures. In more ordinary contexts they are simply evident in the conversations we hold with our acquaintances and with ourselves.[2]

The biblical tradition has been a rich source of arguments about the importance of caring. In chapter 1 I mentioned the role played historically by sermons about love of neighbor such as those of John Winthrop and John Witherspoon. Through the many denominations and faiths that make up the mosaic of American religion these admonitions have continued to play a prominent role in our culture. Variously interpreted, the biblical tradition teaches compassion as a duty to divine law, as a response to divine love, and as a sign of commitment to the Judeo-Christian ethic.

Many of the people I interviewed resorted to biblical language to explain their motives for becoming involved in caring activities. One young man quoted a verse from the Bible (James 3:17) as his reason for caring: "If anyone has the world's goods and sees his brother in need, yet closes his heart against him, how does God's love abide in him?" The conclusion he drew from this verse was simply that "we are commanded to love one another." Another person placed the emphasis less on duty and more on opportunity but still formulated her answer in religious terms: "A good way to show your thankfulness to God is by helping others and seeing your own life as blessed." Another said she thought of Jesus as a role model because he taught: "Care for others and do not expect anything in return."

I shall take up the question of religion's role in reinforcing compassion in some detail in chapter 5. Suffice it to say here that religion figures prominently in the accounts people give of their motives for being compassionate. In one national study "spiritual reasons" was among the top four responses given to an open-ended question that asked people how they came to give to various charities.[3] In my national survey people were asked to respond to a number of possible reasons for trying to be a person who is kind and caring. One of the statements read, "My religious beliefs teach me to be kind and caring." A majority (57 percent) said this was a major reason for them to be kind and caring. Another 26 percent selected it as a minor reason. Only 14 percent said it was not a reason for them to be kind and caring.[4]

Although the biblical tradition has been interpreted in many ways, most of its interpreters have argued that compassion does not spring naturally from the human heart. The familiar biblical stories teach that selfishness is the more human response: Cain's murder of Abel, the lust and avarice resulting in the fall of Sodom and Gomorrah, the jealousy of Joseph's brothers, the selfishness of Jesus' disciples, Jesus' parable about the priest and Levite who passed by the injured man on the Jericho road. There is, however, another tradition in our culture that accounts for compassion by saying it is simply a natural instinct.

· 3 ·

According to a recent article in a popular magazine, this is how compassion may have originated: "Once upon a time, before there was history, some primitive man must have looked up from his fire and observed the approach of a stranger through the empty world. The first man was consuming the gains of a lucky hunt. He paused, saw hunger and fear in the eyes of the stranger, and was moved to something that resembled pity. Then he reached for a charred rib and handed it to the desperate stranger. In that moment, charity was born."[5]

Imaginative as it is, this argument is strikingly unoriginal. It is basically the view that came into prominence during the Enlightenment in the eighteenth century. Rousseau argued that compassion was simply present in the state of nature: just as cows lowed in anguish for a fallen comrade, so humans instinctively felt pity for the suffering in their midst. Adam Smith, the founder of classical economics, offered a similar argument in his *Theory of Moral Sentiments*. No matter who the individual might be, he observed, there were some principles "in his nature" that prompted him to respond emotionally to the fortunes of others. "Of this kind," he wrote, "is pity or compassion, the emotion which we feel for the misery of others, when we either see it, or are made to conceive it in a very lively manner." Everyone, Smith argued, had this capacity by nature: "The greatest ruffian, the most hardened violator of the laws of society, is not altogether without it."[6]

The idea that compassion may in some way be a natural impulse continues to have resonance in our society. Researchers are now studying small children to see if some primary disposition toward empathizing with others' pain may lie at the root of compassion.[7] In the philosophical and ethical literature one finds similar ideas. One author who has carefully examined the ethical basis of compassion argues, for example, that "the impulse to act in behalf of the present other is itself innate." She goes on to explain that "it lies latent in each of us, awaiting gradual development in a succession of caring relations."[8]

In my interviews people expressed the idea that caring is an innate motive in a variety of ways. Jack Casey, it will be recalled, speculated that an impulse to help others was simply a feature of his personality. Another person explained, "I have always had a very weak, soft spot for those not as lucky as I." Others used language reminiscent of Rousseau, suggesting that there is a chord somewhere within us that can be struck by seeing someone in need. An older man summarized the idea this way: "I think there's a degree of compassion in all of us; everyone is touched by need." Another said simply, "I give because that's the kind of person I am."

In my survey 56 percent indicated that "I'm just a sort of person who tries to be caring" was a major reason for them to be kind and caring. Another 33 percent indicated this was a minor reason. Only 8 percent said they did not consider it one of their reasons for caring. In other words, the responses to this question were about the same as those to the one about religious beliefs being a reason for caring. Most of us think the motive for caring is somehow inherent in human naure.

· 4 ·

Another, perhaps more pervasive, tradition in which we understand compassion also hails from the Enlightenment. Although utilitarianism has been popularized in ways that neither its originators would recognize nor its contemporary advocates concur with, its main arguments can be traced to the writings of David Hume, Jeremy Bentham, and John Stuart Mill in the eighteenth and nineteenth centuries. Utilitarianism is an ethical system and a political theory that stresses the consequences of actions for people in general; that is, an action's utility for the common good. Among its more debated tenets is the view that people can and should pursue their own interests, even their own pleasures, as a way of maximizing the good of all.

Like the biblical tradition and theories of natural instinct, utilitarianism has taken many forms. In the philosophical literature it sometimes means nothing more than judging behavior by its consequences. Thus, we might say that someone who helped a handicapped child *in order to* improve that child's life chances did so for a utilitarian reason. But utilitarianism usually implies something more specific than this kind of consequentialist reasoning. I want to limit the term here to motives that emphasize self-interest as well: accounts that focus on what the individual receives as a motive for helping others. A better example of utilitarianism, therefore, would be saying you helped a handicapped child in order to get a good feeling or to advance your career. When I say that utilitarianism is a tradition we use to explain our motives for caring, then, I do not mean that people necessarily draw upon the entire tradition. Rather, it is a legacy that has helped shape arguments about the legitimacy of self-interest, even as a motive for being altruistic.[9]

Well before the work of Hume, Bentham, and Mill, a convenient catalog of the various self-interested reasons for doing good had been provided by Thomas Hobbes. Among the motives he listed for what he called "free-gift" were the hope of friendship, of service, of gaining a reputation for magnanimity, of heavenly reward, and of freeing the mind from pain.[10]

Sometimes, it appears, Hobbes's catalog has become the main inspiration in contemporary appeals for compassion. In a newspaper article encouraging young people to spend their summers doing volunteer work, for example, one reads: "Besides providing a sense of satisfaction and some practical job experience, volunteering during high school can also pay off when going to college." After implying that scholarships might be the reward, the article also cautions against purely selfless behavior: "Doing something that is unfulfilling, and not getting paid to boot, could be extremely frustrating."[11] Another writer, taking a critical view of such appeals, observes that giving and caring are often done "to assuage guilt, to look generous, curry favor, observe a ritual, sell a bill of goods, buy attention or affection, earn a return gift, keep peace in the family; and for darker purposes as well."[12]

Blatant utilitarianism was no stranger to the accounts people gave in the interviews. Janet Russo, we saw, admitted that she volunteered at the women's center in order to make friends. Others saw helping as a kind of bargain, a form of insurance that increases the chances of receiving help from others when you need it. As one person explained, "If you help other people when they are in trouble, maybe someday if you fall into times of distress, there will be someone willing to help you too."

Some admitted their caring had not been motivated so much by seeing a need itself as by realizing that caring could get them something they wanted. A college student who had done volunteer work in high school with disadvantaged children acknowledged that he needed fifty hours of volunteer work to graduate from his high school, so he put in his hours at a center for inner-city kids. Others invoked a kind of reverse utilitarianism. Recognizing they had already gotten something, they gave of themselves as a way of paying their debts. Marge Det-weiler's view of her obligation to help AA illustrates this kind of account.

Utilitarianism also colored the accounts of many who emphasized the psychological aspects of their motivation. These accounts stressed some psychological gratification as the reason for helping others. A desire to feel worthwhile or good about oneself was often emphasized. In some instances guilt reduction served as the primary motive. As one person acknowledged, "Spending time on someone else relieved me of some of my guilt from spending so much time in my own world." In Jack Casey's account, relief from fear and anxiety played a prominent role.

The survey gave evidence of the extent to which the public at large subscribes to utilitarian ideas as reasons for caring. Of the various reasons people were asked to respond to, the one that evoked the most positive reaction of all was the statement "It makes me feel good about myself when I care for others." Two persons in three (64 percent) said this was a major reason for them to be kind and caring. Another 29 percent said it was a minor reason. Only 5 percent said they did not consider it a reason to be kind and caring.

More overt expressions of utilitarian thinking received less assent in the survey, but still evoked supportive responses from a sizable minority of the public. A third (32 percent), for example, indicated that the statement "If I am kind, others will be kind to me" was a major reason for them to be kind and caring. Another third (36 percent) listed this as a minor reason, while 29 percent said it was not among their reasons for caring. An even more straightforward expression of utilitarianism— "Being kind and considerate helps me get what I want in life"—evoked support as a major reason from one person in four (24 percent), while another third of the sample (35 percent) said this was a minor reason to be caring; 38 percent said it was not one of their reasons.

Judging from these responses, a majority of the American public may be unwilling to claim blatantly utilitarian arguments as the primary motive for being compassionate. But a majority does attach some importance to such explanations. There is also wide consensus that some form of utilitarian bargain is implicit in all helping behavior. For example, 91 percent registered agreement with the statement "When you help someone in need, you get as much from it as they do." Only a slightly smaller proportion (78 percent) agreed with the statement "If I help others, it is likely that someone will help me when I am in need."

· 5 ·

One other tradition supplies an important repertoire with which to interpret our motives for compassion. It often mixes with the other traditions we have just considered. But it is also important in its own right (as we shall see). It is a secular version of the religious teaching that loving one's neighbor is of value. It emphasizes the role of desire or will: what motivates one to care is simply the desire, the wish, the decision to show compassion. It gains reinforcement from the fact that so much of our charitable behavior is institutionalized in the so-called voluntary sector—the sector where people presumably care simply because they want to. It is part of the logic that grows from our society's emphasis on freedom, individual autonomy, and willpower.[13]

Some of the interviews contained examples of statements about caring simply because one had a desire to do so. A black woman who worked as a pastor in a large urban church expressed the idea in these words: "When I do volunteer work, nobody tells me to do this or do that; it's what I want to do; it reflects my talents and interests." Another person, a Jewish man who did volunteer work each week with children in a mental hospital, explained, "I wanted to work with young people." More simply, another woman, when asked why she became involved in a prison visitation program, paused for a long time and then remarked, "I guess I just wanted to help them."

The evidence from national surveys on this kind of account is mixed in a curious way that I will try to explain later. When posed with already formulated statements, survey respondents frequently select answers that emphasize a voluntary commitment to altruistic values. For example, 56 percent of the respondents in one study selected "I wanted to do something useful"

56

as the main reason they had become involved in volunteer work. These were higher percentages than those selecting any of the other reasons listed.[14] In my survey 42 percent of the respondents selected the statement "I want to give of myself for the benefit of others" as a major reason for being kind and caring. Another 39 percent selected this statement as a minor reason. Only 15 percent said it was not a reason for their being kind and caring.

When respondents are not given statements to select, though, they seldom voluntarily articulate something that resembles a purely altruistic reason for caring. For example, in the first study I just cited, people volunteered a number of pragmatic reasons for giving to charities, such as the organization being a worthy cause or doing good work or helping the poor. But these reasons focused on the quality and goals of the organization; they were not framed in terms of the respondent's own desires to give, to help, or to care. The only reasons of this kind—well down the list in terms of the percentage of respondents who volunteered them—were remarks about feeling obligated or responsible to help the needy. The people we talked to at greater length about their volunteer activities were also reluctant to offer unsolicited accounts that simply focused on altruistic motivations.

· 6 ·

When those who remembered her paused in 1960 to commemorate the one hundredth anniversary of Jane Addams's birth and the twenty-fifth anniversary of her death, accounts of her motives sprung up like flowers around her grave. Commentators provided reconstructions of why she had given her life to help the poor. Their accounts could in no way influence what she did. But they linked her behavior with the various institutional domains contending with each other to help the poor. Religious leaders searched for clues that she had been motivated by religious impulses, despite her disavowals of religious sentiments; one concluded that "Miss Addams was a theist and a liberal Christian whose motivation came primarily from the ethical teachings of Jesus."[15] Some intimated that she had been more heavily influenced by utilitarianism through her association with John Dewey or socialism through contacts with the Fabians in Great Britain. Others composed narratives that drew on the repertoires of natural instinct, self-interest, and willpower. All their accounts were attempts to associate Jane Addams with some larger tradition—to draw out connections that told how to understand her, but also that reinforced certain cultural traditions by turning her into a metaphor for those traditions.

This, it seems to me, is the cultural significance of accounts. Motive-talk provides connections with our cultural heritage. It associates us with the various values we have been taught to accord prominence. It tells others that we cherish these values. Our ability to care may not depend on giving one account rather than another. But being able to give some account makes it possible to conceive of our behavior as caring. By linking it with broader values we place it in a context. Our accounts define the cultural meaning of our caring; our caring in turn becomes a reflection of our broader values.

In our society we associate caring with the altruistic values we cherish but also with our individualism. We do this as we select from various repertoires to give accounts of our motives for caring. Utilitarian accounts are associated with valuing self-interest, freedom, and success. Accounts emphasizing voluntaristic motives are associated with holding broader altruistic values; religious accounts, with broader religious values.[16] But, just as we saw in the case of values, we also give mixed accounts. Like our values, our accounts combine both altruistic and utilitarian motives. These domains are no less separate in motive-talk than in the realm of values. We need to go beyond repertoires, then, to see how the scores selected are arranged.

· 7 ·

The languages of biblical tradition, nature, utilitarianism, and voluntarism provide only the rudiments, the themes, the categories on which we draw to account for caring. They are the terms of debate but not the debate. They provide only a lexicon; they serve as a pool of terms, not as the structure of what is said. Indeed, the terms of this lexicon create their own deeper problem. They pose dilemmas for their speakers. The meaningfulness of accounts hinges as much on resolving these dilemmas as on mastering an appropriate lexicon.[17]

The vocabulary of motives raises deeper dilemmas because it is too rich, not (as some have argued) because it is too lean. "Motive" in the singular is a word we seldom hear at all, except in murder mysteries where establishing a motive is part of successful sleuthing. And even there, motives are seldom so simple, as Carlo Emilio Gadda has written in one of his novels: "The apparent motive, the principal motive was, of course, single. But the crime was the effect of a whole list of motives which had blown on it in a whirlwind . . . and had ended by pressing into the vortex of the crime the enfeebled 'reason of the world.' Like wringing the neck of a chicken."[18]

We have an overabundance of repertoires to draw on to account for our caring. If large proportions of the population say each of the reasons they are offered provides a major argument for being kind, then being kind is, we might say, culturally overdetermined—like wringing the neck of a chicken. Our problem is not finding one suitable account but deciding among multiple accounts—deciding which one is most plausible or, more likely, deciding which combination to put together and how best to combine them. We saw Jack Casey, for example, wrestling with a plethora of accounts. In the survey data, too, most people selected more than one argument as a major reason for trying to be caring: three persons in four selected at least two as major reasons, more than half chose at least three, a quarter chose five or more.[19]

Why is this a problem, especially when those who pick more reasons for caring are actually more likely to be involved in caring activities?[20] The problem is pluralism. If one can think of a dozen equally plausible reasons for doing something, then what exactly is the status of reasons at all? And even if one can narrow the field to a few reasons, how does one find a plausible way to put them together? Must one choose a dominant explanation in order to persuade? Or does a plurality of interpretations itself constitute a form of persuasion?

Pluralism in our society comes in several varieties, only some of which present dilemmas for us when we speak about our motives. Some readers may remember a television commercial for a foreign automobile. As the proud owner of a new sedan stands beside his vehicle, a voice-over says, "Give me one good reason why you purchased X." The owner responds: "Fuel-injected engine, overhead cam, power brakes, power steering, air conditioning, 5,000-mile warranty. . . ." The voice-over interrupts: "I said ONE." And without hesitation the owner responds jauntily: "Take your pick." This is not the kind of pluralism of reasons that creates problems. We can indeed take our pick because all the reasons given are of the same kind. Any one will substitute for the others. The more reasons we can think of, therefore, the more likely we are to buy. That is the advertiser's point.

A second kind of pluralism that also does not constitute a dilemma—but is often mistakenly thought to—is what we typically refer to as cultural pluralism. Ours is a society in which we celebrate cultural pluralism: racial and ethnic diversity, religious pluralism, a multiplicity of ideologies, tastes, and traditions. This pluralism may be difficult to manage politically at times, but it becomes an ethical dilemma only when it is internalized by an individual in a certain way. I can easily identify myself as a white male Protestant, for example, and still recognize that there are many others who may be black or Hispanic, female, Catholic or Jewish. When pluralism becomes a problem is when I decide that I, myself, want to be all these things.

If I announce to you that I am a confirmed fundamentalist Baptist, but also consider myself a devout Catholic, an observant Jew, a Zen Buddhist, and an atheist, you are likely to have difficulty knowing what to think of me. You may go away with the cynical view that religious identities have become a bit superfluous in my case. Your cynicism seems justified because you still take religious identities seriously. You believe it must matter whether someone is a Baptist or an atheist, and therefore you have trouble seeing how I can be both.

In a less-extreme form, this is why pluralism is problematic in the case of motives for caring. On the one hand, we have been exposed to various repertoires from which to select alternative accounts of our motives and we do in fact choose several of these accounts. On the other hand, we still retain the view that some accounts are better than others, that there are good motives and bad motives, that our motives should in some sense be pure, or at least matter.

A volunteer quoted in a popular book on caring remarked: "If I stop to think about it, I help out for all kinds of reasons. Maybe it's because I should; it's a matter of responsibility. But there's usually a maze of other motives: a need for self-esteem, approval, status, power; the desire to feel useful, find intimacy, pay back some debt."[21] Her tone was breezy, like that of the man in the car commercial. And yet her choice of words betrayed her. Why did she say "if I stop to think about it"? Why did she insert the word "maybe"? And why the curious reference to a maze?

Recall what I reported about each of the three individuals I discussed in the previous chapter. I reported that Jack Casey discussed social and psychological gratifications as reasons for joining the rescue squad. But he sensed that self-interest was not sufficient to account for his behavior. He mentioned other motives as well: the way he had been raised, his desire to help others, his fears, his personality traits, his talents. Unlike the man in the commercial, he did not simply list all these motives and then say, "Take your pick." He worried out loud about the adequacy of certain parts of his account. Having a multiplicity of accounts was important to him but also problematic.

The same was true of Marge Detweiler and Janet Russo, even though both were somewhat better able than Jack to settle on one primary account. Marge was willing to say she gave to AA primarily because she was grateful to it for saving her life; Janet, to say that she volunteered at the women's center for selfish reasons. But both went beyond these primary accounts: Marge talked about selfish reasons for her involvement, Janet discussed other reasons she thought were purer. Like Jack, both distinguished among gradations of self-interest and altruism; both implied that purity of motives was important.

None of the three gave a completely cynical answer to the question of motives. They did not respond that motives were simply unimportant. They did, however, open the door to cynicism in two ways. They did so partly by admitting that the question of motives was unresolved in their own minds. Their self-reflective "I wonder why I do" stood out by virtue of its candor. They also opened the door to cynicism by, as it were, protesting too much. A skeptical listener, especially in Jack's case, could not help wondering if all the talk about complex motives may not have been window dressing for one very simple motive that he was unwilling to acknowledge. As our interlocutor schooled in rational-choice theory suggested in the last chapter, Jack hopes to become a doctor and all this experience will help him get into medical school.

· 8 ·

Whether we wish to impute an interpretation of this kind to Jack or not, the fact is that we live in an era when all accounts of motives have become subject to doubt. Directly or indirectly, we have been deeply influenced by Freud, Marx, Nietzsche, and other masters of suspicion. They have taught us that our motives are not always what they seem. We live in a world of false consciousness, of illusion, that must be, as Paul Ricoeur observes, demystified through an "exercise of suspicion."[22] Our accounts may seem pure and laudable and yet mask a dark side that unconsciously dominates our souls. What we reveal through our accounts about ourselves also conceals. For all our fine rhetoric, our deeds are more important than our doctrines. Thus, it is not any one account that we must treat with suspicion, but accounting itself: the whole currency must be devalued.

Cynicism of this kind was not absent from the remarks of those interviewed. One person, when asked if he had any further comments, remarked that he could have answered some of the questions about motives in ten different ways. Another man expressed his cynicism about motives this way: "Somebody can stand up and say they're doing nice things to pay back their dear old Aunt Edna who's now departed. Who cares? They can say anything they want to. As long as they're doing nice things, it doesn't matter." A young woman expressed a similar view: "I've never been too concerned about motivation as long as some good was done." In the survey there were also signs of widespread cynicism about the motives driving voluntarism.[23] My point here, though, is not so much that voluntarism generates cynicism, but that cynicism is one of the ways in which we respond to motives themselves. If, as I say, you can give me a dozen reasons for doing something, then why should I take any of those reasons very seriously?

But cynicism has never been able to triumph completely. Despite the fact that our culture makes us suspicious of motives, we are unable and unwilling simply to abandon the question. We are not content to say something just to get an interlocutor off our backs when we know this is not at all what we mean. For all the cynicism about motives, compassion is still understood as an act that somehow reflects our inner beings.

We have many ways of distinguishing our inner beings from the world outside ourselves. But we do not believe we can completely separate the two. As one writer suggests, "the one cared-for sees the concern, delight, or interest in the eyes of the one-caring."[24] What lies within cannot be concealed. Our inner feelings come out in subtle ways. And when they do, they influence our behavior, especially when we interact with someone we care about. The very act of caring may be sabotaged by not having the right motives. The same writer argues that bad motives will cause the one cared for to be resentful, whereas good motives will make the recipient glow, grow, and feel "not so much that he has been given something as that something has been added to him."[25]

Pluralism, then, is problematic because of the way our understanding of our selves intersects with the culture in which we live. We are, on the one hand, exposed to a multiplicity of languages about motives. We learn these languages and find them useful in accounting for our behavior because we interact with many different kinds of people and because we are multifaceted individuals. Indeed, it is this multifaceted quality of our selves that constitutes our individuality. We are, on the other hand, unwilling to dismiss motives as being superfluous to our behavior. We believe in an inner self that can find expression in our behavior. This too is part of our individuality. Especially in caring relationships, we want our behavior to reflect our inner selves. And our talk about motives provides the connection between the two.

In short, we need ways to account for our motives that allow us to be both pluralistic and pure—to give multiple accounts and yet to give them in a way that does not diminish their importance. To show how we do this I need to introduce three new voices into the discussion—those of Martin Barnes, Elgin Perry, and Susan Robbins.

· 9 ·

Martin Barnes at age forty is a typical career man who has climbed the ladder of promotions in his company with considerable skill. A tall, attractive man with dark brown hair and mustache, he works as a budget administrator for Cenco, a large utility company in one of the southern states. Seated in the fifth-floor conference room of a downtown office building overlooking the city, he exudes the warm confidence of a man used to dealing with people. Father of two, a member of the Episcopal church, and the owner of a cattle ranch he operates on the side, he seems to know well how to live the comfortable life. But for the past five years he has devoted many of his lunch hours to a community program called Meals on Wheels. Like similar programs in other communities, this one receives federal money to purchase hot meals and relies on volunteers to deliver them to elderly people who are unable to get out or cook for themselves. Martin is currently serving his third term as president of the organization. What he still enjoys most, though, is delivering the meals. Sometimes he has so many that it takes nearly two hours to cover his route. On those days he comes to work at 7:00 in the morning in order to have the time he needs at noon for his deliveries. Why does he do it?

"About ten years ago," Martin explains, "I became involved with Jaycees. They had lots of business and commercial projects I really had no interest in. The project I liked was Toys for Tots. When I turned thirty-four, though, I was too old for Jaycees, so there was about a two-year period when I wasn't involved in much of anything. Then one day I read in the company newspaper that Meals on Wheels needed volunteers. So I joined.

"I remember when I first joined the Jaycees," Martin continues, pausing for a moment to reflect more closely on his motives. "I was working with this guy and he said, 'Come to a Jaycee meeting with me.' I told him no. I said I just don't have the time for it. But finally after his insistence I did go to one meeting. I decided to join, but I wasn't really very enthusiastic about it. After a while I got involved with the Toys for Tots program. And I realized the good feeling and the fulfillment that comes from all that."

Again he stops for a moment to reflect. "You know," he continues, "you can search for wealth, and you can search for fame, and you can search for anything, but I'm convinced that true, true happiness in life comes, I think, from helping other people." Then, changing the tone of his voice slightly, he remarks, "I have people say to me, 'Oh Martin, you're doing so many things.' Or they try to make me seem like such a great guy. But I say, 'Look, wait, I'm not, I'm doing it for a very selfish reason: it makes me happy.'" As if to drive home the point, he thinks for a moment and then concludes: "Albert Schweitzer once said (I've used this a couple of times in speeches, although it's not verbatim), 'I know not which of you will find happiness, but I do know those of you who find true happiness are those who seek and learn how to serve.' That one sentence tells it all."

· 10 ·

As I played and replayed the tape of Martin's interview, I was struck by how ordinary his answer was. It conveyed some eloquence and sophistication: not everyone quotes extemporaneously from Albert Schweitzer. But otherwise the whole account was quite mundane. Martin had joined the Jaycees because a coworker asked him to attend a meeting. He became involved in Toys for Tots and liked it. Later on he became active in Meals on Wheels and enjoyed that too. It all seemed quite ordinary. And then it hit me: that was the point. Yes, it did seem ordinary, but why? What made it, so to speak, a normal account, a story that sounded familiar, that provided an acceptable answer to the question of motives?

Elgin Perry is the same age as Martin Barnes. He also works in an office building in a southern city. But there the similarities stop. Martin Barnes is white; Elgin Perry is black. He has taken some college courses, but was never graduated. At present he works as an assistant in a government-sponsored job-training program. His work consists mostly of routine clerical tasks: keeping records, entering data into the program's computer, paperwork. He is a slender man, below average in height, and wears a small gold hoop earring in his left ear. Although he expresses doubt that he will have very much to say, he talks easily for two hours.

Much of the conversation focuses on his volunteer activities. He is currently tutoring under the auspices of a volunteer program he refers to as LVA. The purpose of the program is to help slow readers and the illiterate learn to read proficiently. For the past four months he has been tutoring one man twice a week, for an hour each time.

When asked why he became involved with literacy tutoring, Elgin explains: "I had the idea at one time of becoming a teacher. I enjoyed the teachers I had in junior high and high school and thought I'd like being one. Tutoring is a sort of teaching. The major thing I do with tutoring is helping people with problems. I got started with literacy tutoring because a young man came into my office one day and said he was interested in getting a job. But more than that, he said he'd like to learn to read. And it sort of got me, you know, it sort of touched a nerve. It made me feel I really ought to do something to help people like that. Here was a person who needed a job and couldn't get one because he didn't know how to read. So where does he turn for help? That's how I found out about LVA and got myself involved."

That is all. Again, I am struck by the brevity, the simplicity of the account. Some of my other questions later on prompt Elgin Perry to say more about motives—how he understands them, how he puts different motives together, what he thinks motivates other people to be kind and compassionate. But for now, this is his account, all he seems to feel it necessary to say about why he became a literacy volunteer.

· 11 ·

The other person I want to introduce is Susan Robbins. She is a remarkable woman, the kind of person who makes doing research worth the experience. Susan is a forty-six-year-old physician. She grew up in the rural Midwest. Her parents were dirt-poor and uneducated. The schools she attended as a child were extremely deficient, she admits as she thinks back. But she was exceptionally bright and worked hard. When she was sixteen she went away to college. After that she went on to medical school, where she met her husband. During their internship they applied to work in Africa but were turned down. She then spent several years working on a residency in pediatric cardiology. Now she has her own practice, heads the pediatric cardiology unit in a large urban hospital, and teaches part-time at the medical school affiliated with a local university.

Susan lives with her husband and their teenage son in a modern, cedar-shingled home nestled in the woods in an exclusive rural area several miles from the city. A large pasture spans the front of the house, and to the rear lies a scenic vista of rolling terrain. Inside, the large, cathedral-ceilinged living room, massive stone fireplace, luxurious carpets, and ample couches all attest to the material benefits to be had from a successful career in medicine. Susan appears barefoot, dressed casually in slacks and sweater, her hair still wet from showering.

Like the others we have met thus far, Susan Robbins prides herself on being "her own person." She believes the comfortable life-style she enjoys is well deserved. Her success came from hard work and she thinks most people could be just as successful if they worked the way she did. She also takes pride in being different. Most people have cats or dogs; she raises goats, letting them graze the pasture out front and tending each one with special, individualized care. As further evidence of her individualism, she points to the fact that she has initiated many reforms at the hospital, including a ban on physicians wearing white "status gowns," as she calls them.

Susan's volunteer work, like Marge Detweiler's involvement in AA, grew out of a series of personal crises. While she was still working on her residency, she gave birth to a boy who died immediately. A few years later, a second baby died shortly after birth. For two years she thought she would never experience happiness again. The fact that she was working with terminally ill children every day in her job made the pain all the more acute. "I was doing follow-up on all our cardiology families who had lost babies or children," she recalls. "Nobody else was doing this; it was obviously a need. We'd call up these people and say how are you doing, been thinking about you, meet with them again if possible."

Susan had heard about an organization called Compassionate Friends (CF) that tried to help bereaved parents. She remembers one particular family whose son died of congenital heart disease. They told her about CF and suggested she get involved. But she did not: "I didn't have enough time and energy to be involved with more families who had lost children at that point." But a few years later she found she had more time and started attending CF meetings. For the past four years she has been an active supporter of the group. She meets formally with the group once a month, helps put out its newsletter, and uses it to talk with other people about their grief. On an informal basis she has cared for a wide range of people, from those suffering stillbirths, to middle-aged parents grieving for teenagers killed in automobile accidents, to families of suicide victims, to elderly people surviving the death of adult children.

Here is how she explained her motivation: "What motivated me in the first place was empathy for parents who had lost children. I'll never forget the first mother. Her little daughter had congenital heart disease and died as an infant. It took me a long time to say to anyone, 'I do know something of what you're going through because I lost two babies.' But that's what I said to her. She wrote me a letter and thanked me for sharing that with her. When I saw her back in follow-up, I said I was really reluctant to say that to anybody because I wasn't asking for sympathy; I was afraid as a physician that they might think I was asking for sympathy, and that wasn't my point. It was more empathy: I understand what you're going through. So that sort of got me started, even before CF was formed. All of this follow-up I was doing for families was just volunteer. It was not part of my job. Then when I had more time to branch out and do it with families other than my own patients, that's what motivated me to do the CF. I knew how important it was already."

Three very different individuals. Three very different kinds of caring activity. Three very different stories. I do not wish to diminish the uniqueness of each or to imply that any of the three is necessarily typical of others. But I do want to compare these accounts to see what makes them plausible, familiar, to see how each one resolves the problem of pluralism and other problems I shall mention later.

· 12 ·

Martin Barnes does not raise the problem of pluralism explicitly, but he very clearly deals with it by the way he frames his account. Rather than establishing one authoritative voice (his own) that carries the full weight of what he says, he constitutes his account as a series of encounters involving dialogue and multiple voices—interaction with a friend, dialogue with coworkers, and finally the voice of Albert Schweitzer. By situating his own voice among multiple voices, Martin is able to present himself in a variety of roles. At first he is the reluctant holdout who has no time; then he is the unenthusiastic apprentice; then the new convert having fun; then (in the eyes of his coworkers) the saint; then the humble pursuer of self-interest; and finally a mouthpiece for Albert Schweitzer. He tells us explicitly that enjoyment is one of his motives. But through the multiple roles he plays we also understand that there are likely to be multiple motives. And rather than having to take only one position among these multiple motives, Martin is able to let all of them have a place in his account.

Elgin Perry's account is shorter and more straightforward than that of Martin Barnes. Rather than presenting multiple voices and casting himself in multiple roles, Elgin Perry reveals how an account can be constructed when only one voice is presented. His account implicitly circumvents the problem of pluralism by completely personalizing the question of motives. Rather than suggesting that there might be other ways of thinking or general rules of compassion to be debated, he focuses the story on his encounter with one individual who came seeking help. The feelings involved, the response, the reasons for responding, then, are entirely idiosyncratic—specifically associated with this situation alone.

Susan Robbins's account falls somewhere between the other two in its style of coping with the problem of pluralism. She is clearly aware of the problem one faces in giving a satisfactory account of one's motives. We know this from other things she said in her interview; we also know it because she says so in the account itself (when she mentions worrying about what a physician can and cannot say). She in fact offers one motive— empathy—and consistently sticks with this explanation of her behavior. She is in a good position to do this because of her own bereavement. Like Marge Detweiler's encounter with alcoholism, this experience makes it possible for her to give a fairly straightforward account. Yet the interesting thing about this account is that she immediately places it in a situation in the same way Martin Barnes and Elgin Perry did. She recalls her encounter with the mother of a child who died of congenital heart disease. And like Martin Barnes, the retelling of this event allows her to introduce several voices into the account. She is able now to objectify her statement about empathy by repeating it as a quote of what she apparently told the mother: "I do know something of what you're going through because I lost two babies." Through the voice of the mother she is able to enhance the credibility of this statement, and the mother thanks her for it. In the rest of the dialogue she is able to confess her own misgivings about the statement and deny that she made it to get sympathy for herself. In this sense she asserts the purity of her motives in the face of a plurality of interpretations.

These three accounts illustrate the complexity of motive-talk. It is not just a matter of selecting from one or more repertoires. Because multiple vocabularies are invoked, they have to be organized in a way that is credible, that does not immediately result in suspicion. Textualizing some of what one says by introducing multiple speakers is one strategy. Situationalizing one's account is another. Subjectivizing it is still another.

Textualization is a particularly effective strategy because it allows one to invoke an authoritative voice, as Martin Barnes did in quoting Schweitzer, without necessarily taking a definitive stand on what that voice says. Textualization also permits one to situationalize statements, rather than having to offer them as generalizations. The following example illustrates both: "I have had somebody say to me that you need to pay back something to the community, no matter who you are, and I think I agree with that. If all you do is take, because a lot of us are very lucky. . . . I know, well, personally, with my daughter, a lot of times she's miserable and doesn't know why, and I wish I could say to her, 'If you'd just help, you'd feel better.'" The speaker establishes a second authoritative voice with whom she can merely agree (but presumably retreat from if challenged). Then she tries to articulate her own motives as a general principle, but finds it necessary to correct herself in midsentence. At this point, she situationalizes the account by posing a conversation with her daughter and then quoting herself.

Another example that shows how situationalizing our accounts deals with the problem of pluralism came from a woman who had recently volunteered a day to help with Special Olympics: "I suppose I became involved for many reasons," she said, "but the main one was Elizabeth. She's eleven years old and has Down's Syndrome. Her family and mine are very close and she's participated in Special Olympics for several years. I went with her and her mother once and saw what a special and exciting day this is for the participants."

It is interesting to observe that this account makes reference explicitly to the problem of pluralism ("I suppose I became involved for many reasons"). The speaker recognizes that she could give a plurality of accounts and probably senses that no one of these would be fully satisfactory to herself or her audience. Thus she singles out, not one of them, but a person. Elizabeth is someone she knows. She has a special relationship with Elizabeth, a personal relationship. She also situationalizes her account by alluding to the feelings she had the day she attended Special Olympics with Elizabeth and her mother. The implication is that these feelings were so highly personal that they cannot be described in any other way, and yet they would be understandable to anyone who had been in the situation or one like it.

Subjective language is present in all these accounts, especially in their emphasis on feelings, but sometimes even in the choice of particular words (the awkward insertion of "I think" in Martin Barnes's otherwise authoritative pronouncement about happiness in life). Here is another example, a rather straightforward, matter-of-fact account given by a college student to explain why she gave support to an acquaintance who

71

was going through a troubled time in her life: "I felt sorry for her and I felt she needed company. I was afraid she might try to kill herself again and I didn't want her to have the opportunity." Nothing is very special about this account: it is composed of four simple assertions, two in each sentence, joined by the conjunction "and." Yet the striking thing is that all four of these assertions begin with the word "I." Three of them link "I" with a feeling, and the fourth links it with a desire. The account is thus totally subjectivized. The speaker makes no assertions that could be contradicted in a pluralistic setting because all her assertions refer to subjective states within herself.

· 13 ·

A second tension that influences the way accounts of caring are constructed in our society is the tension between deviance and normality. We feel compelled to account for our motives because we believe caring is in some ways deviant, the exception rather than the rule. I do not mean it is deviant statistically. If 45 percent of the population is currently involved in volunteer work, this proportion is not deviant numerically—not in the same way a black Muslim of Jewish descent might be, or someone with an IQ of 180. The deviance of caring occurs differently, in ways that are reflections of our culture.

Despite its numeric prevalence, compassion is considered unusual by the majority of the population. As we saw earlier, most of us think people in our society are basically selfish instead of helpful or concerned about the needy. We also think our society is becoming more selfish, not more compassionate. If we think of ourselves as caring individuals, as most of us do, we therefore think of ourselves as being different from the social norm.

The norms of material success and a comfortable life are well institutionalized. Advertising suggests that everyone aspires to them. Our economy operates on self-interest. Helping the needy may be institutionalized, but it is pictured as the exception rather than the rule. Volunteers are unusual, more dedicated than most, people with special gifts—deviant in a positive sense, but deviant nonetheless.

Caring may also seem deviant because it occurs in special settings and under unusual circumstances. Most people work at
their jobs every day. If they do volunteer work, it is at odd moments on weekends or in the evening. They typically give only
a few hours a week compared to the forty they spend at work.
Besides this, caring is popularly associated with crises, accidents, exceptional events—someone stalled on the highway, a
beggar who happens to catch our eye, an illness in the family.
There may be thousands—millions—who respond to these
needs. But they generally do so individually, not in some collective surge that involves the entire neighborhood. For every
person who stops to help someone on the highway or gives a
beggar a dollar bill, hundreds of others pass by.

The relation between motive-talk and the deviance of caring
is, then, complex. There are tendencies in the larger society to
view caring as deviant. Thus it is one of those unusual activities, like refusing to pay one's taxes or shooting a neighbor,
that makes us feel compelled to give an account of ourselves.
At the same time, the way we account for our motives can
make an act seem more deviant or less deviant. One can depict
oneself as the messiah of mankind or merely an ordinary citizen taking an evening stroll. But in either case, some tension
between deviance and normality will remain. Too much deviance and our account fails to persuade; too little, and no account is needed at all.

The tension between deviance and normality was well evi-
denced in Jack Casey's account. Everything about him suggests
the exception rather than the rule: his becoming an Eagle
Scout, his rescue of the woman in the lake, his other daring
feats on the rescue squad, the sheer amount of energy he
seems to have. And yet he also plays up the normality of his
behavior, suggesting that his involvement in the rescue squad
was merely the result of a "normal progression" and picturing
himself as little more than a bystander at the accident he described in detail. The same tension is evident in Marge Detweiler's story—deviance (she knew she was going to commit
suicide), normality (just an ordinary person with limitations,
but one who wanted to help those who had helped her). Janet
Russo's story presents her as the most normal of the three: a
lonely housewife in a new community with experience in the

PTA. But one wonders if it takes this normality to balance the fact that her volunteer work is at a shelter for battered women. Her story would have been quite different had she begun by saying she had been abused too.

What I am suggesting is that accounts of motives for caring have to strike a balance between deviance and normality. It may not be enough simply to say one volunteered for religious reasons or for some utilitarian motive. If one's account makes caring too ordinary, then something special about it is lost. But if it seems too special, it remains unaccountable. How this is accomplished is likely to vary from story to story. It is, however, a tension that lies at the intersection of our individuality and our caring. Even though our accounts are of caring for others, they reflect the uniqueness we associate with our individuality.

· 14 ·

The deviance of caring, like the problem of pluralism, is also managed by situationalizing one's accounts. Martin Barnes's account handles the tension between deviance and normality by revealing the path by which he became involved in Meals on Wheels. The story in part normalizes this involvement, first by showing that it grew out of his work experience (the coworker who asked him to attend Jaycees), then by showing that he did not immediately become an enthusiastic participant, and finally by reporting his denial to his friends that he is doing anything altruistic. But the story also displays the deviance or abnormality of Martin's volunteering. It progressively moves its speaker from the position of simply being one of the gang (an employee with no time to spare) to an unconvinced member of Jaycees, to a person who finds special pleasure in Toys for Tots rather than the more prominent Jaycee programs, to a person who is singled out by his colleagues for questioning and admiration, to an individual who establishes an implicit identification between himself and the stalwart medical emissary to Africa.

Like Martin Barnes, Elgin Perry normalizes his involvement by connecting it with his career interests and his job. He establishes his early career interests in teaching as a frame for the account and then shows that it was an encounter in his office that led to his involvement. At the same time, by focusing on an encounter with one individual, he gives the impression that this may have been an idiosyncratic occurrence. He might still just be Elgin Perry the employee rather than Elgin Perry the volunteer, had this one person not happened into his office. There is even a small sense of mystery about the encounter: a man identified only as "a young man" comes in "one day" and says only that he wants a job and "more than that" wants to read.

Susan Robbins is clearly a deviant—something we soon learn from seeing her goats and learning that she began college at the age of sixteen, but in the context of her account itself, something we immediately realize when she reveals that two of her babies died. That revelation, given in the context of empathizing with a mother whose own baby has died, establishes the unusual character of Susan Robbins and the kind of caring she does. But, like Martin Barnes and Elgin Perry, she also normalizes her behavior by associating it with her work. She could have begun her account by telling about the trauma of the death of her babies. Instead she tells about her work as a doctor. Like both Martin and Elgin, she establishes a frame for her account by going back one stage in her life prior to becoming involved in volunteer work. In Martin's case it was the Jaycees; in Elgin's case, his early interest in teaching; in hers, the work she did with terminally ill patients before joining Compassionate Friends.

Where the balance between deviance and normality is most evident is in accounts that tell of an experience that is both highly idiosyncratic and stylistically commonplace. The story I reported earlier about Elizabeth and Special Olympics provides a good illustration. The story emphasizes the idiosyncratic features of the speaker's relation to Elizabeth: it gives her a name, makes clear that she is an actual person with certain biographical characteristics, mentions the personal tie between families, and focuses on one specific encounter between Elizabeth and the speaker. Yet the story is also commonplace, framed in sufficiently general terms that anyone can identify with it. Elizabeth is eleven years old and has Down's syndrome; otherwise, she has no identifying characteristics. She can be the handicapped child anyone knows—from United Way advertisements or from one's neighborhood. She is also a friend, so even if the listener knows nobody with Down's syndrome, virtually any listener can identify with having a friend. It is notable too that the story concludes on a general note: the speaker saw that Special Olympics was an exciting day, not for Elizabeth, but for "the participants."

· 15 ·

Another axis around which accounts of caring revolve is the degree of voluntarism—the extent to which volition, will, choice, and therefore individual responsibility are involved. Jack Casey calls his caring the result of a natural progression. But is it really? We also come away with the impression that he was an active participant in some of the choices he made. Is it in some way possible to construct an account that preserves both—that takes us off the hook for some of our actions but gives us credit for them at the same time?[26]

This issue arises, I suspect, because we want to take some credit for our actions, but there is also a stigma against taking too much credit for them. On the one hand, caring is supposed to involve choice; voluntarism is, as we say, voluntary. Saying "I just wanted to help" is in some ways the best account we can give. Indeed, it is about the only account in the survey that was consistently associated with higher rates of actual helping behavior.[27] On the other hand, saying "I wanted to help" is a bit too brash. It raises skepticism.

Jack Casey, as I mentioned, sits on a review board that asks people why they want to join the rescue squad. He finds their answers fascinating, but he also registers suspicion of motives that sound too altruistic. "Sometimes they will say something like 'I want to go out and help people,' or 'I feel a need to help the public.'" Jack says he treats these answers with a grain of salt. "That tells me right then and there they aren't telling the truth. I don't think anyone could really sit there with a straight face and tell me that." Basically, Jack believes everybody has an ulterior motive for becoming involved. They might look on rescue-squad work as a noble activity, as a way of helping the community. But "deep down everybody has their own selfish reason; they're really doing it for themselves."

Why does he feel this way? In part it is because we have social norms against sounding too charitable. Compassion, our culture tells us, must truly arise from some selfish motive. Utilitarianism, sociobiology, and many therapeutic accounts explain it away, telling us that altruism is really self-interest. At the popular level, we call people who go around acting too charitable "bleeding hearts," "do-gooders," "Goody Two-Shoes." To avoid these labels, we censor ourselves. We try not to brag about helping someone. And if we give an account, we are likely to downplay our choice in the matter. In the extreme, we may even be apologetic. As one person said in telling about her volunteer work, "I know it sounds silly and irrelevant, but. . . ." Another broke off in midsentence. "This is really corny," she remarked. Several others admitted they were a bit embarrassed because they never talked about their caring with anyone.

· 16 ·

The stories people tell about their motives for caring usually strike a skillful balance between attributions of will and attributions that focus on circumstances. The ones that do not strike this balance stand out. For example, here is an account that adopts a totally passive form, addressing the issue of motivation by placing responsibility entirely on surrounding circumstances. Yong Kim, a man in his twenties, had first become involved in volunteer work as a high-school student. With several classmates he had helped run a soup kitchen on weekends. When asked to explain his motives for becoming involved, he responded: "My teacher, who was also the advisor to the student involvement organization, challenged us. He told us we really wouldn't know what it was like to be poor unless we were confronted with it face-to-face. Safe in our middle-class community we would never understand. Textbooks were no substitute for true experience. He suggested that we help out at a soup kitchen on Christmas Day. As a class we decided it would be an eye-opening experience." Yong's account reveals both that a decision was made and that there was a strong element of utilitarianism in this decision, or at least in the argument the teacher put forward. But by focusing on the teacher and the class, he has to accept very little responsibility either for the decision itself or for the utilitarian motives underlying this decision. As a result, his account conveys little sense of actual compassion or caring.

Accounts that put this much emphasis on circumstances are rare, however. It is more common to situationalize an account in a way that suggests a more dynamic relation between the speaker and the speaker's circumstances. In Martin Barnes's account, the tension between circumstances and volition is established and maintained in two ways. First, by casting himself in the role of a reluctant apprentice, he shows that he was heavily influenced by circumstances (the coworker who invited him, exposure to Jaycee programs), but that he asserted himself by making choices (Toys for Tots, Meals on Wheels). Second, the account specifically addresses the question of altruistic intent by reporting the dialogue he has with his colleagues. By having them say he is doing wonderful things, he implies that the perception of altruism in his case is at least justified. At the same time, by denying the validity of their perception and by calling his own acts selfish, he shows that he does not want simply to adopt the altruistic label.

The question of volition is dealt with in Elgin Perry's story in much the same way. He presents himself as a pawn of circumstances: he is simply seated in his office one day when a man walks in and asks for help. Like Rousseau's cattle moved by some natural instinct for one of the herd in pain, Elgin Perry finds that the man's request strikes a nerve (note the biological metaphor and the connotation of pain). But Elgin Perry also responds. He concludes by saying he became involved. We do not know exactly why; we know only that he acted.

Susan Robbins threads her account between circumstance and volition in much the same way. The happenstance of having two children die and working with bereaved parents was not of her choosing. She can in a sense excuse herself from being too kindhearted by pointing out that she simply happened to have these experiences. She does in fact note that she did not have time for a number of years to work with Compassionate Friends. But her story also shows clearly that she exercised some choice. She reveals this by saying that even though it had been difficult to do so, she decided to communicate empathy to the mother of the child who died.

Accounts that identify a particular person with whom the speaker interacts provide perhaps the most effective way of combining both a high level of volition and a high level of prompting by forces other than oneself. The story of Elizabeth again provides an example. It emphasizes the interaction the speaker has had with one individual and her family. Partly it focuses on external circumstances (the day at Special Olympics). But it also implies that the speaker made a choice. She thought about Elizabeth and decided to give a day as a volunteer the next time Special Olympics came to town.

· 17 ·

There is also the problem of how much rational calculation can be admitted in one's accounts. As we have seen, utilitarianism is a common method of justifying caring behavior in our society. Being motivated by a desire for good feelings, career aspirations, wanting to avoid loneliness, and social recognition were all mentioned in various accounts. Yet there are restrictions on what can and cannot be said about these utilitarian motives.

Some of these restrictions are quite simple. Being motivated by a desire for good feelings is more acceptable to most people than doing something charitable in the hope of gaining monetary returns or even prestige. But these distinctions are usually made in reference to what one receives, not to one's motivations. The two are sharply separated in most people's minds, as we saw in Jack Casey's insistence that "paybacks" were different from motivations.

The more subtle restriction I want to focus on here is between doing something for a utilitarian reason and doing something for a calculated reason. A utilitarian reason acknowledges that one may benefit from caring, but that one does not necessarily foresee this benefit specifically. It merely happens, or it may be desired unconsciously, but one does not plan ahead or try to figure out the balance between costs and benefits. Calculation, in contrast, suggests that one engages in caring with the full expectation worked out ahead of time that one will receive a specific benefit.

Calculation is the issue, not greed. Compassion is never displayed as a means to a greedy end. But greed aside, it is also supposed to involve spontaneity rather than rational planning. As one person explained, "You do what you can, but you don't talk about it and you don't try to count it." You do not count the benefits afterward; nor do you calculate them in advance.

A particularly poignant example of this norm appeared in a local newspaper not long ago. The story was about an elderly woman who needed a kidney transplant. Because of tissue compatibility, the most desirable donor was the woman's daughter. The daughter, realizing this, demanded that her mother sign over a large sum of money to her in advance. The story then quoted the mother's disappointment in her daughter. "What disappointed me most," she said, "was that my daughter could be so—." What? I thought the word was going to be "greedy." "What disappointed me most," she said, "was that my daughter could be so calculating."

· 18 ·

Martin Barnes structures his account in a way that leaves virtually no room for utilitarian calculation. He shows that he became involved at first reluctantly and unenthusiastically because of a friend's insistence. He then makes a point of establishing the correct sequence between involvement and thinking about pleasure: helping with Toys for Tots preceded finding out that he enjoyed it. Thus it is impossible to assume that he might have calculated in advance how to maximize his pleasure. He also truncates the rest of the story, telling nothing of what he may have been thinking about or feeling during the two years before he became involved in Meals on Wheels. It is, again, the prompting of external circumstances (the company newspaper) that leads him to volunteer for Meals on Wheels.

And his decision is presented as a spontaneous impulse: if he went home and calculated the potential costs and benefits, he discloses nothing of this process. Even the Schweitzer quote, which in one way might be interpreted as a utilitarian prescription for finding true happiness in life, contains its own denial of this interpretation. Schweitzer specifically states that he cannot predict who will find happiness.

Elgin Perry's story is a particularly clear example of how utilitarianism is implied but prevented from seeming like a motive involving premeditated calculation. Perry implies self-interest by setting the story in the context of his love of teaching: tutoring is partly a way of gratifying this interest, of obtaining satisfaction. But he rules out any suspicion we might have of calculation by focusing on his encounter with one individual, by having that individual ask for help, by suggesting that his own response was a kind of knee-jerk reaction involving sympathy for the man, by posing a rhetorical question, and then by simply asserting that he became involved. The story is highly truncated. What it leaves out is almost more interesting than what it says. Only after listening to Elgin Perry for two hours did I realize that people come into his office every day seeking jobs, that in all likelihood a large number of them have reading handicaps, that Elgin Perry has thought about this problem on many occasions, that he has actually taught in the past, that he is not entirely happy in his present job, and that tutoring may be a way of opening doors to some other job for himself. He skips over all these details. His account satisfies the bare rudiments of an explanation by focusing only on one encounter and his reaction to it.

In Susan Robbins's account there is no room for rational calculation either. Her report does not give any details about why she happened to specialize in pediatric cardiology. In all likelihood the death of her own infants may have had something to do with it. But she jumps over that, leaving the impression that it was the unexpected circumstance of her own bereavement and her job that forced her to become involved with Compassionate Friends. Nor does she say why she began doing follow-up with bereaved parents or what prompted her conversation with the mother. The account gives the impression of an un-

81

planned remark, an expression prompted simply by empathy. It also makes clear that the gratification received came later and was not anticipated.

In all three accounts what we might call truncation or glossing plays an important role. Here is another example. "I was walking uptown one day in the dead of winter. I saw a bum who was cold. I went up to him and gave him my coat and walked away. It was very spur-of-the-moment. I had several coats and he had none. There was very little thinking at all." For an account this brief it is interesting that two of the five sentences tell us directly that the act was so impulsive that no calculation could conceivably have been present. The speaker could have provided much more detail about the episode. He might have said, for instance, that the event occurred at the subway station just as the speaker was heading for home, that he and a buddy had just been arguing about how selfish it was to walk past all the bums on the street without giving them anything, or that they had just been to see a Broadway play about the poor. Any of this additional information might prompt the listener to suspect the speaker of having engaged in some explicit calculation: about being able to get home without really getting too cold, about making a good impression on his buddy, or about being moved by the message of the play. Instead, the act is portrayed as purely impulsive; no scheming is possible because no thought was present.

One further point. Jack Casey paused in the middle of his account to admit, "I've always wondered, why do I do these things?" His answer: "I don't know." Marge Detweiler caught herself in midsentence trying to explain why she needed people. "Hmm, I wonder why I do," she mused. Is it possible that people in our society just do not have a language to express their motives for caring?

Some observers have argued that the fundamental problem in our society is that we have lost the ability to put our public commitments into words. A closer look at Jack Casey and Marge Detweiler suggests otherwise. They did not simply say they had trouble understanding their motives, and then fall silent. Both spoke fluently and at great length, without prompting, about their motives. Their puzzled statements were, I believe, rhetorical devices. Expressing uncertainty about their motives created distance between them and their accounts. It signaled the provisional nature of their understandings of themselves. It demonstrated their self-reflectivity, thereby establishing a position as speaker that was different from that of the individual whose behavior they were explaining. "I don't know" was itself a valid response, one not to be dismissed, but to be recognized as a strategy for actually linking a conception of themselves with an understanding of their caring behavior.

· 19 ·

What do I make of all this? The problem of pluralism is the predicament of the modern self. The cynicism it sometimes generates in accounts of caring is no different from the cynicism it is capable of eliciting in all realms of modern life—from the cynicism of religious doubt to the cynicism of postmodern interpretation in the arts and literature. And yet life goes on in all these arenas, not so much because we isolate ourselves from this pluralism but because we connect ourselves to it with language. We manage it by situationalizing our accounts, by telling stories that embed values in specific contexts, that frame principles as particulars. We transform the pluralism of larger settings into the particular blend of our personal identities.

The questions of normality and volition and calculation are also the predicaments of our selves. Rugged individualism compels us to be different, to make our own choices, to rely on ourselves, to plan and orchestrate our lives to achieve our desired goals. But caring for others is not the antithesis of individualism. The two are linked narratively. It is in the framing of particularity that we imply the universal. The success of communication itself requires a blend of the two. Choice and constraint do not require separate narratives, but an account that brings them together. The very success of calculation often requires it to be concealed, at least from others, sometimes from ourselves. We define caring in our society as a behavior of choice, a special or unusual activity, one that in some way transcends or eludes rational prediction. Caring is a metaphor for our self-identity.

Motive-talk is the forum in which we work out the relation

between the inner selves of individuality and the altruism of caring. It allows us to have both. We are not compelled to select from either the vocabulary of self-interest or the vocabulary of voluntary compassion. We embrace utilitarianism but hedge our admissions through the dialogue among multiple voices that speak in our accounts. What one acknowledges, the other denies. In the exchange our inner selves remain separate—omnivoices reporting the textualized statements of others. We just as reluctantly acknowledge our altruism, but we contextualize it, limit it, show that it was a reaction rather than a general characteristic that might set us apart from the more self-interested reality in which we live.

It is both necessary in our culture to acknowledge that motives are as complex as our selves and valuable to deny that all motives are equally appropriate. Any number of motives for caring may be conceived, but only some are credited with importance in an account that emphasizes situational specifics. Caring is both special in a way that reflects our individuality and conventional in a way that associates us with the society in which we live. The personalization of our accounts emphasizes the former; their generic and formulaic style signals the latter. We associate caring with moral virtue and therefore with individual choice, but the utilitarianism of our culture limits the extent to which this virtue can be claimed. Our accounts weave the woof of volition through the warp of circumstance. They also truncate and obscure, lest suspicion of calculation arise.

The accounts of our motives, when all is said, are basically stories—highly personalized stories, not assertions of high-flown values, but formulaic expressions of ourselves. It is not the language of religion or philosophy, or of psychology or economics, from which these accounts are constructed, but the language of personal experience. Like all verbal accounts, accounts of motives vary from telling to telling. Yet there is a pattern as well. It resides not in the content but in the rules organizing this content. It consists of rhetorical strategies that make stories plausible within the particular cultural context in which we live.

Jack Casey's account, then, was a paradigm of my own. Although he drew from various repertoires (and my summary imposed themes on his comments), he felt more comfortable telling a story. He had told it before. It brought together the deep anxieties of his inner being and the circumstances demanding a caring response in one dramatic episode. It provided a turning point, an example from which to generalize, yet one that required no further generalization. He preserved his individuality by casting the event decidedly within his own biography. He emphasized his caring by describing his action, but he also disavowed pretension by casting himself as little more than a bystander, an apprentice wanting to learn. So did the others. Their stories scarcely gave a full or logical account of their motives. But they did provide an explanation of how and why these people had become involved in caring. Having stories to tell was a vitally important part of their caring. Their narratives reflected their own individualism and the culture that created it.

CHAPTER FOUR

Finding Fulfillment

HELPING PEOPLE makes you feel good. This is the message we hear again and again from volunteer agencies and fund-raisers. A Christian magazine with a large national circulation recently carried an advertisement by a well-known international relief agency. At the top was the familiar face of a needy child, dark-skinned, with large, sad eyes. Beside her picture in bold, black, underlined letters half an inch high was the word SPONSORSHIP. Below this, filling up nearly a quarter of the page in equally huge letters, were the words *It'll Make You Feel Good.* But in case the reader might have missed this message or not understood it, the ad contained more. Three times in quarter-inch bold section headings the message was repeated. *"You'll Feel Good . . .* knowing that you can help stop her hunger. *You'll Feel Good . . .* knowing that Jesus' love for children has been demonstrated through your compassion. *You'll Feel Good . . .* knowing that you're touching this hurting world." "Please become a sponsor today," it concluded: "You'll feel good about it."

The promise of good feelings is generally more subdued than this, but it is common nonetheless. An article in a popular psychology magazine about caring for the elderly highlighted the following sentence by placing it in the margin in italics with the first letter emphasized in red: "Caregivers experience subtle but sweet rewards for caring for frail loved ones."[1] The article itself described the stress and strain many care givers experience. But it also suggested that care can be better and more satisfying if care givers will only "define their situations more in terms of fulfillment than sacrifice."[2] An article in a local newspaper publicizing the work of a group called Singles Helping Others echoed the same sentiment. "We started as a group of young professionals who wanted to be more than yuppies," explained the group's spokesperson. Some members have lofty goals and put in a lot of time, he admitted, but on the whole "we still want to have a good time."

Research studies show that most people do in fact hold the belief that helping others is a good way of gaining fulfillment for yourself. One study, based on a nationally representative survey, found that virtually everyone regards helping behavior as a vital component of self-worth: 48 percent said their efforts to help others were "very important" to their basic sense of worth as a person and another 47 percent said these efforts were "somewhat important" to their self-worth. This study also demonstrated that those who donated time and money to charitable causes scored higher on various measures of self-esteem than persons who did not donate time and money.[3] In my survey, 51 percent of the public said they receive a great deal of personal fulfillment from doing things for people; another 38 percent said they receive a fair amount of fulfillment. Among those currently involved in charitable or social-service activities, 63 percent said doing things for people was a source of a great deal of fulfillment.

· 2 ·

It probably seems only natural to most of us that good feelings, satisfaction, and a sense of personal fulfillment or self-worth should be associated with efforts to help others. We are, after all, social creatures. Most of us, as we have seen, respond in surveys that we place high value on helping the needy. When we are in fact able to help them, the good feelings that result seem to provide their own testimony to the importance of these values. Yet the emphasis we place on good feelings needs to be examined critically. It is hard to imagine Jesus saying to his disciples, "Take up your cross and follow me—it'll make you feel good." Or a primitive tribesman describing the sweet rewards of inner fulfillment from offering tribal elders the fruits of his hunt. Or the mendicant Franciscans of the thirteenth century saying they still wanted to have a good time while ministering to the poor.

Thoughtful observers of our society do in fact voice concern about the emphasis we have come to place on good feelings. In a published interview, sociologist Robert N. Bellah argues that many of the things we cherish most deeply—family, virtue, religion, freedom—have come to be defended as matters only of personal preference. We have, he suggests, lost our capacity to defend these values in terms of any higher-order principles or universalistic claims. All we have left are arguments about the importance of certain kinds of behavior to the way we feel. But feelings, he fears, may not be an adequate basis for moral reasoning when the chips are down. Indeed, there may be something contradictory about defending impersonal or altruistic values in terms of the personal feelings we associate with them. "When we have to express everything that's loving and caring and socially responsible in terms of 'what it does for me,'" Bellah worries, "that begins to undercut the very nature of those practices."[4]

Theorist Daniel Bell has put the same concern in a broader framework. Our fascination with pleasurable feelings, he suggests, is symptomatic of the fact that we no longer believe in objective truth. Lacking faith, we fight off our fears through the pursuit of emotional gratification. It is evident that we do this in the realm of material consumption, buying adult toys and expensive clothes and gourmet foods that make us feel good. But it is equally apparent, he claims, that this quest characterizes all our social relationships as well. The collapse of our confidence in absolutes results in personal insecurity—a crisis of self-identity. To escape, we attempt to dissolve the boundaries between ourselves and others. We frantically pursue intimacy among friends and family, all the time in hopes of making ourselves feel better. We may do the same in our fleeting efforts to help strangers. We seek them out, offering to alleviate their burdens, but the underlying problem is how we feel about ourselves. We desperately want to be fulfilled, much more so than we desire to be of help.[5]

What these criticisms suggest is the need to probe the question of altruism and individualism from yet another angle. All this talk about good feelings and fulfillment—even if it is seen as a side benefit rather than a motive—suggests that our caring may be located more in the context of what it does for us, as individuals, than in a framework that emphasizes the other, the needy, or community relationships. Perhaps we have not transcended the "me decade" with a new commitment to caring for others; perhaps we have only carried the earlier fascination with ourselves forward to the present. The real question may not be whether we try to help others, but whether the giving we do is still mainly a way of giving to ourselves.

· 3 ·

I used the word "giving" twice in the last sentence. I did so to suggest a way of thinking about the place of good feelings, of fulfillment, in connection with caring. The helping behavior we engage in when we try to care for someone else can be thought of as a gift. We give something—usually an act of service of some kind—to that person. Put differently, our relationship is characterized by a gift that is transferred from the giver to the recipient. The presence of giving defines our relationship by defining our respective roles and the behavior that happens between us. Someone who tutors a person with learning deficiencies provides a service—a gift—that defines the tutor as a giver and the student as a recipient. The same is true when a rescue-squad member saves someone having a heart attack or a volunteer at a women's crisis center counsels someone who has been abused.

The idea of gift applies quite literally in most such cases because no fee is charged: the service is provided voluntarily, without pay. The service given is also like a gift because it consists of something discrete that has real value, symbolic value, or both. A birthday gift comes wrapped up in a box. It is a discrete object, not something amorphous or intangible, like health and happiness. And yet it stands for these amorphous intangibles. In addition to its real value—a sweater that can be worn to work—it communicates good wishes for health and happiness. The same is true of most acts of compassion. Given voluntarily, they take shape within a limited space and time dimension. Elgin Perry's tutoring happens twice a week for an hour or two and will continue only for a limited time. This discrete commodity or object that he transfers to his student has both real and symbolic value. It helps the student learn to read and enables him to find a job. It also expresses goodwill— it symbolizes one human being's care and compassion for another.

I emphasize that acts of compassion are discrete gifts that have real and symbolic value in order to suggest that they also embody, like any good or service, an investment of time and energy. Susan Robbins had to find the time in her busy schedule as a physician to give support to bereaved parents. Jack Casey had to invest a great deal of physical energy and even risk his life to pull the drowning woman from the lake. In some cases, like Jack's, the actual time and energy spent helping someone also represents many years spent acquiring the appropriate skills. But even in the most superficial acts of compassion, like tossing a quarter into the lap of a blind beggar on the street, some small investment of time and energy is involved. Gift giving, in short, is like purchasing a candy bar or spending an evening watching a baseball game: it requires an investment, an expenditure, of time or money or energy that might have been devoted to something else.

The analogy with buying candy or watching baseball seems crass, compared with helping a beggar or saving a life. But it seems crass only because in the former cases we can immediately see the return, the payoff, from our investment. A dollar invested at the vending machine brings out the candy and with it the nutrition or calories or satiation one expects to get in return. Gifts seem to defy this quality of other economic transactions. By their nature, they are given freely, without expectation of payment or other return. The dollar given to a beggar is not advance payment for some service you expect him or her to render; it is simply a gift. And yet anthropologists and sociologists who have studied gifts argue that something usually is in fact received in return.

In a valuable article written some time ago, sociologist Alvin Gouldner formulated this observation about gifts in what he termed "the norm of reciprocity."[6] Citing a wide variety of evidence from philosophy, literature, history, and anthropology, he argued that giving creates an asymmetry or imbalance in social relationships that people feel compelled in some way to rectify. In some contexts the norms of the situation may require only that you say a sincere "thank you" to the person who has given you a gift. In other circumstances you may be expected to give that person a gift of equal value sometime in the future. Other examples include performing menial services in return for a monetary good (as a serf might to a lord who had paid the serf's taxes), responding with deference or obeisance (as a subject might to a king), or living up to someone's expectations or carrying out his or her mission (as a child might for a parent). The transaction—which is now seen as a two-way exchange—defines the roles of each party to the exchange and, indeed, depends on each party having a separate and definable identity.

The idea of good feelings may be understandable within this framework of gifts and reciprocal exchange. Someone expends time and energy giving someone else the gift of tutoring or emotional support, and in return receives a good feeling, a sense of satisfaction, fulfillment. The service is, we might say, exchanged for a feeling. Or, viewed differently, the feeling provides compensation for the time and energy invested. This may be one way to understand what people mean when they say they derive fulfillment from caring for others. If so, we can see what else this understanding implies about our culture, and we can consider how good feelings compare with more traditional meanings of reciprocity.

The idea of reciprocity is indeed a common way in which people make sense of the good feelings they receive from helping others. But there are at least two other distinct ways in which people talk about these feelings. Comparing these three cultural motifs is thus a way to consider more carefully the relation between individualism and altruism in our society—and whether the critics are right when they accuse us of being more interested in ourselves than in the people we serve. Although the language of fulfillment is common to all three motifs, they differ significantly in the way they depict the self relating to others.

· 4 ·

Martin Barnes clearly exemplifies the logic of reciprocity in the way he talks about his volunteer work for Meals on Wheels. Although he is a humble man who, as we saw, chafes at the praise his coworkers sometimes heap on him, he has a clear sense of his own identity. He prides himself on the responsible position he holds at Cenco and takes delight in describing his cattle ranch. His sense of identity also comes through when he objectifies himself: his speech is sprinkled with references to "Martin Barnes." Having a distinct sense of himself also makes it possible for him to relate to the persons he cares for as distinct, separate individuals. Indeed, much of his conversation consists of stories about the various people to whom he has delivered meals. "The reason I've kept the same route," he explains, "is that I've established a friendship with the people on the route. I'd really hate just to leave one day and never get to see them again." They are individuals with distinct identities with whom he interacts.

Caring for people is, in Martin's view, a social transaction. He interacts with the people on his route, they interact with him; he gets to know them as individuals, they get to know him. "There's always some time for pleasantries, like: 'Have you seen your son recently?' Each time, as you grab a few sentences with them, it's like you have one long conversation with them and you get to know a lot about them. And likewise, they get to know things about you also."

When Martin speaks of what he receives from his volunteer work, he focuses on a feeling of fulfillment. Sensitive to the fact that he has been in the public eye as local president of Meals on Wheels, he discounts publicity as a meaningful reward. Just as he did in describing his motives, he does this by voicing the words of his coworkers and then disagreeing. "People here sometimes talk in a joking way about the television shows I've been on. They do it in a joking way, but I often sense they are showing their true feelings when they say it. I have gotten a lot of personal publicity—too much, in fact. No, the real thing I've gotten out of it is just that feeling inside when you've gone out and done something."

Not surprisingly, he situates his description of this feeling in the context of his interpersonal transactions with those he cares for. "You finish that day's work and you're worn out and tired, but there's just such a good feeling way down inside. To walk away from that elderly person who's very feebly standing there and says God bless you or the sincere thanks that radiates from their faces, it's hard to explain but it's the inside reward really." The sense of fulfillment is an emotional epilogue that completes the transaction. The fact that he gave something is evident from the comment about being worn out and tired. The fact that his recipient gave something in return is equally apparent. The elderly person stands there, speaks, expresses thanks, says "God bless you." "I remember this one particularly feeble lady and the way she said 'God bless you' was just so sincere I just wanted to reach out and hug her." The feeling evoked is prompted directly by the recipient's physical presence and her attitude. It signals symmetry, balance, closure in the exchange.

· 5 ·

To say that one feels fulfilled implies that one at some point must also feel empty. The giver must experience a deficit of some kind in order to become the recipient and complete the reciprocity of the transaction. In Martin Barnes's case a candid admission of such a deficit was an important feature of his biography. "About five years ago I think I came very close to suffering a nervous breakdown," he observed. "I'm convinced it came from job pressures and maybe even from civic pressures, because it was about the time I was chairing the Toys for Tots program. In any case I was spiraling downward, taking a nosedive. I felt really vulnerable and really helpless. I wanted to scream for help and was embarrassed to do it openly. I've never told anybody about it."

The upshot of this experience was that Martin felt he knew what it was like to hit bottom. It gives him a place, as it were, to put the good feelings he receives. It is a place that existed before his current involvement in caring activities. But he also creates an additional space through the caring itself. In following the logic of reciprocity he regards his caring behavior as a kind of investment. There is a return, but the return requires an initial payment. "I'll go hard at it for a while, and then just feel so drained that I want to relax."

Besides relaxing, Martin focuses on the good feelings he receives from his volunteer work. He believes he is compassionate enough that he would try to help people whether it gave him a good feeling or not. But good feelings help compensate for the time and energy he spends. On balance, he feels rewarded, fulfilled, but his fulfillment is indeed something he weighs in the balance.

· 6 ·

In many of the other interviews some notion of giving and receiving, exchange, and reciprocity also seemed to provide the framework in which people understood the fulfillment they received from caring. But "framework" is my word. The stories people tell are in their words. The words themselves have a kind of tangibility. They have color and texture. They consist of little formulas, like coins that people pull out of their pockets and insert in meters to keep their conversations running. The language of fulfillment and good feelings has this formulaic quality. It is a socially acceptable way of bringing closure to a story.

Consider the following: "I helped a girl at eight o'clock every morning in a sewing class who had a serious nervous disorder. She needed special help because she really wasn't able to keep up with the rest of the class. So I would go in and help her and she actually completed three different garments. It gave her a new lease on life because there's a lot of time when she can't go and be with others, so by being able to sew, she has an outlet. And I enjoyed meeting her and getting to know her. So it was a good experience for me that way."

The person speaking is a college-educated woman who has taught school and now volunteers several hours a week to help handicapped children like the one she describes in this account. The speaker is an articulate woman. She says she receives a great deal of enjoyment from the volunteer work she does. But enjoyment is not simply something she feels. It is also a formula she uses to bring an end to the story. Like some of the other phrases of which her narrative is composed, such as "new lease on life," and "she has an outlet," it is a recognizable commodity.

Good feelings play an important role in the telling of stories about caring as well as in the experience of caring itself. Reciprocity may be present in the relationship; it is certainly present in the story about the relationship. Having set the story up as a gift transaction, the speaker seems compelled by the narrative itself to bring the relationship described into a state of equilibrium at the end. Rather than simply letting us understand the event as altruism, the speaker completes the transaction by claiming to have enjoyed it. Thus we run no risk of concluding that the gift was given grudgingly or for an ulterior motive; the giving was made worthy by the receiving.

· 7 ·

I have suggested that good feelings about ourselves are often understood as part of a reciprocal exchange with the persons we care for and I have tried to identify some of the conditions—in life or in stories about life—that make this understanding possible: a distinct sense of our own identities, a clear sense of the person cared for as a separate entity, a service rendered at some cost to ourselves, an emotional payback associated with the recipient's thankfulness or attitude or sheer humanness, and a void of some kind into which that payback can enter as a sense of fulfillment. Drawing on what we saw in the previous chapter, the ability to distinguish paybacks from motives is essential to this understanding. Good feelings are not the primary motivation for helping in most cases; they are a payback, a result, a by-product.

The idea of reciprocal exchange not only allows us to understand good feelings as fulfillment but also helps us communicate our understanding to others and experience the feelings again. Further reflection on this idea suggests that good feelings may almost be implied by the kind of exchange much of our voluntary caring entails. It occurs between strangers, as voluntarism, not within the family or a tightly knit community such as a primitive tribe or a rural village. Contrary to what Gouldner and others have written about the norm of reciprocity in such settings, the giving we offer in broader, more open settings does not involve a specific sense of duty or obligation. We feel, as the surveys show, that it is important to help others in general, but we do not feel obligated to give a specific service to a specific individual. Our giving is not legitimated by a lan-

guage of duty. It has to be legitimated by a language of fulfillment. I give freely, voluntarily, without obligation; therefore,
the experience should also be pleasurable for me.

Perhaps an example will make the contrast clearer. Here is a
woman talking about an experience she had at the age of four-
teen, when she was called on to care for her dying grandmother. The setting was one of obligation for a loved one. It
still involved giving, an act of genuine caring, but the woman
did not resort to a language of personal fulfillment to give closure to her account. Indeed, the pain of seeing a loved one die
outweighed any sense of fulfillment. "Because it was painful to
see her die, I didn't really feel self-gratification or good about
myself." Instead, the experience consisted of an obligation. "I
never considered doing anything but caring for her." It required sacrifices, the woman admitted, but it was a decision
she chose to make because her "love outweighed the burdens
by far." She spoke primarily of the bond she had with her
grandmother, rather than any immediate sense of gratification.
What this example suggests is that fulfillment may substitute
for the deeper bond of love that is inevitably lacking in caring
for strangers. It provides compensation when a sense of duty
might not be sufficient to sustain the caring relationship.

But there are problems with the reciprocity model of fulfillment. One is that the real goal of one's helping behavior is
sometimes obscured. In most of the cases I have mentioned
people talked about fulfillment as a payback, a side benefit, a
return that kept them going, a reward that made it possible for
them to continue giving care. Fulfillment was a facilitating factor, a means to an end, rather than the end itself. For some,
though, fulfillment was the end; helping people was merely
the means to attaining that end. One of the other members of
Jack Casey's rescue squad, for example, admitted: "I don't do
this to help people. I do it to make myself feel good about helping people." Another person made a similar observation: "If I
stop and help somebody cross the street, I do that because I
want to feel good. It gives me that feeling that I've done something good for the day." In his view there was nothing wrong
with pursuing a good feeling for its own sake. When it comes

right down to it, he ventured, selfishness and compassion "are really the same thing."

The more serious weakness of the reciprocity model of caring and fulfillment is that caring becomes only one—and perhaps not even a very important—source of fulfillment. If we extend the logic of the reciprocity metaphor to all realms of life, then we can give to our families, and receive fulfillment; give to our jobs, and receive fulfillment; even give to ourselves, and receive fulfillment. To the extent that we receive fulfillment from all these other sources, we may simply be filled up. We may have no need to care for anyone else, no need to get the good feelings that come from sponsorship, because we are already fulfilled.

Quite a bit of evidence in fact supports this criticism. In the first place, we do as a society seem fairly happy with our lives and we receive fulfillment from many sources, not just from caring. Ninety-five percent of the public report being fairly happy or very happy when asked directly about their current level of happiness—57 percent say they are very happy. When asked about sources of fulfillment, eight in ten say they receive a great deal of fulfillment from their families, half say this about doing things for people, and more than four in ten say it about their leisure activities, their work, their religion, and just being good to themselves. Most of the remainder say they receive a fair amount of fulfillment from all these sources.[7]

It may seem that doing things for people is one of our most important sources of personal fulfillment, judging from the fact that more people say they receive a great deal of fulfillment from this source than from any source other than their families. But how much of a contribution do these various sources of fulfillment make to our overall happiness? That is more the issue. And the answer is: the fulfillment we receive from doing things for people does not figure very importantly in our overall happiness. In order of importance, the sources of fulfillment that best predict differences in individuals' levels of happiness (taking into account differences in their happiness as children) are: fulfillment from family, fulfillment from leisure activities, fulfillment from religion, fulfillment from being good to themselves, fulfillment from doing things for others, and fulfillment from work.[8] Caring behavior does not rank high on the list. Even when this kind of analysis is restricted to people who are heavily involved in charitable and other volunteer activities, caring behavior still ranks near the bottom as a predictor of overall happiness.[9]

These results run contrary to what one would expect from advertisements and news stories, such as the ones I mentioned earlier, that emphasize the importance of fulfillment and other good feelings associated with caring. Admittedly, the questions at hand are a little crude. So, just to see if this was the problem, I obtained another set of data with better questions and explored the whole issue somewhat more thoroughly. This set of data was also drawn from a nationally representative sample of the American public. It included extensive measures of self-perceptions among more than 1,400 respondents. Among these measures was the sophisticated Rosenberg self-esteem scale—an index widely used to assess variations in levels of individual self-worth. Other items in the study made it possible to see whether generosity, helping behavior, and other characteristics contributed positively to people's levels of self-worth.[10]

I performed three tests with the data. The first examined the relationships between overall self-esteem and a dozen pairs of personal attributes, such as talented/untalented and friendly/unfriendly. Among these attributes was generous/selfish. If caring is a significant source of personal fulfillment, this attribute should be one of the strongest predictors of self-esteem—but it was not. Indeed, it was one of the weakest. Of the twelve pairs, it ranked tenth in importance.[11]

The second test examined the relationships between self-esteem and a set of eleven items that the respondent rated in terms of their importance to his or her basic sense of worth as a person. One of these items was "your efforts to help others." Other items on the list focused on moral standards, "efforts to fulfill your potential as a person," family, friends, social status, and work. I thought helping behavior might be one of the most important predictors of self-esteem because one person in two rated it as very important to self-worth, but I was wrong. It ranked fifth of the eleven items—below moral standards, "efforts to fulfill your potential as a person," family, and friends.[12]

The final test examined the relationship between self-esteem and another set of eleven items that asked people to say how satisfied or dissatisfied they were with each. The items covered the same range of activities and interests as in the previous test. I thought the level of satisfaction people expressed with their helping activities might be a good predictor of their overall self-esteem. Again I was wrong—very wrong. Satisfaction from helping others ranked at the bottom of the list, below satisfaction from hobbies, finances, and work, and far below the items at the top of the list: satisfaction from fulfilling one's potential as a person, moral standards, social status or prestige, and family.[13]

On the whole, these results fairly strongly confirm the criticism I mentioned earlier: that we may not find appeals to good feelings from caring very compelling because we are already fulfilled. Many of us say our helping behavior is an important source of fulfillment and self-worth. But set against the other things in our lives that give these feelings, helping behavior seems relatively insignificant. What this means, I suppose, is that good feelings may not be a very strong incentive for most of us to become more caring. We might send a check to help a sad-eyed orphan, but we probably would not do anything serious that would impair our relationships with our families, with ourselves, or even with our other leisure activities. What it does not mean is that caring individuals like Martin Barnes should be faulted for the good feelings they do receive from helping others. These feelings make their caring a positive experience. They can help people and they can make sense of their caring by putting it in the framework of a gift, a reciprocal exchange that benefits both parties. But there are limits to the value of thinking about fulfillment as a reciprocal exchange.

· 8 ·

In contrast to the exchange metaphor that sees good feelings as the final stage of a reciprocal transaction, there is another, completely different metaphor that some people use to describe their fulfillment in relation to their caring. This understanding locates fulfillment at the start of the process rather than at the end. It identifies fulfillment as something you already have, rather than something you receive in return for your giving. It is an understanding that seems to fit better the results I have just reported: it says in effect, yes, we are already fulfilled; indeed, that is the way it should be—take care of your own needs first and after that you will be able to serve others. It allows people to acknowledge that they are already quite happy and that they receive fulfillment from many realms of activity, not just from caring; it is consistent with the data that satisfaction with one's efforts to fulfill one's potential as a person is the best single predictor of self-esteem.

In many of these cases people used language they had learned in therapeutic contexts, so for convenience I will label this framework the therapeutic motif. It certainly could and does spring from other roots within our cultural tradition as well. But in recent years it has gained a sharper, and in some views, a more problematic identity from being articulated in therapeutic settings. Like the exchange metaphor, it appears to be a fairly common way of understanding fulfillment. Despite being given a rather crudely worded question, for example, 66 percent of the people in my survey said they agreed that "you have to take care of yourself first, and if you have any energy left over, then help others."

Ellen Steinberg provides a number of useful insights into the therapeutic mode of understanding. She stresses self-determination and supports her image of the self with a sophisticated array of therapeutic arguments. Her views about fulfillment reflect these arguments. She knows them well. She is in fact a therapist.

As a young woman in the 1950s Ellen had been active in community politics. Like most women at that time she married early and devoted herself to raising a family. This occupied her during the 1960s. Then the women's liberation movement came along and Ellen was prompted in middle age to go back to school. She finished her college degree and went on to earn a Ph.D. in clinical psychology. For the next seven years she ran her own practice as a therapist. Meanwhile, her husband's business was becoming more and more successful. Eventually she decided to scale back her practice because it was no longer financially necessary for her to work full-time. As she regained more free time, she devoted most of it to the synagogue of which she and her husband are members. Now, at age fifty-six, she serves as education chairperson for a Jewish women's organization, does the monthly bulletins for a Jewish retirement home, and belongs to a variety of Jewish voluntary agencies. She estimates she spends between ten and fifteen hours a week doing volunteer work.

When asked to explain why she became involved in volunteer work, Ellen, like the other people we have met, frames her account by going back one stage in her personal biography and then offering a variety of motives to account for her behavior. "When we lived in the Midwest," she recalls, "I became involved because it was about the only way to meet other Jewish people. I was on the state board of Hillel and the state board of our Jewish women's organization. We only had twenty-one people in our synagogue. It was a very small community. So the only way to get to know other people was to get involved at the state level." When she and her husband moved to a large city on the West Coast, things changed. "We're just delighted with the Jewish community here. Because my husband is an executive in the Jewish community, those are the people we met first, and we've made some wonderful friends. I got involved in the Women in Power conference last year because somebody asked me. I had a good time doing that and out of that was invited to be chairman for education. I got involved because I think Jews who are fortunate enough to be, not affluent, but to not have to work, need to pay back. I think you owe it to the community. The Jewish community has been good to us, and we want to repay it."

In repaying her debts, Ellen has always received what she regards as ample payment in return. She candidly admits that friends and prestige have been among these rewards. "I've gotten to know some interesting people. I've gotten to support some causes I really care about. I would be dishonest if I didn't say I've gotten some status in the community. I've gotten to be known much more quickly than I otherwise would have, not just as my husband's wife, but as myself."

If these remarks make Ellen Steinberg sound at all like a shallow suburban socialite who does volunteer work simply for the social status involved, though, let me interject a bit more about her religious beliefs. She was not raised Jewish. Her background is what she describes as "New England white Protestant Anglo-Saxon." When she married a Jewish man, it was easy for her to convert, though, because she had never been very committed to Christianity. "I tried to work out a relation with Christ for many years and I just couldn't see that this was a world to which the Messiah had come. I don't understand what he was all about." Judaism makes more sense to her because of its emphasis on community. She likes the way people in the community help each other. "All Jews are tied to each other and all of them are obligated to each other. The Hebrew word that is usually translated as charity doesn't mean charity, it means righteousness or justice. It is just that we take care of each other and that we take care of those who don't have the material things they need. The whole notion is to live 'rightly,' because you are called to live that way. We take care of our own. That's just part of it." And she feels she is part of it, not only because of her volunteer work but also because she and her husband faithfully try to observe the Sabbath and other customs that bind them to the community. She feels her religion is "the beginning and the end of my life; it's central to how I live."

Ellen Steinberg, then, is clearly someone who takes her involvement in the community very seriously. Yet, curiously, she is not the kind of person who considers herself interdependent at all. She does not use a metaphor of reciprocity to describe her relationships. Unlike Martin Barnes, she does not think of caring as an exchange with another individual—an exchange involving the giving of some tangible service and the receiving in return of some inner sense of fulfillment. For Ellen, the good feelings that come from volunteer work are generated from within herself. She talks about herself in terms of strength, fortitude, taking care of herself, not being vulnerable, not being in need of care. Asked if her involvement in Jewish organizations had made her more dependent, for example, she responded, "No, more independent." And then, correcting herself, she added: "But I was already independent."

· 9 ·

Ellen Steinberg's view of caring differs from Martin Barnes's exchange model in a number of important ways. For one, she does not admit that any sacrifice is involved. Martin said that on balance he felt fulfilled rather than drained, but he did acknowledge times when he felt he was making a sacrifice. Ellen, in contrast, denies that she ever gets drained. She says she learned not to when she was a practicing psychologist. She learned how to harden herself to the pain people were experiencing so that she could help them without becoming emotionally involved. "To overidentify with their pain and their problems," she observes, "doesn't help them a bit and it makes you less effective."

She also believes the very idea of sacrifice is mistaken. It is not enough, in her view, to be like Martin Barnes—to sacrifice yourself as long as you get enough fulfillment to make up for it. In her mind the whole notion of sacrifice is anathema, dangerous, perverse. "If being compassionate means I have to sacrifice myself, I'm not going to do it. I don't think most people would. And if they would, they should come to me in therapy and I'll work with them on it. The notion that people should be smarmy and self-sacrificing and all doesn't fit with my ideas. Watch out for bleeding hearts; they'll kill you, they really will."

Another difference between Ellen Steinberg and Martin Barnes is that she does not tell her story in a way that creates a void needing to be filled. Ellen had experienced a crisis in her life similar to Martin's, but note how differently her story ends: "There was a time in my life when everything had gone wrong. There just wasn't very much that was right. And I got into therapy with a therapist who saw me without pay for seven years. His support and encouragement helped me get through school, and helped me raise my kids, because I had four who were adolescents at the time. As a psychologist, I have always made it a point that I will see people who can't afford care because that's an obligation I have to him." It is not the continuing vulnerability that encourages her to be caring, but the strength she now has, a privileged position that makes her feel she has ample resources to use in paying off her debts.

From her training as a therapist, Ellen is convinced that you must be fully in charge of your own life before you try to do anything for somebody else. "I really hate it when women get involved in volunteer organizations to take care of the great unwashed because they aren't taking care of business in their own lives. We do terrible things to people who already have enough problems without wanting them to also meet our needs." Fulfillment is something you must have in your life first, not something you get from helping others.

She also denies that you can ever really help others. They have to help themselves. She found this was true in her counseling practice. She did not view her role as that of a helper, although she did regard herself as showing compassion. Her role was not to care or even to empathize, but to "understand with them." "I wanted to understand with them what got in the way of doing what they wanted to do with their lives." This is also a dictum she tries to apply in her everyday life. "I try to listen. I try not to jump in with my solutions. I try to help people figure out what they need to do for themselves." And then, chastising herself for even using the word, she explains: "I don't like the word 'help.'"

In effect, then, she denies the existence of both halves of the exchange that people like Martin Barnes view as a reciprocal relationship. She does not receive fulfillment from other people, nor does she actually give them anything. Individuals ultimately have to be autonomous. You have to feel good about yourself already before you can relate effectively to people in need. You can listen to their problems, but they are the ones who must find their own solutions. Community remains important, but apparently its importance is chiefly as context, as setting, not as a dynamic network of interaction. Community is an aggregation of strong individuals.

· 10 ·

Among other things, the view of sacrifice that Ellen Steinberg illustrates is especially worth underscoring. Consider how different her negative view of sacrifice is from the value that caring people have generally associated with sacrifice in the past.

Take Martin Barnes's hero, Albert Schweitzer, for example. Although it is Schweitzer's statement about happiness that Martin chooses to remember, Schweitzer argued that true compassion required not only a sacrifice of one's time and energy but of the usual happiness and joys of life as well. He wrote, "Anyone who experiences the woes of this world within his heart can never again feel the surface happiness that human nature desires." The anguished faces of the poor and the cries of the sick, Schweitzer explained, would always remain with him.[14] Mother Teresa of Calcutta has expressed the same view: "Real love is always painful and hurts: then it is real and pure."[15]

But Ellen Steinberg's view of sacrifice seems more common in our society than Albert Schweitzer's or Mother Teresa's. Caring is supposed to be fun, like playing tennis, not an act that costs you dearly, certainly not some drudgery, like Tolstoy's bread labor.

To see just how widespread the denial of sacrifice is I built a little experiment into the national survey I conducted. I mentioned in chapter 3 that 42 percent of the public said "I want to give of myself for the benefit of others" was a major reason for them to be kind and caring people. In a subset of the survey, I changed the wording of this question to "I want to sacrifice myself for the benefit of others." With this minor modification in wording, the number who said it was a major reason to be kind and caring dropped from 42 percent to 15 percent! Sacrifice seems to be an unpalatable concept in our society.

But why is it a problem if the language of sacrifice has dropped out of our nomenclature? Because caring often does in fact require sacrifice. It necessitates giving up some free time. It can involve the administrative hassles Jack Casey complained about or the emotional drain of seeing someone in pain that the woman who cared for her grandmother described. To say that it does not require time and energy, to deny that one can become worn out in doing good, to obscure the fact that real dangers and risks may be necessitated, is simply to lure people into a false understanding of caring that is unlikely to prove enduring. Furthermore, if caring does not entail sacrifice, it may result only in token support that does less for the recipient than it does for the giver. One's caring becomes like that of the Los Angeles priest, Father Maurice Chase, described in national news media as the minister of dollar handshakes: his way of helping the poor was to pass out dollar bills and handshakes each Sunday afternoon on the city's Skid Row. It was a kind of caring that, in the words of a local social worker, "does nothing for the people but does a lot for Father Chase."[16]

The notion of reciprocity that Martin Barnes employs is at least honest with respect to the reality of cost. Part of the exchange of service for good feelings is in fact a serious expenditure of time and energy. The reward—the amount of fulfillment received—presumably bears a direct relation to the extent of one's investment. In focusing on the importance of taking responsibility for oneself, the therapeutic understanding can limit caring by restricting it to activities that require no serious depletion of one's personal reserves. But there is a third metaphor people sometimes use, a metaphor that differs from both the exchange model and the therapeutic motif. It provides a place for both sacrifice and fulfillment, but situates them in a larger and more dynamic context.

· 11 ·

Helping people has been part of Ted Garvey's experience for as long as he can remember. As a small child he went around with his mother and sat on people's laps while she visited senior citizens and took them meals. When he went away to college he lived in a co-op in order to get by as cheaply as possible. It was a time for him of exploring alternative life-styles and rethinking his politics as well. After graduation he joined the Peace Corps. For three years he worked in Africa as a beekeeper. His mission was to teach the natives how to raise honey as a cash crop. Now, at age twenty-seven, he is living in a co-op again. The house is a drafty old structure furnished with odds and ends from the Salvation Army and decorated with peace-movement posters. He has a full-time job working as a residential aide in a shelter for the mentally ill homeless. In his spare time he devotes about twenty-five hours a week to various kinds of volunteer work. Some of it is for the co-op. Some of it has a political focus, such as working with a statewide public-interest group on ballot initiative campaigns. The remainder is for a refugee-resettlement project. Each week he tutors several refugees on a regular basis, teaching them English, telling them how to handle job interviews, and helping them find work.

Ted Garvey is similar to Martin Barnes, Ellen Steinberg, and others in deriving fulfillment from the caring he does. He talks about special times when he felt good about himself, and about a more general feeling of satisfaction and worth—"a sense of having done more with my life than just earning a wage." He believes people who genuinely care about others and take the time to show it are basically happier than people who get locked into more structured lives. Even when he gets discouraged and feels as if he is not accomplishing very much—a feeling he says he had during much of his time in the Peace Corps—he still gets a lift from knowing he is at least trying to be helpful.

In a curious way his understanding of fulfillment is a blend of two themes, one we saw in Martin Barnes and one we saw in Ellen Steinberg. Like Martin Barnes, Ted Garvey realizes that genuine caring requires a real investment of time and energy. Working as many hours a week as he does with the homeless, drug addicts, and refugees, he often finds himself seriously drained. The previous week, he recalls, "I really had a severe case of just being wrung out, drained, feeling depressed. It was an acute case of burnout. It hit me over a twenty-four-hour period and took about five days to go away. It was the pressure of the work and a lot of other things that just hit at the same time. I guess it sort of tripped my circuit breaker." He also talks about times in the Peace Corps when he became overwhelmed with the pain and suffering he saw.

The idea of sacrifice is something to which he can relate. It is not a dirty word, as it is for Ellen Steinberg. He sincerely admires people he knows who are sacrificing themselves to help the needy. For example, he talks at length about a nurse he knows at the shelter. "She's getting extremely poor pay but she's down there working with the most serious cases involving drugs, sexual abuse, and mental illness. She's there because she really cares and she's just committed to sacrificing herself in that way."

Like Martin Barnes, Ted Garvey locates the fulfillment he receives in the context of an exchange relationship. The happiness he receives is associated with a sense of giving something away, even of sacrificing himself. But, as with Ellen Steinberg, the fulfillment he receives is primarily something he generates from within. It is not contingent on someone saying "thank you." The relationship does not in some way have to close back on itself in a reciprocal way so that the giving he does is balanced by the fulfillment he receives.

Nor does his sense of fulfillment depend on special moments of being in touch with another person's humanness. These moments are important, but only as context. For example, Ted talks about learning during his years in the Peace Corps to look beyond the pain and suffering, becoming detached enough from it "to see more about their whole lives and realize that their lives weren't all just pain and suffering; to see that they were very real human beings." But the ability to see people in this way requires knowing yourself first. You have to have a sense of worth already. And if you are beginning to feel too drained or burned out, you have to take control of yourself.

Being strong, knowing who you are, and not helping others in order to meet your own needs is Ted Garvey's recipe for genuine caring. He says he has seen lots of people who were not effective because they lacked this inner strength. "They're too insecure or they have too many needs of their own to be met. To be able to care for other people, you have to have your own strength. You make a poor helper if you're a weak person. You can't just go out and work with the homeless and the mentally ill. It's pretty demanding."

In this respect Ted is like Ellen Steinberg. He describes himself as being emotionally self-sufficient. Fulfillment precedes caring, rather than deriving from it. But his view of fulfillment also differs from Ellen Steinberg's in a significant way. He does not view himself as someone who is strong, confident, fulfilled, blessed with a stalwart personality and therefore able to dole out good deeds without depleting his resources. The fact that he gets burned out betrays this kind of self-sufficiency. His self-image is more dynamic. Its central theme is *growth*. Caring for others does not give him good feelings, period. It presents him with challenges, teaches him lessons, makes him stronger so that he is better able to care the next time than he was the time before.

Ted Garvey's idea of caring is a lot like his view of muscle building. Each time you care you become a little stronger, a little more capable, a little better at helping others. Also, you do not build up your muscles as an end in itself. You build them up in order to accomplish some other end. No accomplishment is simply an end in itself. It should instead be a growth experience that enables you to do something better or more effectively in the future.

· 12 ·

Donna Frylinger is the same age as Ted Garvey. She is like him in having a sharply honed social consciousness. To earn a living she works for a public agency that treats drug users on an outpatient basis. On the side she donates about five hours a week to a volunteer agency concerned with child abuse and sexual assault. She also gives time periodically to an organization that distributes food to the homeless. Donna is the youngest of five children. Her religious background is Seventh-Day Adventist. What distinguishes her from the people we have met thus far is that she is legally blind.

Donna acknowledges that most of her volunteer work was inspired by a need to gain experience in order to become a social worker. Her interest in social work, in turn, was inspired by her handicap and by her religious background. Both led naturally toward a career in one of the helping professions. But for Donna the continuity between past and present was also a tether. She found herself constantly struggling to break free of her past and try new things. The protective environment her parents had created for her had become her prison. She wanted more freedom than her parents thought best for their visually impaired daughter. Her religious beliefs also wanted to break out of their Adventist mold.

Exposing herself to the raw problems of battered women, rape victims, abused children, the homeless, and drug users was a way for Donna Frylinger to grow. In addition to broadening her social horizons, helping people has also forced her to become more independent. "When you're in a position of helping someone else out, you tend to take the stronger-type role.

When you are dealing with someone who is trying to get away from their husband, and they can't think, you sort of have to do the thinking for them. So I think I've been able to carry some of that over into my own life."

Like Ted Garvey, she admits there are times when she becomes very drained. For example, she recalls a recent weekend when she was in charge of the crisis intervention center's hotline and received sixty calls. At times like this she finds she has to pull back from the people she is helping. She realizes the importance of identifying with their pain. But to help them, she says, "you have to maintain a little bit of distance. You can't get sucked into it. Then you have two people who are so carried away by the problem that nobody can do anything."

The good feelings she receives from helping people, therefore, do not come from a sense of intimacy—from the kind of humanness-touching-humanness that Martin Barnes described. Nor are they somehow a gift from the recipient of her care, a payback that fills her up after she has been drained. Like Ted Garvey and Ellen Steinberg, she realizes that taking care of herself is her own responsibility. The good feelings must come from within. She has to protect herself from becoming too involved, too drained, too dependent on the caring relationship. Donna's motto is that you have to take care of yourself before you can help anyone else. She says she learned this from her mother, whom she describes as a caring woman who survived by being very interested in herself. Donna has also been in therapy and regards the therapeutic relationship a valuable prerequisite to helping others: "One of the best ways of learning how to care for other people is to get yourself a good therapist who knows how to listen and help you sort through things."

Donna Frylinger is like Martin Barnes to the extent that she has a clear sense of her identity and a clear sense of the separate identities of those she tries to help. There is no blurring of the boundaries. She is a distinct enough entity that genuine exchange can take place. But she is like Ellen Steinberg insofar as she has adopted a therapeutic model of inner strength. How much she has been influenced by being in therapy and undergoing training in social work is especially evident in a comparison she draws with her religious background. Having attended

Seventh-Day Adventist schools through high school, she was steeped in a kind of Christian tradition that emphasized self-sacrifice, yet she now feels that view is wrong. "You think you are supposed to be real selfless, that what you do doesn't count, and you should be putting everything into helping others." But now she feels "that's gotten carried too far; you need to care enough about yourself so you can care about other people. If you think you aren't worth anything, then you are likely to wonder how come everybody else in the world is so much better than you." In other words, you will then feel sorry for yourself and feel that others have all the advantages, rather than being able to focus clearly on their needs.

Donna Frylinger differs from Ellen Steinberg, though, in understanding inner strength as a means to an end rather than an end in itself. Her fulfillment does not involve self-sufficiency to the same degree as Ellen Steinberg's does. It is not something she already has, a constant in her life; it is something that expands and grows. Her views in this respect resemble those of Ted Garvey. Inner strength helps you serve. As you serve others, your inner strength grows. You are then better able to help others. The whole process is a kind of upward spiral. In her words, "the longer you do caring things, the more good feelings you will have; it will just kind of mushroom, and then you will be even more able to help other people."

If Ted Garvey is a secular version of the Puritan ascetic, if his helping others is a kind of body-building exercise, Donna Frylinger represents a different, more domestic, more communal strand in American culture. Her ability to care for others also depends on strength of character. The more she helps, the stronger she becomes. But she does not slip off to the woods to regenerate herself. She does not prepare for the day's struggles by working out at the gym. She sustains herself through the support of family surrogates and friends.

Donna Frylinger is thus an example of someone who has married the therapeutic mode of self-determination to the concept of an enabling support group. She takes responsibility for her own happiness, rather than depending on those she tries to help to supply it. Fulfillment is not a matter of replenishing herself or of compensating for her deficiencies. It is a learning experience, a challenge, a way of broadening herself so she can

111

be a more effective helper in the future. But she is not without needs either. Her strength does not come heroically, stoically from within. It arises in the community of friends on whom she depends for support.

An emphasis on personal growth, combined with and in service to an ethic of caring, is a prominent motif in our culture. It is, as we have seen, evident in public-opinion polls that show widespread consensus on the importance of living up to your potential as a person *and* helping others. It is also part of the way we have understood individual responsibility historically. As we develop our own potential, we grow, and as we grow, we become better able to help others. John Stuart Mill once put it this way: "In proportion to the development of his individuality, each person becomes more valuable to himself, and is, therefore, capable of being more valuable to others."[17]

· 13 ·

Having described several understandings of personal fulfillment, I can now reopen the question that I have tried to tiptoe around since initially raising it in the first chapter: what exactly do people mean—people who care deeply about others—when they describe themselves as individualists? I talked earlier about our emphasis on personal freedom, individual success, and self-interest as a working definition of American individualism. But this takes us only so far. Individualism is a concept we understand only in relation to other dimensions of our culture. When some critics say we are becoming too individualistic, for example, they put this criticism in the context of ideas about community. For them, individualism somehow means a breakdown or an absence of community. We can see individualism differently when we set it alongside caring. When caring people say they are individualistic, they reveal some other connotations of the term, equally valuable and far more positive.

One woman, a volunteer tutor for handicapped children, defined individualism this way: "[It] involves developing my own unique self, growing in my own way." In her view, a black box, a void, a nothing, can be of little use to anyone else because people cannot interact with a nullity. Being an individualist means having a strong, clear identity, being an entity with whom another person can interact. "If you are a strong individualist and know who you are and what you believe, then someone can relate to you. They can't if you more or less have your hand over your face." Besides this, self-knowledge is a prerequisite for helping others. "If you don't understand yourself, you aren't likely to be able to understand other people."

Ellen Steinberg, as we might expect, emphasizes the capacity to be different, to stand up for what you believe, as the main ingredient of individualism, but she also thinks this means that you can be compassionate in your own way. Find your own strength and you will be able to serve best because you will be most in touch with your own needs as well. Half-jokingly, she admits "on good days I see myself as unique, on bad days as eccentric and weird." In either case she says her impulse is never toward the crowd. "If everybody is doing something, I'm pretty sure not to want to do it. I'd rather do something and have other people do it a year later."

Her prescription for others is patterned on her own experience. You can be compassionate, but you have to be true to yourself first. The main thing for anyone, she argues, is "that he is comfortable in his own skin, that he knows his own strength and his limitations." Recognizing this can be terribly liberating, she maintains, because it means you can express your caring in a way that is best suited to you. It may not even be in a way that is obvious to other people.

Although they place greater emphasis on growth, Ted Garvey and Donna Frylinger also talk about individualism in many of the same terms that Ellen Steinberg does. For both, nonconformity is a key ingredient. In Ted's case the self-esteem that has grown with his caring activities has also made him less dependent on receiving approval from other people. "When I look at myself, I'm happier with what I see. I don't have to be concerned. It frees me from having to be concerned with what other people think of me." And this means he can live a more caring life-style. "I feel like I can get away with living in a house like this and dressing the way I want to if I'm doing good work that helps other people." In Donna's case, she has also discovered that part of growing and becoming stronger is getting over being concerned about what other people think. She mentions that her choice of a profession is different from what her family would have chosen for her and that she has been able to work through her religious beliefs, keeping some of them and throwing out others. She especially admires caring people like Mother Teresa and Gandhi because they were individualists who did what they thought best. "They were single-minded in what they set out to do; they were very strong; they knew what they wanted; they didn't let other people pick them apart and tell them this isn't possible." Part of her definition of individualism also involves making a distinction between being compassionate and needing to be involved with a community of people all the time. She insists that compassionate people often "need distance." "They can be there for someone and then they have to get away." She says she is like that and she believes a lot of other people are too.

The individualism that can be reconciled with caring, then, might be summarized as follows. It embodies a sense of nonconformity, of being different, of being able to live and act as one chooses, even if one's choices violate social norms; willing nonconformity is often necessary in order to be caring because, as we saw in the last chapter, compassion is understood as a kind of willful deviance from the conventional. Individualism also embodies inner strength, a strong and clear sense of personal identity. It is this self-confidence that allows one to give. There is also a sense of balance, of give-and-take, of sacrifice and growth that requires interaction with others. It is, therefore, possible to live in community without giving up one's individuality.

· 14 ·

With all the emphasis we place on individualism in our culture it is not surprising that fulfillment is such a central theme in our understandings of caring. We believe the individual, first and foremost, is responsible for caring—not the government, not some organization, not society in the abstract, not even the family. But for the individual to care, it must have resources. It must be strong, have a clear sense of its identity, take care of itself, love itself. It cannot be an empty space. Fulfillment is the strength, the identity, the self-esteem needed for the individual to care.

Fulfillment is also the handle on caring that fits most comfortably in our cultural grip. In the past one might have felt compelled to be caring because of religious injunctions or because it was befitting one's station in life. Responsibilities to the poor, the stranger, the hungry, as well as to one's family and community, were carefully defined by social norms and closely monitored in the daily life of kin and polity. In our day both the absolutes of sacred belief systems and the pressures of tightly knit communities have waned in importance. We may, as the survey evidence suggests, still feel that we should help the needy in some abstract sense. We hold compassion as a value. But we do not have value systems or social pressures that tell us we *should* show compassion at specific times and places to specific individuals in specific ways. As Ellen Steinberg put it, "'should' is not a word I like."

And so good feelings become the acceptable alternative for justifying our compassion. Motive-talk is, as we saw in the last chapter, largely situational. In stressing the volitional dimension of caring, motive-talk turns specific acts of compassion into arbitrary episodes in one's biography. "Should" drops out; choice predominates. To explain why we are involved, it is then easiest to assert simply that it feels good. How do you validate your choice, whether to buy candy or to tutor the disadvantaged? Not that it was the right thing to do, but because it felt good. Elgin Perry spoke volumes when he remarked, "I don't feel I SHOULD be doing volunteer work right now; there's no obligation, I'm simply doing it because there's a good feeling involved."

It is perhaps not surprising that the language of sacrifice has dropped out of our vocabulary with the triumph of fulfillment. We are at least honest enough with ourselves to realize that our investments in caring often do not in fact cost us much. Elgin Perry again: "I'm not really losing much with those two hours; I can't even think what I'd do with that time." Most of our voluntarism is of this kind. It does not involve raising bees in Ghana or living in a co-op to sustain ourselves on a minimum wage so we can help refugees and drug addicts in our spare time. It consists of a casual donation, an evening at Little

League, baking pies for the fire company. It is still service that matters, but it is service that can be performed with a minimum of sacrifice. It is the voluntarism characteristic of an affluent society.

The bright side is that fulfillment still provides a more acceptable reward for caring than many of the more concrete benefits people mentioned in passing. We may feel embarrassed to admit that our volunteer work got us a new job, made us friends, earned respect for us in the community, and so on. But having a warm feeling in one's chest as a result is perfectly acceptable. The fact that we emphasize fulfillment means we still respect the purity of caring. A good feeling is nothing one can display publicly. It is not something one can necessarily calculate ahead of time how to get. It simply happens, spontaneously, inwardly. It may even depend on having the right motives and being genuinely concerned for another's well-being. One person stated it well when she said, "If you are sincere and do a good job at it, or even just try to do a good job at it, the feelings will come."

I will return to these observations in later chapters. I want to underscore here, though, that our emphasis on fulfillment as a central feature of caring may be less useful *socially* than it is psychologically. Its psychological consequences, as we have seen, amount to relatively little when all the various commitments that contribute to our self-esteem are compared. What it provides is a language that helps justify caring when other values or circumstances already commit us to voluntary service. It makes caring a positive experience and gives us an acceptable way to talk about it, all of which is valuable, but good feelings carry no special appeal when we are already overwhelmed with promises of good feelings. The social limitation of focusing on personal fulfillment, though, is more severe.

Our emphasis on fulfillment consists ultimately of a gift we give ourselves, rather than a true gift that forges social bonds through its exchange. In anthropological studies of gifts the fulfillment of the transaction always depends on the other person. He may give something back almost in the form of barter. His obligation to give a return gift may not need to be fulfilled for some time, perhaps not until his eldest son marries or the chief of the clan dies. In the meantime, the society is bound together in small ways by the fact that he owes something to somebody else. He may not even owe directly the person who helped him. His obligation may be to that person's children, or to a neighbor who at some later point helps the original giver.

Fulfillment from caring, in contrast, is instant gratification. It creates no long-term or indirect obligations. It does not even depend on how the recipient of the gift responds. He or she does not have to say thank you. The recipient does not even have to be a person. It can be an organization one gives time to, an animal one takes in off the street, a goal one sets for oneself as a kind of challenge. The caring associated with this kind of fulfillment may still be of value. Organizations need to be run, stray animals need shelter, goals need to be pursued. But the social value of the gift is lost. Lasting social bonds are neither created nor reinforced by the transaction. The fulfillment from giving does indeed come from within. It may be just as well to acknowledge that it does.

PART III
THE ROLE OF FAITH

CHAPTER FIVE

Conviction and Community

D EBBIE CARSON began doing volunteer work in high school. Much of it was organized by her youth group at church. She visited inmates at the county jail and sang hymns at local nursing homes on Sunday afternoons. She also worked as a candy striper at a hospital. Volunteering became a habit. So did caring for the needy. In college she majored in special education. After college she worked for a year in an inner-city program for disadvantaged families. After that she taught children with learning disabilities.

Now in her late thirties, married, and the mother of two children, Debbie Carson still devotes much of her time to helping others. For the past four years she has served on a committee that plans activities for international families—just little things, like an outing to pick apples in the fall, a kite-flying party some windy Saturday in the spring, a square dance. Twice a month she invites some of the international women to her home for three or four hours in the morning to work together on crafts. Many of these women are new to the community and more isolated than their husbands. A morning like this helps them get to know each other. It gives them a chance to speak English. It gives her a chance to learn from them too.

I was curious about the role of faith in Debbie's efforts to be kind and compassionate. She said her work with international families was "not really a church activity." It was just something she enjoyed doing. The woman who had helped her organize it, though, was someone who went to the same church, and the two of them were involved with an outreach program their church had started for international families. Debbie's choice of words showed she did see this activity as a ministry. She also told about another experience that revealed a deeper aspect of this ministry. "We had one man from Afghanistan and he was interested in Christianity and had not really had it explained to him. So he came to our home and we spent about two or three hours just talking to him. He was just amazing. Just to be the first person to explain something like that to him, that was a really special time."

· 2 ·

The world's major religions all encourage their followers to be compassionate. The Hebrew Scriptures teach that men and women are created in the image of God and are for this reason deserving of all the caring and kindness that can be given them. The Scriptures also teach that loving others is a duty we owe to God. The Koran teaches that those who give charity guard themselves from evil. Buddhist thought, particularly in the Mayahana tradition, elevates compassion above all other virtues. And Christianity has emphasized love of neighbor, deeds of mercy, and charity for the needy.

In our society the biblical tradition has been a major inspiration for helping behavior, both formal and informal. Although reality often fell short of ideals, it was the spirit of love and cooperation that inspired many of the early colonists and settlers. As John Winthrop's sermon from which I quoted in chapter 1, reminded them, Christians in the New World could prosper materially and socially only by setting an example for all to see of God's mercy and justice. Care was to be extended to those within the community who worked hard and yet suffered from misfortune. Care was also sometimes extended to those beyond the community through the work of itinerant missionaries and amateur physicians. Hospitals and almshouses were established. Much of the early work concerned with juvenile delinquency, foundlings and orphans, and prison reform owed its origins to religious leaders. Religiously sponsored colleges, medical schools, and nursing orders helped pave the transition from informal voluntary service to paid professional expertise. And the various denominations and faiths competed actively with one another to provide their members with everything from life insurance to retirement communities to mutual-aid societies.

The strength of the biblical tradition is evident in the lives of many individual volunteers. Like Debbie Carson, many became involved in volunteer work because of their exposure to religious teachings. Over the years, though, the role of faith appears to have weakened in our society. Although most people still claim to believe in God, growing numbers express doubts about this conviction. An increasing percentage of the population takes a relativistic view toward the Bible. Actual knowledge of the Bible is quite low. And, even though it is still a small minority, the proportion claiming to have no religious affiliation or identity is growing.

In other ways the clout of organized religion has also diminished. In the field of higher education, for example, the virtual monopoly that religious bodies once held over the nation's colleges and universities has been greatly reduced by the enormous expansion of public universities and community colleges. Hospitals, orphanages, homes for the elderly, and social-welfare services that were once provided by religious organizations have also shifted largely to government or nonsectarian auspices. Religion may still be an important component of the nonprofit sector on the whole, but enough change has taken place that many people have begun to question whether religion and caring are as closely linked as they once were.

On one side of the debate, some people still argue that religious convictions encourage compassion. They do not deny that nonreligious people can be compassionate too, but they think it is more likely for people with genuine religious convictions to live out those convictions by loving their neighbors. One elderly man, for example, believed strongly that religion and caring went hand in hand. "All religions teach one basic precept: be kind to your fellow man. If you learn that as a child, it's bound to rub off in later life." But the view has also become widespread that religious convictions do not make people more compassionate. The spectacle of greedy television preachers siphoning off charitable donations to pay for their own vices is one reason for the cynicism about religion. As one person noted, the kind of theology that simply emphasizes making converts and getting people to mail in donations often seems to be devoid of genuine Christian love. "Conservative religions basically—the evangelistic ones—say that if you just accept Jesus into your life then you are saved. I really wonder about some of those people. They don't seem to be caring to me. I don't mean to lump them all into one group—I'm sure there are some very compassionate evangelistic people. But I wonder about their motives."

Others simply believe that altruism springs from so many other sources that one need not be religious to be caring. Several people recited some of the utilitarian arguments I presented in chapter 3 as evidence that religious values were not necessary for someone to be altruistic. Many argued that compassion was just a natural impulse that some people had even though they might not be religious. A school psychologist who had been raised in a Jewish home, for example, stressed this theme in questioning whether her own caring sprang from religious sources or other influences. "I remember learning the Golden Rule, but I'm not sure that motivated me any more than just being the kind of person I was and watching how other people behaved and treated each other."

In the survey only 30 percent of the public thought religious people are generally more compassionate than those with no religious convictions. Forty percent thought religious people *should* be more compassionate, but often are not. Twenty-four percent simply felt that religious people are no more compassionate than anyone else. Church people held a somewhat more positive view of the compassion of religious people than people who themselves were uninvolved in religion. But even among regular churchgoers opinion was divided: 40 percent thought religious people were more compassionate, 41 percent thought they should be but often were not, and 15 percent thought there were no differences.

· 3 ·

What then is the role of faith? Does it inspire caring and compassion? Or has helping behavior become a virtue in itself, freed from its historic roots in religious tradition? Beyond this, do different religious traditions encourage different kinds (or levels) of charitable involvement? Is it possible to see the effects of secularization on charitable behavior in our society? And, most important, has individualism penetrated religion itself to such an extent that compassion is endangered?

No single study provides answers to all these questions, but I have been able to piece together evidence from a number of different sources. Some of it points in one direction, some of it in another. We must, therefore, consider the various pieces in relation to one another. Consider the following, all of which bear simply on the question of whether religious involvement in some general way reinforces charitable behavior.

Item. Among individuals who say that having a deep religious faith is absolutely essential to them, 89 percent say that helping people in need is very important. This figure drops to 52 percent among people who say having a deep religious faith is not very important to them.[1]

Item. In a national study that isolated volunteer activities done informally and individually, apart from any organization or agency, church members were more likely to have been engaged in such activities within the past year than nonmembers, and members who were involved in small religious fellowship groups that met regularly were significantly more likely to have been engaged informally in volunteer work than other members who were not involved in such groups. The same study distinguished among a large variety of organized volunteer efforts, one type of which was specifically concerned with social services and welfare. Church members were more likely than nonmembers to have donated time to these efforts, and members involved in small fellowship groups were much more likely to have donated time than members not involved in such groups.[2]

Item. The likelihood that an individual will be involved in charitable or service activities increases with the frequency of an individual's church attendance. It does so even taking into account differences in the charitable behavior and churchgoing patterns of various age groups, men and women, people who live in various regions of the country, and educational categories. The effect of church attendance on charitable behavior is stronger than the effect of any of these other characteristics.[3]

These items all suggest that religious conviction and involvement in religious communities do encourage altruistic behavior. But consider the following:

Item. Individuals who attend church every week are no more likely than individuals who seldom attend church to give money when they see a beggar in need, stop to help someone having car trouble, lend money to a friend or relative, help someone through an emotional crisis, try to get someone to stop using alcohol or drugs, or care for an elderly relative at home.[4]

Item. Regular churchgoers are no more likely than less-frequent church attendees to exhibit caring in the workplace. Within each group, virtually the same proportions say they do (or are likely to) visit fellow workers who are in the hospital, bail a fellow worker out of a jam, give a birthday present to someone at work, or discuss personal problems with people at work.[5]

Item. Positive relationships between individual religious commitment and charitable orientations may be limited to particular social contexts, rather than reflecting something general about the impact of religion on values. For example, data collected from surveys in European countries do not show consistently positive relationships between frequency of church attendance or individuals' subjective assessments of the importance of their religious attachments, and willingness to give money or time to help the poor.[6]

· 4 ·

What can we conclude? Participation in religious organizations, it appears, has a genuine, but limited, effect on charitable behavior. In some studies this effect is exaggerated by the fact that participants in religious organizations appear to be referring to those organizations when they say they are involved in volunteer or charitable activities. What they mean is simply that they take part in religious services. Beyond this, there is some evidence that religious participation encourages people to become involved in activities that actually benefit the needy. The kinds of activities that are encouraged seem to be ones closely connected with the church itself. Some of these may be organized activities, such as going door-to-door to raise money for some charitable cause or signing up to visit members of the church who are in the hospital. Others, such as caring for a sick friend or relative, may not be formally organized by the church, but are encouraged as part of the informal norms of fellowship and community that exist within the church.

There is, however, a wide range of caring activities that does not seem to be encouraged by participation in churches. These include the relatively spontaneous acts of kindness, such as giving money to a beggar or helping someone with car trouble, that are likely to occur when one is not around the church and that involve needy persons who are not fellow church members. They also include activities that could conceivably become part of the formal or informal norms of religious communities, such as helping people with emotional crises or drug problems, but which apparently have not become an interest of religious organizations. In some cases it appears that these kinds of caring are happening as frequently outside the churches as they are inside. In other cases needs are not being met in either context.

What the evidence on religious participation suggests is that churchgoing does not seem to generate convictions about caring that carry over into all realms of the believer's life. People do not, for example, see caring acted out in their churches and then go out with such conviction about the importance of caring that they help the next person they see. Instead, their caring is channeled by what they see and hear in church. It is channeled, above all, into programs the church as an organization is trying to promote. After this it is channeled informally among members and into certain kinds of traditionally acceptable behaviors. One's definition of what constitutes a need and of when it is appropriate to care is, in short, shaped by the organization one attends.

· 5 ·

Is it simply participation in a religious context that makes certain kinds of caring more likely? Or do specific beliefs and teachings make a difference? Theologians and religious leaders have long contended that certain kinds of religious beliefs or imagery are more conducive to caring behavior than others. The question is, which ones? In some schools of thought the decisive factor is what one believes about the nature of God.

For example, a God thought to be loving and caring might serve as a role model for the believer to imitate, more so, say, than a vengeful or angry God. Or such a God could be seen by the believer as a resource or an enabler. Receiving divine love and care might make the believer better able to care for others. In addition to arguments of this kind, some students of religion have suggested that picturing God in more feminine or androgynous terms, as a mother-God of divine mercy and forgiveness, instead of in the more harsh, traditional masculine way, might be conducive to caring behavior. Others have argued that fine distinctions of this kind might pale in their effects beside the simple fact of whether one believes or does not believe in a personal God who watches what one does and says.

To the extent that one can measure such things in empirical studies, the perception that one is receiving love from God does in fact seem to be associated with a greater willingness to care for others. Among people who said they had felt during the past year that God loved them all the time, 83 percent indicated that helping the needy was very important to them. This figure declined to 73 percent among those who said they had experienced God's love many times during the past year, 57 percent among those who said they had felt God's love only a few times, and 55 percent among those who had not felt God's love. The proportions who were actually involved in charitable or service activities were also highest among those who felt God loved them all the time (36 percent) and dropped to only 16 percent among those who did not feel God loved them.

Evidence from other studies also lends support to arguments about the effects of different images of God. Believers who describe God as caring are in fact more likely to attach high value to helping others than believers who say God does not care. They are also more likely to have donated time in the past year to helping the needy. The same is true for believers who say God is loving as opposed to those who see God as an angry being.[7]

About five out of every six persons, though, think of God as caring and loving. So one does not gain strong purchase on the religious underpinnings of care giving by knowing that people think of God in these ways. It is also the case that perceptions of other divine attributes, such as powerful, watching, and existing, are just as highly related to helping people. In other words, believing that God exists and is aware of what you do and say seems to be as conducive to caring as picturing God as a loving and caring being.

There also seems to be little support for the idea that feminine or androgynous images of God are associated with caring. Those who think God is forgiving are a little more inclined to value caring behavior than those who picture God as vengeful. But those who picture God as male are also somewhat more likely to value caring behavior than those who think of God either as female or as a combination of male and female.[8]

A somewhat different way of getting at the relationships between specific views of God and caring is available from a set of questions (asked in the same national study) about feelings that people may or may not have had in church or synagogue. Among these were "afraid of God," "guilty as a sinner," "close to God," and "that you are a wonderful person." The first two were intended as manifestations of an austere kind of religious orientation that focuses on obedience and fear; the second two, as a more personally affirming kind of religious orientation. Saying that helping others is very important was positively associated with the latter two; it was not associated positively or negatively with the former two.[9] Thus, it appears that a personal God one can feel close to and a belief system that affirms one's personal worth may be the religious beliefs most conducive to care and compassion.

· 6 ·

If religious participation and religious belief in general make some difference to the likelihood of people being compassionate, it is nevertheless the case that American religion is enormously diverse. From the beginning, Puritans did things their way; Episcopalians did things a different way, as did Quakers, Baptists, Methodists, and Presbyterians. Each might have touted charity, but each manifested it in a different way. Beyond the sometimes minor distinctions among Protestant denominations and sects, there were also the major differences that divided Protestants and Catholics. Each had its own institutions for encouraging voluntarism and for doling out the benefits of charitable contributions. Even now, many of these institutions remain separate.

When it comes to the individual believer, Protestants and Catholics still show some signs of living in different subcultures. For example, when asked who best illustrated compassion, Catholics were more likely than Protestants to mention other Catholics, such as Mother Teresa and Pope John Paul II. In turn, Protestants were more likely than Catholics to mention the Reverend Jesse Jackson, evangelist Billy Graham, or their own minister. Another difference between the two emerged when individuals were asked who they could depend on if they themselves were in need. Although both traditions have emphasized caring among fellow believers, Protestants were somewhat more likely than Catholics to think they could depend on members of their congregations if they were in need.[10]

The two are basically similar, however, in their beliefs and values and in the relationships between these beliefs and values and involvement in charitable activities. Protestants and Catholics are about equally likely to place high value on the importance of helping the needy (77 percent and 71 percent, respectively, said this was very important) and of giving time to help other people (66 percent and 62 percent, respectively).[11] The two are also quite similar with respect to the motives and values that are most conducive to becoming active in charitable work. Within both traditions, those who are involved in charitable activities are distinguished from those who are not involved by wanting to help others, by wanting to make the world a better place, by the belief that caring for others makes them stronger, and by the importance they attach to their faith.[12]

· 7 ·

In recent studies of American religion the main cleavages are no longer between Protestants and Catholics, though. Nor are they between Presbyterians and Baptists, Episcopalians and Methodists, or even Christians and Jews. The historic conflicts that separated these various denominations and faiths have been superseded by a new dividing line in American religion. The major division is now between religious conservatives and religious liberals.

On the conservative side, public figures like Jerry Falwell, Pat Robertson, Jimmy Swaggart, and Jim and Tammy Bakker have greatly colored the public's perception of what an evangelical Christian believes. And the public scandals that have surrounded some of these figures have created strongly negative impressions in many sections of American society. But religious conservatism extends well beyond the television broadcasts of these leaders. Millions of Americans—Protestants, Catholics, and Jews—take a traditional, orthodox stance toward their faith. They do so for both religious and secular reasons. Their religious views include a strong conviction about the existence of God and an emphasis on the divine inspiration and inerrancy of the Scriptures. They believe in the value of participating faithfully in their chosen religious communities. And some of them believe in proselytizing unbelievers and members of other faiths. On secular issues they are often vexed about the decline of traditional moral standards, devoted to strengthening the nuclear family, strongly opposed to abortion and pornography, and distrustful of government efforts to provide social-welfare services.

The liberal side is defined by a more relativistic orientation on both religious and secular issues. Religious liberals are more likely to view the Bible as a book of ancient myths or human wisdom or, if divinely inspired, as a text that requires heavy philosophical interpretation to be understood rather than as a book to be taken literally or at face value. Religious liberals are about as likely as religious conservatives to believe in God. But they are less sure of God's existence; indeed, they sometimes take pride in their willingness to express doubts. And the God they believe in may be a blend of naturalistic, scientific, and philosophical ideas rather than a focused being. Religious liberals for the most part claim some affiliation with organized religious bodies, but a minority of them claim no affiliation, and many others attend sporadically. On secular issues liberals are more inclined to emphasize individual freedom on questions of morality than to favor laws imposing moral standards on the whole society. They are likely to voice this position on issues such as abortion and pornography. And they are notably more inclined than religious conservatives to favor government welfare programs for the poor and needy.[13]

· 8 ·

Rancor between religious liberals and religious conservatives has been so intense that some observers have questioned whether both might be endangering their capacity to speak to deeper religious values, such as reconciliation, love, and fellowship. It is ironic, therefore, that compassion appears to be one thing about which religious conservatives and liberals can agree. People in both categories stress the importance of helping the needy about equally, and are about equally likely to view themselves as a generous lot. Three religious conservatives in four, for example, said it was very important to them to help people in need; 72 percent of the religious liberals said the same. Approximately half of the conservatives (54 percent) and half of the liberals (50 percent) claimed they received a great deal of fulfillment from doing things for people. Thirty-five percent of the former and 32 percent of the latter were currently involved in some charitable or social-service activity.

On more specific kinds of caring, religious conservatives and religious liberals also appear quite similar. Approximately the same numbers of each, for example, had visited someone in the hospital during the past year, given money to a beggar, or cared for someone who was ill. Conservatives were somewhat more likely to have gone door-to-door raising money for various causes. Liberals were a bit more likely to have lent money to someone, saved a person's life, stopped to help someone having car trouble, or donated time to a volunteer organization.[14] But all these differences were quite small.

· 9 ·

Despite these broad areas of agreement, religious conservatives and liberals do differ in their basic understandings of compassion. Their overall value structures differ, and different values and motives underlie their involvement in charitable behavior. Both claim to be religious, but conservatives' faith is much more central to the way they understand their lives than are the religious convictions of liberals. Indeed, part of what people seem to be saying when they identify themselves as religious conservatives is that faith as traditionally understood is something they hold dear.

Not only are conservatives more likely in surveys to answer that religion is very important to them and that they attend religious services regularly, but they are much more likely than liberals to say they try to be caring because their religion teaches them to be caring. Not only do they testify to the importance of religion in these ways; they also emerge as more religiously guided when subtler ways of examining the strength of their values and motives are employed. To be specific, among conservatives the value that discriminates best between those who are involved in charitable activities and those who are not is having a deep religious faith, and the reason for being kind that best discriminates is believing that one's religious beliefs teach kindness and caring. Among religious liberals, neither of these statements about religious belief is as strong a predictor of who becomes involved in charitable activities and who does not.[15]

In other ways, the underlying values and motives that promote charitable activity among religious conservatives and religious liberals also differ dramatically. Conservatives are more likely to be driven by the desire to give, even to sacrifice, themselves. The feeling that one has debts to repay is also a better predictor of charitable behavior among conservatives than it is among liberals. And, consistent with both these emphases, conservatives are more likely to register an antimaterialistic view—a rejection of money—as a correlate of charitable behavior.

In contrast, liberals who become involved in charitable activities differ from liberals who are not involved by the importance they attach to values of self-improvement and social betterment. With faith and a sacrificial orientation less important as predictors of charitable involvement, liberals seem to be motivated most effectively by the belief that caring for others will make them stronger, that caring is and should be an important

133

part of their personal identities, that it is important to take care of themselves, and that charitable activity is a way of making themselves feel good. But these personalistic orientations are also balanced by views about the importance of altruism for the society and the world. Religious liberals who are involved in charitable activities differ from fellow liberals who are not involved by placing higher value on doing things to make the world a better place and in believing that being a caring person makes society better.[16]

On balance, then, the high regard in which both religious conservatives and religious liberals hold compassion would suggest, on the surface, an area of agreement, even of potential reconciliation. If they cannot agree on biblical interpretations or social programs, at least they might be able to cooperate in sponsoring charitable activities and helping the needy. They might even learn to show more compassion to each other. But the likelihood of such cooperation working out is diminished by the fact that the two wings of American religion differ so greatly in their underlying perspectives. Even if both tried to serve the needy, they would be motivated by different values and use different language to legitimate their activities.

This at least is the view one gets from looking at patterns in the whole population. But often these very patterns obscure similarities that may be present at the individual level. Like all stereotypes, the images that divide religious conservatives from religious liberals contain some truth. And yet these stereotypes also mask similarities and areas of agreement. Conservatives are generally not so bigoted and are more kindhearted than liberals are willing to admit. Nor are they quite so naive as they are often portrayed. Especially with the advances they are making in higher education, many of them are exceedingly sophisticated and capable spokespersons for their point of view. By the same token, liberals are neither so shallow nor so secular as conservatives sometimes think. There are, to be sure, differences. But understanding across the divide can be nurtured when each side listens more intently to the other. Individual conservatives and liberals who share a deep commitment to compassion are particularly worth listening to in this respect.

· 10 ·

Debbie Carson is a religious conservative. But she defies most of the stereotypes of religious conservatives. She is not a bigoted fanatic who prays five times a day. She is not a simple-minded bumpkin who uses her faith as a crutch to make it through a difficult life. And she is not a dogmatic moralist bent on converting the heathen and taking away their rights to have abortions. Debbie Carson is one of the so-called new evangelicals. She is a sophisticated, articulate member of the upper middle class who nevertheless believes strongly in the vitality and importance of an orthodox biblical faith. She typifies both the historic continuity in American evangelicalism and its most influential and rapidly growing sector in America today.

As I mentioned earlier, Debbie is a college graduate. She majored in special education. She also holds a master's degree in the same subject. Her husband, who also describes himself as a committed Christian, is a doctor. They live in a comfortable, and by no means modest, house in the suburbs of a southern city that specializes in high-tech industry and government contracting. Debbie was raised in the South, but she has also lived on the West Coast and in the Northeast. She has traveled extensively, both domestically and abroad.

Debbie and her husband are not part of the fundamentalist fringe. They belong to a Presbyterian church. Like other Presbyterian churches, it subscribes to the mainstream of Protestant theology that was born during the sixteenth century, especially the doctrines of John Calvin and John Knox. Also like other Presbyterian churches, it attracts many of the more affluent and better-educated members of the community. The church building is a large, modern structure located in a nice part of town. The minister has a Ph.D. Many of the men and women in the congregation have graduate degrees. But unlike many Presbyterian churches, this one has been growing rapidly in recent years. It now has a membership of more than three thousand. Its members attribute this growth to an aggressive program of evangelism and clear biblical preaching. They consider it an evangelical church. Indeed, its affiliation is not with the main body of Presbyterian churches in the United States, but with a smaller Presbyterian denomination that was founded by leaders disturbed by liberal tendencies in the larger body and committed to a more conservative program of religious, moral, and social teachings.

There is no question about Debbie's commitment. "Christianity," she says, "has shaped my whole worldview. I take the biblical view and that has shaped a lot of what I do. I believe the world is not innately good, that it was created good, but is in a fallen state, and that it is a value—that it is eternal—to give and to care for people and to help them. With a Christian mentality, each individual is so important that if you help one person then that matters and it will matter forever."

Religious convictions surface freely in Debbie's remarks on other topics as well. For example, when asked to name some public figure who exemplified compassion she was one of the few to select Christ. She said he came immediately to mind "because I am a Christian and have studied his life since I was quite young." She also noted that she has lots of relations with other Christians. Expanding on why Christ impressed her so much, she explained: "He didn't have education or an influential position, but in the way he lived and the way he taught, in just a short span of thirty-some years, he had a tremendous impact. The values he expressed are to me very fundamental to a world that is going to be caring."

She also selected her pastor as the individual she knew personally who best exemplified kindness and caring. "I remember once after church when everybody was kind of running here and there saying hello and talking, and I saw him standing over in the corner with one person talking quietly and all of a sudden he seemed to be overcome with emotion and tears welled up in his eyes. I didn't know him very well at the time, but just observing his life made me think he was someone who really cared." As she talked more about him it was clear that she saw him as a kind of Christ-figure, not a hero she looked up to like Mother Teresa, but someone she knew personally who modeled the life of a compassionate Christian. "He has an ability to care, and I think people know that in a way that sometimes overwhelms him. He has such a way of letting someone know his concern, even if it's the first time he has talked with them. I've thought how nice it would be to have that characteristic. He's so transparent."

These role models and her basic Christian beliefs play an important role in Debbie's understanding of her own efforts to be kind and compassionate. The main reason she feels it is important to care for others is that individuals have eternal worth. When you show compassion that also has eternal value. "In the Christian view," she explains, "there is a life beyond this one, eternal life, so if you live a life that is compassionate, it has implications forever. If I didn't think life had any more meaning than just this life, I'm not sure I'd be doing the same things. I might, but it wouldn't have the same significance."

Besides the larger significance her beliefs give her caring behavior, they also reinforce an ethic of equality in the here and now. She does not care for others simply because it has eternal value. Like many other contemporary evangelicals, she is very much oriented toward the world of today. Christianity tells her how to think about herself and how to relate to her neighbors. "The Christian teaching is that we do care for ourselves. God made us and we're important. But we just need to realize that it's easy to think of ourselves as better than or more important than others. So we need to see others as equal to ourselves and care for them just as much."

Her beliefs about caring also reflect some of the other emphases among conservative Christians that I identified earlier from the survey. She is, for example, convinced that compassion should involve giving of yourself, and is even comfortable, up to a point, with the language of sacrifice. She also remarked that Gandhi was someone she admired chiefly because of his willingness to sacrifice himself for his beliefs. At the same time, she is sophisticated enough to recognize the dangers of developing a martyr complex. Her faith has taught her that even sacrifice can become a matter of pride. She admits that there have been times when she cared for others just because it made her feel good about herself. She believes you have to have a strong sense of who you are and that you get this from yourself and from your faith, not from those you try to help. "I began to realize that I need to learn better who I am and not have to define myself in terms of what I'm doing or whether I'm involved in this, that, or the other thing."

Like other religious conservatives, she also associates compassion with a de-emphasis on money. She is concerned about the level of materialism in our society, and is genuinely committed to devoting her life to something that will benefit the poor. She says she often enjoys interacting with people from other countries better than with her own neighbors because so many Americans are "materialistic" and not "relationally oriented."

Debbie does more than pay lip service to these convictions. A few months after she was interviewed, Debbie, her husband, and their two young children left the United States to become medical missionaries in Africa. Her husband started a clinic and she took a job teaching in a Christian boarding school. If the world was perfect, she explained, there would be no need for people to do such things. But it isn't. "There are needs, and as long as we can do something, we want to be willing to do that."

When she was interviewed, she realized that the caring she did for international women was relatively painless when compared with, say, some of the difficult cases her husband dealt with as a doctor. But it was also clear that she felt very deeply for the women she had gotten to know. Hers was not simply the casual contact of some volunteers that involves nothing of themselves. She became personally attached to these women and she experienced pain when they moved away. Indeed, she said the hardest part was when they left. "Then I just feel like a part of my heart's been torn out and it takes me a couple of months to get over it."

· 11 ·

What I found most intriguing about Debbie Carson was her ability to transcend the special language and beliefs of her evangelical tradition. She is not one of the faithful who can speak only to the faithful. It is almost as if she were speaking to people who in fact spoke a different language. She puts things in words familiar to them, and then translates back into her own Christian vocabulary. In describing the value of volunteer efforts, for example, she drew on the Christian metaphor "ye are the salt of the earth." But she avoided the Christian jargon itself. "I think of [volunteer work] like the idea of seasoning in food. You put a little salt in the soup and it makes the soup taste better, even though the whole soup isn't made of salt." She also drew on the biblical metaphor of being a light to the world, again translating: "It's like a candle in a dark room. Maybe it's just one tiny little candle, but it's still more than nothing." And then she switched back to an evangelical idea, but recognizing that it was an idea not shared by everyone, signaled its origins: "I guess thinking about it in Christian terms, with the idea of the Fall and all, there isn't going to be any great solution to society's problems. But if one person helps another, it can be a step toward changing the hearts of individuals."

She knows the special language of evangelical Christianity—knows it so well that she can articulate her beliefs in stylized words and phrases. But, like many others of the educated evangelical elite, she has learned how to translate her beliefs into a more universal language. Note again what she said about the man from Afghanistan: "He was interested in Christianity and had not really had it explained to him." She did not say he was interested in Christ or the truth. She objectifies Christianity. She makes it a religion—one of many. And she concludes her story, not with something laden with evangelical terms (like "he received Christ"), but with a very truncated phrase that does not even mention Christianity again: "Just to be the first person to explain something like that to him, that was a really special time."

In the same way she objectifies Christianity, she objectifies and personalizes her faith. In talking about the relation between her volunteer work with internationals and her faith, for example, she said: "It's broadened my horizons and really made me think through my own values. It's reinforced some and made me realize some aren't ones I really want to pursue. So it's really encouraged me to think about other values and other ways in which people live." She turns the particulars of her evangelical faith into "values"—a word more likely to be used in diverse, cosmopolitan settings. And she refers to a selective process. As she observes others and as she watches herself in diverse settings, she decides to emphasize some values and not others.

In describing herself as a Christian she also went out of her way to translate Christ into a figure that someone who was not a believer could appreciate. Rather than simply stressing her belief in the absolute truth of Christianity, she contextualized her convictions by noting that she had studied Christ all her life and interacted a lot with other Christians. She went on to say explicitly that "Christ is a very controversial figure." And then she defended him on pragmatic, rather than religious, grounds. "If you think about how he's affected history, quite apart from whether he's a religious figure or not, he's the one person who has really influenced people's morals and principles. Christ is a very important figure, no matter how you feel about his claim to be God."

Debbie Carson has also learned, from interacting with a wide variety of people in school, in the places she has lived, and in her travels, when to talk the special jargon of evangelical Christianity and when to speak a secular language. I noted earlier that she disavowed any direct connection between her volunteer work with internationals and her church. That was after she was asked. The way she explained her involvement initially just hinted politely at a church connection and mostly relied on the kind of scripts others without religious leanings employed. "It seems that all through my life I've really enjoyed getting to know other cultures," she opened. Then elaborating: "In college there were several internationals and I was helping tutoring and that kind of thing. When we moved here I had more free time and just wanted to get involved in volunteer work. I found out about these programs through some people in the church and that provided a kind of nucleus to get some things going."

When she talks like this Debbie Carson requires the listener to engage in his or her own decoding process. If the listener is sensitive to her evangelical subculture, he or she can pick up the cues, recognize that a kindred spirit is speaking, even probe for more detail. If the listener is not familiar with evangelicalism, Debbie's speech will sound ordinary and inoffensive.[17] Here is another example. Asked what she had gotten from working with international families, she remarked: "I always feel I get more than any service we give to these people. I just find these people fascinating and I feel that for our family it's been a broadening experience. I don't feel that I'm sacrificing or in a way giving out more than I'm getting. Usually it's the other way; we receive a lot more than we're giving out." Nothing here to signal the outsider that an evangelical is speaking. And yet to an insider, the phrasing of this comment would seem familiar. It is in fact a standard evangelical way of describing one's life in Christ more generally. Sacrifice is an issue, whereas it is not for many other people. It is an issue because the born-again experience requires one to give up one's former life, to repent and be different, to quit going it alone and trust in Jesus. But the sacrifice is always compensated for by the blessings one receives. So Debbie Carson talks about how much she has gained from serving these people. In her theology they stand in quite literally for Jesus. As she serves them she serves her Lord. It is a way of realizing the blessings of the Christian life. "We receive a lot more than we're giving out."

Sometimes the cues that color her language are even more subtle. She uses a lexicon that anyone in the broader society can understand, but her speech employs a deep structure—a rhythm, a cadence, a manner of phrasing—that reflects the subculture and signals familiarity to other evangelicals. Here is what she said about Mother Teresa: "She has nothing materially, not even a normal life; all she's done is just be faithful to what she thought she should do, and yet she's been called the most powerful woman in the world." Mother Teresa is a Christ-figure. Debbie says they both illustrate compassion in its highest form. But we also know Mother Teresa is a Christ-figure for Debbie because this phrase is a typical evangelical way of talking about Christ. He was born in a stable, had nothing, not even a family, and yet he has been called the most influential figure in history. It is simply the theme of the lowly being exalted. And then, in case we did not get the connection, she makes it for us: "I think of the verse that says if you lose your life, you gain it. That's really true for her."

· 12 ·

For all the devotion she has to her God and to other people, Debbie Carson has developed a language that also allows her to function well in the relativistic, individualistic culture in which she lives. Contrary to popular stereotypes of evangelicals, she is an extraordinarily tolerant person. Perhaps she has to be to work effectively with people from other cultures. But she is not the stereotypic missionary of the past who knows all the right answers and goes out to convert the heathen. When she says she learns a lot from other cultures, she means it. Her personality and the gentle manner in which she speaks convey an openness to the values and beliefs of other people.

But it is again her adeptness in the use of language that best enables her to live in a relativistic and individualistic society. Consider one particular word that occurs repeatedly in her speech, the word ability. In relating a story about her best friend in Alabama, for example, she concluded: "She really has an ability to care for people." She used the same phrase in describing her pastor: "He has an ability to care." She used it again when she talked about admiring Mother Teresa's ability to show compassion. She also talked about her own abilities, including being a "people person" and having a capacity to relate to others.

"Ability" is an interesting word—interesting for its ambiguity. It is something a person has, is, received at birth, or achieved. One is never quite sure. The dictionary itself waffles, saying that an ability can be either a natural talent or an acquired proficiency.

When she is pressed to do so, Debbie Carson can articulate her views about the relations between nature and nurture with considerable skill. She does so, for example, in describing why some people seem more compassionate than others. "I think selfishness and compassion are both innate qualities," she observes. "Which one comes out kind of depends on how a child is brought up. A lot depends on what values are put before a child and what examples he sees. If they are nurtured and cared for, then they'll be able to care for others." Elaborating, she invoked a hierarchical theory of human needs that she had probably learned as a major in special education: "I think a lot of selfishness as adults comes from needs that haven't been taken care of as children. So it's hard to take somebody who's a selfish person as an adult and try to get them to think about being more compassionate." In this sense, she thought the die was cast. She had to excuse people who acted selfishly because they probably had unmet needs. "Those needs have to be met somehow before they are free to develop that other nature. I see that in my own children."

But when she uses the word in ordinary conversation, "ability" has the same ambiguous meaning it does in the dictionary, and for that reason it serves her well. Insofar as it is something she admires and aspires to, it is an acquired proficiency. But to the extent that some people just have it and others do not, it connotes a natural talent. Sometimes it is just a gift, a personality trait, as she says of the people in her fellowship group at church: "We have people who are funny and are clowns, some people who are outgoing and some who are more serious; it's nice to have a group of people with different gifts." In this sense caring is a natural talent as well, as in the case of her pastor, who has an ability to be transparent, or her husband, who she says has an ability to help people in pain. At the same time, ability can be learned and developed, as she notes when she talks about wanting to become more caring herself. It requires agency, a decision, an act of will, as Debbie remarked about her friend: she was willing to be vulnerable. Ability is a convenient word: it allows her to say what she values in herself and in other people at the same time that it allows her to excuse people for their differences.

Ability is also one of those words that has a dual meaning that connects her evangelical subculture to the larger society. The dictionary says someone who has an ability is able and that being able means having sufficient power, skill, intelligence, competence, or resources to accomplish something. All this makes sense both in the evangelical tradition and in American society more generally. Evangelicals talk a lot about being able. There is a popular evangelical hymn, for example, that affirms the believer's faith in Christ with the refrain "I know that he is able." As the believer follows Christ, he or she too becomes able. The believer learns Scripture, becomes stronger in the faith, is able to withstand temptation, gains the capacity to live a moral life, and cultivates the skills necessary to lead others to Christ. Evangelicalism is like doing math. It is a religion of skill, competence, discipline. But so is American culture. We value our abilities, whether they are natural talents or proficiencies we work hard to cultivate. When Debbie says "ability," then, it serves her as a bridge word. It selectively emphasizes something common to her tradition and the society in which she lives.

As an abstraction, ability is something we all value. We want people to have abilities and we expect them to use their abilities. It is a value we share. But it is a value that we can also experience differently. It is like mothers. We all have them—motherhood is universal—but each one of us has our own mother. We are united in our diversity; diverse in our unity. In the conservative religious tradition Debbie Carson exemplifies, this is how faith and caring are understood. She values her religion very deeply, just as she values showing compassion to the needy. But both are in large measure abilities; you should cultivate them, but you should not be critical of others who may not have the same abilities. It is a way of being a committed, conservative Christian in a pluralistic society.

· 13 ·

The Reverend Cranfield Holmes, the rector of an Episcopal church, illustrates much of what typifies the liberal perspective in American religion. Born of American parents, he spent much of his childhood in England where his father was stationed as a government liaison during World War II and after the war ran a prosperous business specializing in foreign trade. When his parents eventually returned to the United States, Cranfield stayed in England; he attended an expensive boarding school and later was graduated from Cambridge University. Upon graduation he spent a year traveling before settling down in New York City. At first he entertained notions of following in his father's footsteps by pursuing a career in business, but after several years in various lower-management positions he decided to attend law school. A year later his studies were interrupted by the escalation of conflict in Vietnam. When he was drafted, Cranfield declared himself a conscientious objector and spent the next three years working as a noncombatant in military hospitals. More than anything else, he says, it was that experience that convinced him to enter the ministry.

When I met him, Mr. Holmes had just turned fifty and was in the seventeenth year of his ministry as an Episcopal priest.

He was a handsome man who looked younger than his age. His beard was still the same ruddy color as his hair and I could imagine from the friendly manner in which he spoke that he was well liked in his parish. He also introduced me to his wife Pat, an attractive woman in her early forties. I learned later that she and Mr. Holmes had married about five years before, after his first marriage broke up. There were three children from the first marriage with whom Mr. Holmes still kept in close contact.

The church they serve—a parish of about three hundred members, half of whom attend regularly, located in an older neighborhood not far from a disadvantaged section of a middle-sized city in the Northeast—is an all-encompassing community for Mr. and Mrs. Holmes. In addition to his preaching he spends much of his time doing pastoral counseling for his parishioners. She has a full-time career, but spends much of her spare time at the church. For the past several years she has taught a Sunday school class for teenagers, worked on various committees, and sung in the choir. Both describe the church as the place where they have seen compassion most vividly illustrated. Mr. Holmes observes that the people in his church are not particularly notable, but have taught him a lot. "I've listened to them talk, and they've had an extraordinary impact on me; in fact, I think the strongest impact on my attitudes has come from very ordinary people. I've been very impressed especially with people who've cared for others and shown me how to care." His wife echoes the sentiment. At first she found it hard to be involved in the church because people cast her in a stereotypic "pastor's wife" role. But as she worked in smaller groups she became better acquainted with specific individuals, learned from them, and learned more about her own abilities to serve. "They separate me from my husband's role in the church, so I get a better sense of my own personhood. People respond to me as me."

The parish is a focal point, but Mr. Holmes and his wife both reach out from that point to be of service in the broader community. He serves as Director of Family Services for the city and heads a local peace group. He also counsels people from the wider community who have drug addictions. He values these broader involvements, not only because they are ways to

share his ministry, but also because he is freer than in his parish to do what he wants: "I feel I'm not beholden to that community, although it's in line with their aims and objectives."
Mrs. Holmes heads a committee that oversees a day-care center
for working mothers in the inner city and babysits two evenings a week at a center for abused women. Both convey a genuine sense of concern for the needy and disadvantaged. Mr.
Holmes describes it as a conviction that you have to sit where
someone else is sitting in order to understand the depths of
that person's experience. "Sometimes people aren't very attractive, and if you're able to enter into their experience, you begin
to understand the reasons for their unattractiveness. People
who have been suffering from homelessness or some kind of
disablement can become very sour; to understand this, you
have to suffer a little bit with them." Mrs. Holmes says she has
a special feeling for abused women and neglected children because she was once in a similar situation herself.

· 14 ·

Because of his training in theology I expected Mr. Holmes to
give an elaborate theological rationale for his involvement with
the needy. Instead I found him cautious in his use of religious
language. Indeed, there was a kind of reluctance on his part,
almost an embarrassment about using words that might seem
too pious or too peculiar to a religious tradition—the kind of
reluctance one sees among many religious liberals. He explained that his first sense of religion had come from his
nanny. His remarks about his parents suggested that he had
not been particularly close to them. But his nanny had been a
model of kindness and had also imparted some of her religious
values. For a long time, he thought of compassion as kind of a
religious duty, as a way one should behave because one owed
something to God. But during his years as a minister he has
modified that view. He now thinks of caring more as an experiment. Helping the needy is something you choose to do, often
as a way to learn about yourself, or to gain some satisfaction.
   This emphasis on personal growth and fulfillment is, as I
noted before, a characteristic that seems to distinguish the mo-

tivational language of liberals and conservatives in survey studies. It is clearly an important motif in the language of both Mr. Holmes and his wife. In his experience, caring for others has been a significant way of increasing his ability to tackle difficult problems. He puts it simply: "I'm better able to cope with things." Mrs. Holmes elaborates: "I think I've grown, because I'm working on projects I've never done before. I'm accustomed to working in business and being the head of departments and things like that where I'm more or less able to mold a group and get them to go in the direction I want them to. I find that is impossible in a church committee. Everybody has their own idea about where to go. So I think I've learned a lot about group dynamics and how to fit into a group and to know when I should open my mouth and when I should just be quiet. I've also learned that everybody has something to offer." Like many of the people I quoted in chapter 4, she feels she has gained as much as she has given: "You don't stand aloof and say you have no weaknesses. There's a great deal to be learned from people in need. You need to be open to the good and positive things that might come in unexpected ways."

But there is also a healthy balance between personal growth and social betterment in the language the Holmeses use to talk about caring. For example, Mr. Holmes admits that being in the ministry and doing volunteer work has not only made him feel stronger but has also made him feel more dependent on others. "I've learned how much a part of everything else I am and that I need help from other people as well; I'm part of the social organism." He also believes caring is somehow diminished if people care for others strictly as a way of gaining personal satisfaction. When he was younger, he recalls, he found that working with handicapped people gave him a tremendous sense of self-satisfaction. "Looking back, I really feel my main motivation at that time was the sense that I was doing good, and that I was a great guy in consequence." He reflects that this may be a necessary stage for people to go through in learning how to care. But he thinks it is unfortunate if people never move beyond that stage. In his own case, he feels he has. Those who do not, he worries, may actually wind up hindering the needy rather than helping them, because their commitment is too shallow. Instead of staying long enough to form lasting relationships and learn what the problem really is, they simply move on.

· 15 ·

Debbie Carson also talked about personal growth and social betterment as reasons to be caring. But what distinguishes the more liberal discourse of the Holmeses is the way they objectify religion. From Debbie Carson one gains the feeling that the human world is embedded within a larger, transcendent, supernatural cosmos—a divine reality to which religion points. From Cranfield Holmes one gains the sense that religion is instead embedded within a larger reality that is basically secular—the reality of human culture, or what he calls "society." He in fact pointedly uses the word "religion" instead of "faith" or "Christianity," and "society" is a word that does not simply mean the United States; it has more inclusive, almost mystical connotations. Indeed, Mr. Holmes prefers to describe his faith by translating religious language into something one might associate with some of the great social philosophers of the nineteenth and twentieth centuries. When asked to explain the religious beliefs that motivate his caring behavior, for example, he had this to say: "Religion, it seems to me, points to the teaching that society is served best when people serve others—when they love their neighbors as themselves. Some people clearly get a lot of their inner drive from the sense that they're pleasing an Almighty Creator. Others of us get more from a sense of the process between birth and death that our maturity and the maturity of all those who are sharing our time is best served by mutual interconnectedness and mutual service. Salvation in that sense comes from within the society and leads us toward a more mature society."

Debbie Carson's emphasis on sacrifice is also missing in Cranfield Holmes's arguments. It is not the selflessness of Mother Teresa that he admires, but her perseverance. In his own case he says he seldom feels he is doing anything self-sacrificial. "There are occasions on which I say, oh damn, do I have to go and do that. In that case perhaps it seems like it's a sacrifice of myself, but I don't in fact say it's a sacrifice. I see it entirely as being something that I've asked myself to do, for my own benefit." He also denies that a proper understanding of religion teaches one to be self-sacrificial. He says he used to think of himself needing to repay his debts to God, or to society, by giving until it hurt. But now he uses the metaphor, as we saw, of an organism. "I feel that my volunteer service is part of an organism, and that a healthy organism involves giving. An unhealthy organism is self-centered. I see it as a natural way of living. It's the one that gives me the most pleasure."

So from Cranfield Holmes's perspective, life necessitates give-and-take. Debbie Carson would hardly disagree. Her emphasis on the interdependence that exists among all of God's creatures is similar to what Cranfield Holmes means by an organism. She too acknowledges the pleasure that comes from giving. What she would not do is subsume God within this concept of organism. The divine transcends the natural and commands people to be self-sacrificing. It would, therefore, not seem quite right to her to say that giving is a *natural* way of living. Nor would she be comfortable with associating this way of living so directly with pleasure. In her view, selfishness is the natural way; to be selfless requires the obedience and inspiration that comes from following God.

· 16 ·

Often, though, it is not so much some deeper philosophical difference that divides Cranfield Holmes's liberal orientation from Debbie Carson's conservative viewpoint as it is a choice of words. It is not a fundamental clash of worldviews, at least not one that either can formulate explicitly, but a matter of emphasis. Both recognize the relativism, the pluralism, the basic secularity of American culture. But Debbie Carson struggles to maintain the priority of Christian symbols within this context, while Mr. Holmes struggles to make them more contextualized. The outcome is not always terribly different, despite the fact that some people might feel more comfortable with one way of speaking than with the other. For example, we saw in Debbie Carson's case that she pointedly selected Christ as the person who best exemplified kindness and compassion. But she wound up talking in as much detail about Gandhi, Mother Teresa, and Martin Luther King, Jr., as she did about Christ. She was in this sense pluralistic. She was able to draw inspiration from a variety of role models, including some outside the Christian tradition. Mr. Holmes was pluralistic in the same way. He too mentioned Christ, Gandhi, and others. It was just that his account made more of a point of being pluralistic. "Years ago, I would have immediately said Jesus; now, I'm less convinced that that is a fair statement. Clearly there've been other outstanding individuals. I think of Gandhi and Martin Luther King. They are religious-type leaders. Florence Nightingale and Dorothea Dix would be others. I have been impressed at various different times by various different lives." To the sensitive ear, listening for signals of orthodoxy, Debbie's remarks were probably more comforting than those of Cranfield Holmes. But the differences are actually suggested by rather subtle cues rather by the main arguments of either speaker.

How these subtle differences show up is also evident in Mr. Holmes's answer to my question whether religious people are any more likely to be compassionate than nonreligious people. Like Debbie Carson, he waffled. Wanting to give religious people the benefit of the doubt, she pointed out that some nonreligious people were also very caring. Wanting to keep religion in its place, he observed that "sometimes people who have a deep religious faith are actually more self-centered than others because they're looking to save themselves rather than anybody else." He said he doubted that faith necessarily saves people from self-centeredness. But then he also backtracked, qualifying the negative tone of his remarks, by observing that "some of the greatest examples of caring have come from people who have had a deep religious faith and have understood the implications of that faith." In short, one said the glass was half-full; the other said it was half-empty. The main difference was a matter of emphasis.

Part of what Mr. Holmes is saying differs very little from the view someone like Debbie Carson might take. He is saying that religious convictions in our society are—and have to be— highly personalized. They have to be a matter of personal conviction; otherwise, we might wonder how sincerely held they are. Religion must be something you work out in your own way. This is what the Christian tradition itself has always taught. It is just that some people emphasize "your own way" more than others. Debbie Carson would call it faith. She believes in her own way, believes with personal conviction, but in doctrines that are fairly orthodox. Cranfield Holmes has a more open, more broadly defined sense of what may be orthodox. Thus he does not talk so much about his faith as about his philosophy. When he describes caring as an experiment, for example, he says he usually becomes involved in a specific group or activity simply because someone asks him to, but it is his "philosophy" that tells him the work these groups do is worthwhile. "I am committed in my own philosophy to the work these groups are doing—working for peace and counseling the disadvantaged, especially in the area of drugs."

The main difference is that Cranfield Holmes has subjectivized his beliefs to a greater extent than Debbie Carson has. She sees herself in a relationship with God. Her faith is highly personal, but it still involves something outside herself. She recognizes that each person must find God individually, perhaps even in his or her own way. But the search involves attaching oneself to something transcendent, a divine being with a distinct identity. Mr. Holmes's God is also transcendent, but it is more metaphoric, a state of being that is constructed symbolically. And because it is created symbolically, it is more purely his own. It is within his own heart, in the same way Debbie's God is within her heart, but it is more nearly contained there. It cannot be separated from his own biography and the language he has developed to describe it.

After the interview was over, Mr. Holmes gave perhaps the most candid assessment of how his faith and his efforts to be caring intersect. "If you asked me the really blunt question, why do you do such things, I'd say the answer is that I'm really not sure. Is it that it's become habitual? In a sense it has become habitual with me to be involved with caring and to be interested in people's problems. In a sense I don't see it as caring, it is simply the way my life is lived now. Ask me where the wellspring comes from? I know historically some of the influences, but basically the wellspring comes from inside my heart. I would give honor to those who've shown the way, but basically it seems to just be part of the goodness of life that I should respond as best I can and encourage other people to do so as well."

· 17 ·

In the end we return, then, to the question of individualism. Cranfield Holmes and Debbie Carson each illustrate in his or her own way the extent to which religion in our society has been colored by individualism. Despite the important differences that separate one from the other, that make one a religious conservative and the other a religious liberal, each of them spoke about faith in a very personal way that, to be sure, made it sound like a serious and sincere conviction, but in personalizing it to this extent, also rendered it completely inoffensive to someone who might have different beliefs. Despite the fact that they placed their own beliefs at the center of their lives, they were reluctant to impose those beliefs on anyone else. This was especially the case with Mr. Holmes, but it was true of Debbie Carson as well. Although she was in a sense trying to be a Christian witness to people from non-Western cultures, she spoke in a way that bestowed respect and autonomy on these cultures and emphasized the blessings she herself received more than any of the traditional evangelistic rhetoric about saving souls from damnation. In both instances, exposure to many different belief systems and theological perspectives had resulted in sharply idiosyncratic religious worldviews. What both believed was the unique outcome of their own journeys. Indeed, both were proud of having thought through theological and moral issues for themselves.

Surveys reveal how widespread these individualistic tendencies in American religion are. One question that was posed in a recent national study asked people whether they agreed or disagreed with the statement "A person can still be a good Christian or Jew if he does not attend church or synagogue." Seventy-six percent agreed. They might have been thinking of someone confined to a hospital because of illness or perhaps a scientist stationed at the South Pole. But the same study included an even more individualistic statement: "An individual should arrive at his or her own religious beliefs independent of any churches or synagogues." This statement actually evoked more assent than the first: 80 percent agreed. And on both, younger people were more likely to agree than older people.[18] The norm is clearly toward people gaining spirituality on their own. You do not have to be part of a religious community. In fact, you had better block out that influence. Start with a tabula rasa and write your own religious script.

And does this kind of individualism in religion erode its power to encourage caring and compassion? Or do people find ways in religion, as in their values generally, to reconcile individualism and caring? The evidence is not conclusive, but it does point in a worrisome direction. Some of it does suggest that privatizing one's religious views in this way may have a dampening effect on the value people ascribe to caring for others. For example, there is a statistically significant negative relationship between saying that a person can be a good Christian or Jew and not attend religious services and agreeing strongly with the statement that people have a responsibility to give to the needy. People who said they feel it is important to develop their own religious beliefs independently of any church were also less likely to value caring for the needy than people who took issue with this popular form of religious individualism.[19]

· 18 ·

But there is also a deeper connection to be found in the complex relationships among religion, caring, and individualism. It is not just a question of whether individualism erodes religion's power to inspire caring. It is the fact that caring itself becomes a kind of object lesson in religious individualism. It illustrates—and legitimates—religious individualism.

You know someone who is very compassionate and yet without religious faith. You know others who attend church every Sunday and seem to be utterly without compassion. How do you make sense of it? You distinguish spirituality from religion. You decide that what is truly important is the invisible, interior, entirely individualistic variety of faith that people call spirituality. That, you say, is different from religion—the external shell, the public form that may be an actual community embedded in the framework of society, but vacuous nonetheless. And you not only distinguish the two; you clearly prefer one to the other. Spirituality results in caring; religion often does not. The individualistic dimension occupies the higher ground. It gains credence. Pragmatically, it seems better.

The only question is, how can spirituality of this kind be sustained? Can it long survive if elevating individual spirituality above organized religion also means nonparticipation in any community of kindred believers? For Ellen Steinberg, as we saw earlier, it could not. A healthy spirituality required her to participate in her religious community. But for many others, spirituality seemed to be something they wanted to unplug from any broader network of believers. So, for them, and for our culture more broadly, we must ask how well this works. Does personal faith promote caring apart from involvement in a religious community? Or does one need the support and encouragement of fellow believers?

Please do not confuse the question I am asking now with the question I asked at the beginning of the chapter. I asked then whether religious people are any more caring than nonreligious people. I presented evidence that gave a very qualified yes. Now I am asking a different question. Suppose someone claims to be moved by a deep sense of spirituality. Is this faith likely to compel caring activities if it is held apart from involvement in any religious community? Or does it yield results only when it occurs in the context of a supportive community?

I recognize how difficult it is to answer a question like this. But research studies involving large numbers of people do make it possible to draw some inferences. The strategy I use is to separate those people who are actively involved in churches or other religious organizations from those who are not involved in such communities. Within each of these groups it is then possible to compare those who place a lot of importance on their faith with those who do not value having a deep faith. From these comparisons we can see whether faith and caring are related in the same way or differently in the two contexts. Here is what some of these comparisons suggest.

First, as I reported earlier, the more often an individual

claims to experience divine love, the more likely that person is to spend time on charitable activities. But this effect is limited to individuals who attend church regularly. Among individuals who attend church infrequently or who do not attend, how much or how little they feel God's love has no effect on the likelihood of their being involved in charitable work.[20]

Second, a more detailed analysis of the motives and values that facilitate charitable behavior shows very different patterns among those who are active participants in their churches or synagogues and those who are inactive. I compared the reasons people gave for wanting to be kind and caring among regular weekly churchgoers and among less-frequent churchgoers. Faith was a strong predictor of charitable behavior among the former but not among the latter. "My religious beliefs teach me to be kind and caring" was the reason that discriminated most strongly between churchgoers who were currently involved in charitable or service activities and churchgoers who were not involved in these activities. Among the less-frequent attendees, this reason ranked seventh (out of nine) as a predictor of who was involved in charitable activity and who was not.[21] I also compared the values of regular churchgoers with less-frequent attendees to see which values in each case were the best predictors of whether or not people were involved in charitable activities. The values that discriminated best in both populations, not surprisingly, were placing importance on giving time to help people and valuing helping the needy. After these, the value that best discriminated between those involved in charitable activities and those not involved *among churchgoers* was placing importance on having a deep religious faith. Among persons not active in church, valuing a deep faith did not relate strongly to charitable behavior.[22]

Comparisons made possible by other studies also suggest that spirituality begins to move people toward being compassionate only when a threshold of involvement in some kind of collective religious activity has been reached. This evidence comes from making comparisons within two sets of people. The first comparison involves people who are *not* currently involved in any kind of volunteer religious work. It compares persons who have donated time within the past year to helping poor, disadvantaged, or needy people with individuals who have not donated time to such activities. The second comparison involves people who *are* involved with religious work, and again is between those who also give time to helping the poor or disadvantaged and those who do not give time. In the first comparison, intensity of religious commitment does not seem to make much difference: people who help the needy are not any more religiously oriented than people who do not help the needy. In the second comparison, though, intensity of religious commitment does make some difference: those who donate time both to religious work and to the needy are more devout than those who donate time only to religious work. The kinds of religious orientations that make a difference in this second case, but not in the first, are: saying that your relation to God is very important to your sense of self-worth, saying that your relation to God is a source of a great deal of satisfaction, attending church more than once a week, and feeling close to God when attending church.[23]

I interpret these results to mean that religious inclinations make very little difference unless one becomes involved in some kind of organized religious community. Once you are involved in such a community, then a higher level of piety may be associated with putting yourself out to help the needy. But if you are not involved in some kind of religious organization, then a higher level of piety seems unlikely to generate charitable efforts toward the poor or disadvantaged.

If religious values have been an inducement for people to care for their neighbors historically, then the spread of individualism within modern religion is likely to have a dampening effect on charitable behavior. The evidence from empirical studies suggests that many individuals who are heavily involved in caring for their neighbors consider themselves spiritual even though they are not involved in any religious community. They distinguish between spirituality and religion. But the evidence also shows that spirituality is conducive to caring activities only when it occurs within the context of such communities.

CHAPTER SIX

Along the Road

A CERTAIN MAN was going down from Jerusalem to Jericho; and he fell among robbers, who both stripped him and beat him, and departed, leaving him half-dead. And by chance a certain priest was going down that way: and when he saw him, he passed by on the other side. And in like manner a Levite also, when he came to the place, and saw him, passed by on the other side. But a certain Samaritan, as he journeyed, came where he was: and when he saw him, he was moved to compassion, and came to him, and bound up his wounds, pouring on them oil and wine, and he set him on his own beast, and brought him to an inn, and took care of him. And on the morrow he took out two shillings, and gave them to the host, and said, "Take care of him; and whatsoever thou spendest more, I, when I come back again, will repay thee."[1]

· 2 ·

Theologians and religious ethicists have devised elaborate doctrines to explain the Judeo-Christian understanding of compassion. The Bible itself has given them ample justification for doing so. In addition to the passage describing the Good Samaritan, compassion is mentioned 41 times in the Bible, the word "kindness" is used 45 times, and love is referred to more than 450 times. With so much material to work with, every denomination and faith has produced its distinctive interpretations of why and how people should love their neighbors. Jewish scholars have honed the doctrine of *zedakah* to a fine art. In the Middle Ages the Roman Catholic tradition distinguished numerous types of mercy, stewardship, gift giving, and alms, each with its own eternal reward. Each branch of the Protestant Reformation taught its followers a particular combination of faith and works. Since that time countless sects and religious movements have emerged with new ideas about how best to spread the gospel, promote charity, heal social ills, and store up merit in heaven.

But Americans are a fairly simple lot with respect to such teachings. Despite the fact that we buy more Bibles per capita each year than any other country, and despite the fact that more sermons are preached in more churches on any given Sunday than in all the rest of the industrialized countries combined, we know little about theology and religious ethics. Our great commitment to knowledge and expertise in the secular fields, especially in science and technology, has not carried over to the religious realm. Pollsters, who find nearly universal belief in God among the American people, are repeatedly surprised by the large proportions of the public that cannot identify even such rudimentary biblical facts as the names of the four gospels or the town in which Jesus was born. It seems, as the religious observer Will Herberg argued some years ago in his book *Protestant—Catholic—Jew*, that our faith is often continentwide but only an inch deep.[2] Our faith may be a vast and fertile plain verdant with life, but its roots are shallow. We subscribe to one religious tradition or another as part of our identity—as part of what it means to be an American—but we have little understanding of what those traditions teach. If asked to say how the Lutheran doctrine of compassion differs from (or is similar to) the Calvinist doctrine or the Baptist doctrine, we would be at a loss for words.

People were in fact at a loss for words when asked to describe any specific religious teachings that might be relevant to their efforts to be kind and compassionate. Those like Debbie Carson and Cranfield Holmes who could put their efforts in some broader theological perspective were the exceptions. Most were lucky if they could remember some vague paraphrase of the Golden Rule—like the woman who said, "Do unto others—how does it go?" Many drew a blank entirely. They were involved in volunteer work themselves. They knew religious organizations that sponsored charitable activities; some of them were involved directly in these activities. They knew compassion was part of what their religion taught, but they could not say why or how. This was particularly true of those who were uninvolved or only nominally affiliated with some religious tradition. Jack Casey, for example, said he really had no idea what religion taught about compassion. But having no idea about religious teachings was not uncommon even among those who were heavily committed to their faith. A woman in her seventies who had attended church faithfully all her life, for example, said it was very difficult for her to say exactly what her church taught about caring. "I guess it reinforces my volunteering and helping, but that's all I can say." Another person who said he attended church regularly noted that his church provided many opportunities for people to be caring and compassionate, but when asked what his church taught about such activities, he admitted: "I can't think of anything specific."

· 3 ·

If questions about religious doctrines cause our brains to short-circuit faster than an essay on fractal geometry, we are nevertheless a surprisingly intelligent people when it comes to the story of the Good Samaritan. A man who spent much of his spare time doing volunteer work at a local Presbyterian church, for example, was unable to say exactly why he thought religious people should be compassionate, but then recounted the story of the Good Samaritan to illustrate that Jesus had taught us to be caring. The woman in her seventies who could not say what her church taught about caring also became suddenly articulate when asked about the Good Samaritan parable. "It's the story of a person who is put upon and beaten along the roadway and left for dead," she began. "Several people, very religious people, come along and pass by on the other side, and then the Samaritan comes along and takes care of him and takes him where he can be helped and pays for everything." Similarly, the man who could not think of anything specific his church taught noted that the important thing for him was being exposed to stories like the parable of the Good Samaritan as a child: "If you grow up going to Sunday school and hearing about the Good Samaritan and the miracles of Jesus and the beatitudes, you can't help but have some of it rub off on you."

Even people who disclaim having had a religious thought in their head for decades can often recite the story of the Good

Samaritan with ease. Martin Barnes, the businessman who directs Meals on Wheels, mused for a moment when he was asked about religious teachings and then remarked: "You know, what I'm flashing back to are the Bible stories I learned as a kid—with the pictures and all." The story of the Good Samaritan was one such story that stood out in his memory. He was able to summarize it in these words: "There's this man who's traveling and he's robbed and beaten and left in the ditch, and I think many people pass and he's obviously quite ill and no one will stop, and then there's this one person who did stop; that was the key to the story, the fact that he did stop and help."

Another woman said she had difficulty with religious teachings because they seemed too absolute and abstract. Like several of the people I quoted in the last chapter, she was more comfortable defining spirituality in her own way. But she could relate to the story of the Good Samaritan because it was a story. It did not try to make a theological point. It simply presented a character who showed compassion. She said she had identified with the good in this character since she was a little girl. As she thought back, she said: "This was something that was brought into our own home when I was growing up. There used to be a lot of hoboes around and they'd come to the door asking for food, usually dressed very badly. And my mother would always invite them in and give them a cup of coffee and fix them up with a great big sandwich. So [the Good Samaritan] was something I saw as a girl."

Like the stories of being cared for that most of us have tucked away in our personal biographies, the story of the Good Samaritan is a common feature of our collective tradition. It is a simple story, and so, even with all our sophistication in science and technology, we hark back to it. We can remember it and retell it. We see examples in our daily lives that bring it to our minds. It is taught by religious institutions, along with all the subtle doctrines and theologies we cannot remember. It is also reinforced in the secular media through television stories and literary narratives that build on its simple outline. Jim Casey in *The Grapes of Wrath* is the Good Samaritan. So is the Lone Ranger. Mother Teresa in the dusty streets of Calcutta and Albert Schweitzer on the muddy trails of Africa are too. The Good

Samaritan is the legendary figure who helps someone else along the road. The story is one of those ancient myths that embodies the deepest meanings in our culture. In learning it and reshaping it we define what it means to be compassionate.

· 4 ·

In my survey 49 percent of the people interviewed said they would be able to tell the story of the Good Samaritan if asked to do so, 45 percent said they would not be able to, and 6 percent were unsure whether they could tell it or not. Among those who attended religious services every week, the proportion who thought they could tell the story rose to 69 percent. It was also higher among better-educated people than among people with lower levels of education. Despite the fact that younger people are generally better educated than older people, however, there was a notable decline in the proportion who thought they knew the story among younger respondents: only 35 percent of those in their twenties or thirties thought they could tell the story, compared with 55 percent of those in their fifties or older.[3]

There was also a positive relationship in the survey between knowing the story of the Good Samaritan and being involved in charitable activities. Two-thirds of those who were currently involved in charity or social-service activities knew the story, compared with only four in ten among those who were not currently involved. Viewed differently, among those who knew the story, 40 percent were involved in charitable activities, but among those who did not know the story only 21 percent were involved. Individuals who knew the story were also more likely than individuals who did not know it to have donated time to a voluntary organization during the past year, cared for someone who was sick, given money to a beggar, donated money to charity, or helped someone they knew personally through an emotional crisis.[4] Which came first—knowing the story or becoming involved in charitable activities—is of course impossible to know. That knowing the story came first seems most likely in many cases, though, because people often mentioned learning it as children.

The value of the Good Samaritan story was also evident in the survey from the number of people who saw it as a part of their experience. Besides simply being able to tell the story, many indicated that they had experienced something personally, or read about something, that reminded them of the Good Samaritan. Indeed, the proportion who said this—59 percent— was higher than the proportion who thought they could actually tell the story. Again, there was a strong positive relationship between having an experience of this kind and actually being involved in charitable work. Among those who were involved, for instance, 72 percent said they had experienced something that reminded them of the Good Samaritan, compared with 53 percent of those who were not involved in charitable work.

Of the two—being able to tell the story or having seen it lived out—it is the latter that is most important. If you have witnessed the story in your own experience, then being able to tell it is conducive to becoming involved in charitable activities yourself. If you have not witnessed it personally, being able to tell it makes no difference to your own likelihood of being charitable.[5] So what is going on? Apparently the Good Samaritan parable is like other stories: it cannot just be a part of historic lore to be relevant; it has to be revitalized, updated, put in your own context, for your actions to be influenced by it. Fortunately, most people—85 percent—who can tell the story have also experienced an example of it in their lives.

· 5 ·

Freddie Jackson Taylor is one person who has seen the Good Samaritan story enacted repeatedly. He has not heard the story preached since he was a child, but he has seen compassion many times at the Burnside Center where he volunteers, and this compassion makes sense to him because it reminds him of the Good Samaritan. A typical case, he says, would be "a poor soul, usually a male, who'd be sitting on the stoop and not be able to get up. He needs assistance, needs to get across the street, because if he doesn't get there the shelter will close and he'll be outside all night. Someone comes along and sizes up the situation. They help him by taking him across the street and delivering him to the shelter." This sort of thing happens all the time, he observes. "I've seen a lot of strangers do this. I've done it myself. It's like the story."

But one does not have to be a Freddie Jackson Taylor and do volunteer work at a shelter for the homeless to have vivid examples of the Good Samaritan in one's personal experience. The small acts of kindness we observe in everyday life can also stand out because they remind us of the parable. The kindness itself strikes a chord, but the chord is amplified when it resonates with the sounding board of the Good Samaritan story that is embedded in our minds. A homely example was given by a man who helps from time to time with Boy Scouts. "The other night I was driving home and I came across an accident— two cars had run into each other and an elderly man in one of them had collapsed. A guy I knew was there helping them. He'd gone and called for help, which was all he really had to do. But instead he came back and tried to do what he could to help out. To me, that was an example of the Good Samaritan." Then he added: "The Good Samaritan story says it all: anybody you walk past who needs help, that's your neighbor."

For some people the Good Samaritan story actually seems to provide an underlying pattern, a deep structure, for telling their own stories about caring. Its presence is evident like Debbie Carson's evangelical framework: in the rhythm, the cadence, the pattern of phrases as people tell their stories. This influence is particularly evident among individuals who have been taught Bible stories as children. Something inside them draws them back to these stories when they interpret their own experiences.

A social worker in her early forties provided a vivid example of how the Good Samaritan story can be relived in one's own experience. Her upbringing as a conservative Baptist had steeped her in biblical stories from earliest childhood. She remembers one time in particular when her life seemed to parallel the story of the Good Samaritan. It happened one Sunday morning when she was about eighteen. "I was driving to church, late as usual, and probably speeding. I saw this family alongside the road and I think they were in a station wagon. It was the whole family, you know. And walking, not too far from the car, was a man carrying a gas can to the nearest station. All sorts of thoughts raced through my mind: do I stop, do I not stop? I'm a woman. This has nothing to do with me. I've been told not to stop and pick up people. This is a stranger. I'd be late for church if I stopped and helped this person. So, I ended up not stopping. I don't think I'll ever forget it." When asked if she thought she had done the right thing, she replied emphatically, "No!"

In a more positive way, a young man recalled an episode when he had been on the road and had an opportunity to show compassion. "One day on the way home from a friend's house I saw a woman walking barefoot on a dirt road carrying a crying baby. I stopped the car and asked her what was wrong. She explained that her car was stuck. So I drove her to the nearest phone. She called her husband. He came and I helped them move the car." When asked what prompted him to stop, he mused that it was probably "the Good Samaritan effect."

Sometimes people do not even get the whole story quite right—in fact the main thrust may be rather skewed. But something in their experience seems to fit. It resonates with something in the parable. And that resonance gives the story a larger meaning. It ceases to be a trivial event and becomes an example of how compassion recurs as part of the human journey.

Janet Russo, the woman we met in chapter 2 who volunteers at a women's crisis center, said she always thinks about her mother whenever anyone mentions the Good Samaritan. It was a time when her mother helped someone on the highway that stood out most in her memories. "My mother was always big on helping others," she recalled. "One time—I'll never forget this—we were driving along and there was this family on the side of the road and they had a flat tire. My dad had driven by and my mom said we had to turn around and help them. There were the children and it was late at night. So we turned around, and she was going on about how every good you do on earth is going to be repaid in heaven."

For Janet, the story had an ironic ending. About two o'clock the next morning, there was a knock at the door. When her father answered it, a policeman announced that their car had been found with all its tires missing. They had indeed been repaid, her father laughed, not in heaven but right here on earth, and not with kindness, but with evil. Nevertheless, Janet has always remembered her mother's kindness and has tried to be kind herself. The story was more than just an episode from her childhood. It was a paradigm about how to live.

Jack Casey acknowledged it was for him as well. Despite the fact that he claims no understanding of religious teachings, he does picture himself sometimes as the Good Samaritan. He remembered one time when he was called to pick up an elderly man who had passed out in his bedroom. "His skin was just putrid and he was doing a lot of coughing and he wasn't pleasant to see or hear or smell. I didn't even want to go in where he was. And I felt bad that I didn't want to get in there and be willing to touch him. That kind of destroyed the Good Samaritan spirit I'd tried to show. To be a Good Samaritan you've got to be able to go that extra mile. I'd like to think that I'd be able to go to any extent to revive someone."

· 6 ·

As with any story, we bend the way we understand the parable of the Good Samaritan to fit our circumstances. Indeed, the story's simplicity makes it malleable in our imaginations. We may keep the motif of a traveler being injured alongside the road, but we move the road from Israel to Illinois and add motor vehicles. Because thieves prey less on motorists now than they may have on the road to Jericho, we picture people simply having a flat tire. We see the significance of the two figures who pass by, but change them so they are no longer a priest and a Levite. They become a stockbroker and a used-car salesman. We selectively keep some features and change others.

The story has always been embellished in different ways to absorb the distinctive meanings of various cultures and circumstances. There is, for example, a beautifully preserved drawing from the tenth-century German empire ruled by Otto III that depicts the story of the Good Samaritan in a series of cartoon-like frames. At the top is a small image of a walled fortress that looks more like a royal castle than the city of Jerusalem. At the bottom an innkeeper receives money from the Good Samaritan. But the center of the drawing is dominated by the fierceness of battle as the bandits set upon the traveler. It is an unusual portrayal of the parable, but one that fits well with the military order of the society in which it was created.[6]

In other contexts different features of the parable have been emphasized. The seventeenth-century English theologian, Matthew Henry, in his commentary on the Bible which was published in 1710, for example, gives to the story a staunch moralistic flavor that was characteristic of the Dissenting tradition to which he belonged. He notes, for instance, that the man traveling was doing so "peaceably" and was going about his "lawful business." The thieves, in contrast, were exceedingly "barbarous." After elaborating on their barbarity, Henry exclaims: "What reason have we to thank God for our preservation from perils by robbers!"[7]

When asked to tell the story of the Good Samaritan in a contemporary setting, people generally focused on rather different features of the story than those emphasized in these historic portrayals. Elgin Perry, the black man who volunteers as a tutor for a community literacy program, for example, put the story in a political context. Suppose for the moment, he ventured, that an average American citizen is walking down the sidewalk. "He stops one of the presidential candidates and asks him for help, but the candidate is busy and doesn't have the time to help. Then the other candidate comes along and helps the person. And the person goes to the polls to vote and remembers that this person gave him kindness." For him personally, he continued, Jesse Jackson was the true Good Samaritan.

Ted Garvey, the former Peace Corps volunteer who now works with the mentally ill homeless, knew the story of the Good Samaritan well despite the fact that he had not been to church since childhood. It was easy for him to retell it in a way that related directly to the kinds of people he works with every day: "A man is lying on the sidewalk in the grip of some psychosis or drug-induced catatonia, and he's asking people for help, and people pass him by, and then someone comes by who recognizes the man as suffering from what he's suffering from. They see certain psychotic symptoms. And through compassion or whatever, and through a certain amount of knowledge and information about community resources or whatever, can try to help the man out, walk him down the street to a project or call a detox center. Those would be little steps, but do anything rather than just walking by."

· 7 ·

Preachers do the same thing when they give sermons about the Good Samaritan. Remembering that Jesus told the parable in response to the lawyer's question about how to inherit eternal life, they sometimes turn the story into a lesson in appropriate theological doctrine. Rather than stressing the importance of showing compassion toward one's neighbors, they emphasize the "Christian" motives that must have inspired the Samaritan to show kindness. One pastor, for example, went so far as to turn the Samaritan into a Communist who had somehow become born again in order to associate kindness with the right religious credentials. Setting the story on the Ho Chi Minh trail, she imagined a local Vietnamese being attacked by robbers. A Protestant clergyman passed him by in his Land Rover. A Buddhist monk passed by on his bicycle. Then a "good Communist" came along—the kind of person she thought her American audience would despise in the same way Jesus' Jewish audience hated the Samaritans. The good Communist stopped and was at first overwhelmed with anger because he discovered that the injured man, covered with dust, was actually not a local villager at all, but a Westerner, an enemy. But then the Communist gained control of his feelings. This servant of Marxist-Leninist doctrine was somehow "a worshiper of the One and only Jehovah, God in heaven." Indeed: "He had turned his back on the gods of the temples to serve Jesus Christ. He now believed that all men and women were his brothers and sisters. So just that fast his excuses dissipated, and his anger melted. He stooped down to examine the injured man."[8]

I mentioned before that the Lone Ranger is the Good Samaritan. He is. In the beginning episode of the original film series he and four other rangers are out along the road, actually a dusty trail in western Texas, tracking a gang of thieves. The thieves are clever. They plan an ambush, circle around, and hide behind the rocks overlooking the trail. When the rangers come by, these treacherous thieves fire on them, shooting them all in the back. Some time later, the ranger who is to become the star of the series regains consciousness and crawls inch by inch under the scorching sun in search of water until he passes out. At that point an Indian finds him, drags him to the shade of a nearby tree, gives him water, and bandages his wounds. To this point the story follows the script of Jesus' parable almost exactly. As I said, the Lone Ranger is the Good Samaritan. But it seems as though the Good Samaritan is really Tonto. Except—except that Tonto helps this white man because he recognizes him. Suddenly Tonto has a flashback. It is now he as a youth who is lying injured. His village has been sacked by bad men. And then a compassionate ranger comes along and helps him. He cradles him in his arms and gives him water. As they part, the injured youth gives the ranger an amulet. Now, years later, Tonto recognizes the ranger because he is still wearing the amulet. At the hands of its Hollywood producers, the story of the Good Samaritan has taken an interesting twist. Ultimately, it is the Lone Ranger who is *both* the victim and the savior. It is his inexplicable individual heroism that in a sense saves him.

· 8 ·

Like everything else it touches, the individualism in our culture paints its colors all over this ancient parable. Observe how Patrick Tishel, a Roman Catholic priest, modifies the story in a recent homily on the meaning of the Good Samaritan: "A man was going from Atlanta to Albany and some gangsters held him up on the way. They robbed him of his wallet and his brand-new suit; then they beat him up and left him unconscious on the side of the highway. Passing by in his car, a preacher saw him, turned away, stepped on the gas, and went back to thinking about a sermon he was going to give his congregation. Later a gospel singer drove past without stopping because he was late for a rehearsal. Finally, a poor old black man came up to the site in his car and saw the man on the side of the road. He was struck with pity, tears came to his eyes and he stopped. He got out of his car and helped the man as much as he could; in spite of his age, he managed to lift the man into his car and took him to some place that could help him further, a hospital of some sort. When he was leaving, he gave the nurses and medics some money and said, 'If this doesn't cover it, I'll be back later when I get my next check.' The moral of the story is: 'Help your neighbor and stop being so apathetic!' "[9]

Father Tishel's version of the story probably seems about as authentic as one could hope for. He has preserved all the ingredients of the original parable, simply translating them into our own context. The injured man is still on a journey; he is still attacked by thieves, beaten, and robbed. The two coldhearted passersby are still members of the established religion. The man who stops is a poor member of a minority group. He cares for the injured traveler, takes him to the hospital, and offers to pay the bill.

But note that a few embellishments have been made. In the biblical account the priest simply sees the injured man and passes by on the other side of the road. In this version the clergyman goes off "thinking about a sermon he was going to give." We somehow have access to his subjective consciousness. The problem has to do with his thoughts. We do not know what the priest's reasons were in the biblical account (although many commentators have conjectured about them). Then, when the black man stops, he is not simply moved to compassion, as some versions say, and he does not just have compassion, as other versions state. His compassion is not immediately, at least, an act. It is an emotion. "Tears came to his eyes." The camera zooms in on his face. We see the evidence of his subjective feelings. Another minor feature of the story that seems interesting is the vagueness associated with where the injured man is taken: "a hospital of some sort." Why a hospital of some sort? Why not just a hospital? Every other detail is made explicit—from the wallet and the new suit that the robbers take, to the fact that the black man is elderly and has difficulty getting the injured man into his car. Even the biblical version states simply that their destination was an inn. By adding "of some sort," this version leaves the destination more mysterious than is necessary. Finally, the new version does not end with Jesus saying "Go thou and do likewise." Instead, it makes a point of calling this admonition a "moral." And it elaborates: "Help your neighbor and stop being so apathetic!"

These embellishments may seem trivial, except that Father Tishel added them intentionally. He did so because he wanted to show how we ordinarily alter the story ever so slightly to fit better with the way our culture thinks about such things. What he has tried to do is turn the parable into a moral tale. By shifting the emphasis even in these minor ways toward the individual, and especially toward the subjective and emotional state of the individual, he has placed the entire burden of doing good on the choice, the willpower, the moral fortitude of the individual. There is nothing in the story, except a very large unspoken "should" or "you ought to," to empower the individual to make the right moral choice. As he says, he has taken a multidimensional story and stripped it of the larger wisdom that once was able to transform and empower the soul.

· 9 ·

To show what might be done with the story, he tells it again, the way it was told by the church fathers from earliest times through the Middle Ages. "The man who was beaten while going from Jerusalem to Jericho represents mankind descending from the conscious paradisal state of Jerusalem to the materially minded state of Jericho, a very worldly city. While traveling from Jerusalem to Jericho, he was beaten by robbers on the side of the road. The robbers are the fallen spirits playing on the unchecked passions within us. The man left wounded and bleeding represents the state of all mankind, wounded in soul by the Fall and by sin at work in us. A priest came by, looked at him and passed by; and a Levite, a lay religious, came by, looked at him and passed by. These representatives of the old covenant passed by not only out of their hard-heartedness, but because of their inability to render effective help to the man. The old covenant, though it pointed man in the right direction, in its essence was unable to save fallen man. But the Good Samaritan who came riding on his donkey had compassion on this stranger. Even though to the Jews Samaritans were considered outcasts worthy of ridicule, this Samaritan had compassion on the Jew and stopped. He bound up his wounds and cared for him."[10]

Like the other elements in the story thus far, the Good Samaritan is also a figure that requires interpretation: "The Good Samaritan in the teachings of the Fathers is Christ Himself, who even to the Jews was a stranger. He came to heal the soul of man deadened by sin by pouring in the oil of gladness, the oil of chrismation or of regeneration as we might call it. And he also poured into the wounds wine, the symbol of fruitfulness, the wine of the Eucharist. Then he put the man on his donkey, symbolizing man's lower nature which Christ has mastered and uses for God's work, and he took him to the inn."[11]

The inn, not just a hospital of some sort, also has special meaning: "The inn is the Church, and it provides the place where a man who has been beaten and healed can regenerate until Christ comes again. The two denarii given to the innkeeper for the care of the man are the two great commandments given as the basis of participating in the heavenly life while here on earth: love the Lord your God, and love your neighbor. In this you can clearly see the symbolism of the Church and the Second Coming of Christ, and of Christ Himself, the great gift and minister to humanity."[12]

This of course is an allegorical way of understanding the parable. Every detail has a deeper, specific, theological meaning.[13] It is no longer a common way of reading the parable. Indeed, to contemporary ears, it sounds foreign, archaic, strained, tedious. Yet the very fact that it sounds strange speaks loudly of how different our culture is from the medieval culture in which such readings were commonplace. The allegorical reading is possible because of the institutional authority of the medieval church. It provided the resources from which to give an authoritative interpretation of this kind. In our society no such institution exists, neither in the church nor among the intellectual elite generally. The story can have no authoritative interpretation, just a pared-down retelling that leaves its meaning up to the imagination of every individual listener.

The medieval reading also supplies the listener with a large stock of cultural and institutional resources. One does not have to see only the good example of the Samaritan and resolve to be more charitable oneself. In the medieval reading the listener is in fact not asked to identify with the Good Samaritan, except insofar as the Samaritan is a figure of Christ. The listener may identify with the example of Christ, but if so, he or she has all the additional teachings about Christ to provide strength and encouragement. Within the story itself, the listener is actually asked to identify with the injured person, the one who stands for humanity in its descent from the spiritual realm of Jerusalem to the material realm of Jericho, the one who is victimized by unchecked passions, the one who is rescued and rejuvenated with symbolic oil and wine. The affluent, white, middle-class listener does not have to make the difficult leap of identifying with an elderly black man or some other outcast who differs dramatically from his own social position. Both the listener and the injured person are members of the established culture.

But most significant in the medieval version is the fact that the injured person is taken to the inn, which is given the prominence of representing the church itself. This teaching was emphasized especially by St. Bede, who saw the church as the place where the injured man could recover from the worldly passions that had led him into harm's way in the first place. It was not that the listener simply resolved to follow the example of the Good Samaritan; instead, the listener was encouraged to become part of a supportive community that would provide daily guidance, instruction, and opportunities to practice a new set of values. Moreover, as St. Maximus taught, the two denarii or shillings were the two great commandments: to love God and one's neighbor. These were the way to overcome one's selfish instincts. They were not simply admonitions, such as "help your neighbor" and "stop being so apathetic." They were teachings given in the context of the inn, the church, the supportive community. As the injured man recuperated at the inn, these were the teachings that would gradually enable him to become more compassionate. The story was thus not so much a moral tale that worked by playing on the sentiments of the isolated individual as it was a parable about community and social support. It was in fact this meaning that still struck Rembrandt when he painted his great interpretation of the Good Samaritan: his portrayal is not set along the road, as most contemporary sketches are, but in the warm light of the inn.

· 10 ·

The average person today has little more awareness or appreciation of the medieval allegorical reading of the Good Samaritan parable than of other recondite theological teachings. One would not expect otherwise. But, in addition to the subtle allegorical symbolism having dropped out, the role of institutions and communities has also faded from view. Ted Garvey's rendition, emphasizing the Samaritan's knowledge of community resources, was a rare exception. It at least suggested that care givers do not simply act from some inner compulsion and act alone. To be caring, in his story, one had to be a part of a community. Otherwise one would not know how to be an effective care giver. Most other stories simply left institutions out of the picture entirely. The story became a lesson in doing good, but it gave the individual no resources on which to draw.

Consider the following attempt to put the parable in contemporary language: "A Mexican laborer who'd been picking beans in a field in Arizona runs across a Caucasian daughter from a family in a big city and she's been struck by a truck and thrown off into the ditch and been lying there in the dust for a while. Nobody's stopped for her because of the traffic, and so he stops and takes her to a nearby house, and then he just quietly walks out the door and goes back to work in the fields. He doesn't leave his name or anything. Reporters come on the scene and talk to the girl and she just knows he helped her. To me that would be a genuine act of compassion."

This is in many ways an extraordinarily clever scenario. It was told by an older man who knew the biblical story well and was able to capture all its essential points—the difference in social origins between the injured person and the helper, the passersby who fail to stop, even the humility of the helper. He does not have to stretch the parable at all to tell it in this way. Yet the message the story reinforces is one of individual heroism. The care giver is a nonconformist, the individual with some inner virtue that compels him to help when nobody else does. It would not occur to the storyteller to embellish the story by adding something about the laborer's tightly knit community and how he had learned to help because others helped him.

Here is another example. It too is a creative application of the story to a contemporary setting. "There is a white South African who is somehow in need. And a member of the cabinet came by and wouldn't help. Then another white person, a member of the aristocracy, came by and didn't help either. But a black man who had been abused his whole life by these white people came along. He was willing to go the extra mile and help the white person in need." This story even recognizes the larger injustices that are likely to be associated with showing compassion in a setting like South Africa. But it does not turn the story into a political statement, for example, by arguing that the black man needs to organize a vigilante committee to protect himself from being lynched while helping the white person. It simply emphasizes that this individual was "willing."

The importance of individual virtue in renditions such as these is not at all surprising, given the way we understand goodness in our culture, for the most part, and the way in which religious leaders themselves interpret the parable of the Good Samaritan. Sermons I have examined routinely stress individual virtue in interpreting the parable. One pastor, for example, explained that the reason the Samaritan was able to stop and help the injured man was that he had a good image of himself. The priest and Levite had probably been raised in a way that made them insecure about themselves. But the Samaritan had high self-esteem. If we simply let our faith massage our self-esteem, he implied, we will become able to love our neighbors. Another pastor turned the sequence around. In his view, the compassion of the Good Samaritan was important in its own right, but more interesting as a means to a personal transformation. Reciting the parable, he concluded that it was "clear as a picture." It raised "no further questions." But then he went on to explain that the intent of the story was to show the lawyer to whom Jesus was speaking how to gain eternal life. This, he said, is a transformation inside us that is already in progress: "God is providing us now with endless opportunities to discover who we are and why we are. God is providing us now with the answer to our deep longing for fulfillment as a human person." Helping those in need was a good way, in his view, to secure this inner fulfillment. "If you want to experience a miracle of transformation in your life," he concluded, "simply take your neighbor's hand in yours and offer him or her your loving heart."[14]

Theologians, writers, and social scientists who have examined the Good Samaritan story have also, by and large, stressed its subjective, individual, and moralistic aspects, rather than connecting it with larger institutional resources the way medieval thinkers did. Finding themselves distressed by a purely ethical interpretation of the passage, theologians have often emphasized its spiritual meaning. Theologian Karl Barth, for example, argued that Jesus was really asking the lawyer to trust in him, as the physical embodiment of the Good Samaritan. Other biblical interpreters have drawn the same conclusion, but in so doing have sometimes turned compassion into something that only a God-figure like Jesus could be expected to manifest. The Samaritan's love becomes unexpected, costly, and totally without explanation. One writer puts it this way: "[The Samaritan] appears dramatically on the scene to bind up the wounds of the suffering as the unique agent of God's costly demonstration of unexpected love."[15]

Writers drawing on the parable for literary inspiration are also prone to turn compassion into something inexplicable that rises unexpectedly from the human breast. Former and longtime dean of the chapel at Princeton University Ernest Gordon, for example, loved to recall an event that reminded him of the Good Samaritan during World War II. As a prisoner of war, Gordon and his companions were being transported by the Japanese across Thailand on a train. At one point they came across several truckloads of wounded Japanese soldiers. Without a word, most of Gordon's group went over to the wounded soldiers and offered them rations, water, and rags to bind their injuries. When they were chastised by the ranking Allied officer in their midst, Gordon reminded him of the Good Samaritan and of Jesus' commandment to show love to one's enemies.[16] The story is moving, but it leaves the listener wondering what compassion really is. In emphasizing that no words were spoken, the story in fact suggests that each individual was simply moved by something internal.

This is another example, like those we saw in considering the language of motivation, of the idea that compassion is not really compassion if it can be understood. It has to come from within. It cannot involve calculation: the men move to help their enemies without a word, thus indicating that they have not talked the situation over, discussed what the consequences may be, or thought about possible rewards or punishments; they merely act spontaneously. Indeed, no influence of any kind can be admitted. As psychologist Raymond F. Paloutzian has noted in a perceptive analysis of the Good Samaritan story as ordinarily told, all the attributions are internal.[17] The Samaritan is on a journey, but he interrupts his trip, so his actions seem spontaneous, unpremeditated, but voluntary. He gives his own money voluntarily. There is nothing to suggest that he received any reward or was moved by any ulterior motive. Because he is a foreigner, we know nothing of his cultural background; indeed, the contrast with the priest and the Levite suggests that he had not been taught to act ethically in the same way they had been. In focusing on these aspects of the story, we come to define compassion itself as something purely spontaneous, voluntary, inexplicable, and individual.

What I am suggesting is that we are drawn to the story of the Good Samaritan with special magnetism because it is essentially, in our modern view, a story about individual virtue. We do not interpret it as a story about the impossibility of living according to divine law. We forget that Jesus told it to a man who had just answered that keeping the law of God perfectly was the only way to inherit eternal life. Nor do we pay much attention to the role of the inn or the symbolism of the two coins, the oil, and the wine. We do not ask the listener to identify with the injured man or show him becoming part of a community that collectively supports charitable behavior. Instead, we think of the story as a moral lesson. The person who cares with compassion is the person who goes and does likewise. He simply gives help because it is the right thing to do. We fail to ask what sort of upbringing or social support or institutional resources that person may need to perform acts of compassion.

We also fail to see institutional connections with the kind of care that is given. Despite the fact that social services often require organized efforts, we still dwell on the Samaritan sitting there alone on the Jericho road pouring oil on the injured man's wounds. It would certainly be possible to retell the story in a way that has the Samaritan petitioning the Jericho highway department for better police patrols. Or, as a black minister I spoke to in Los Angeles put it: "If I were preaching from that passage, I'd talk about a neighborhood where people were always getting mugged when they walked down the street. I'd ask people what ought to be done—like maybe put in some better streetlights." But his interpretation was the exception. It showed only the possibility of rethinking the story to give it a more collective emphasis. For most of us the story remains an illustration of individual compassion. We let it reinforce our individualism because we neglect even the institutional focus it once had historically.

· 11 ·

As the authority of the church and of other traditional communities has declined, we are left without the institutional support for doing good that was an integral part of the medieval interpretation of the Good Samaritan. In the future the further erosion of religious institutions many social observers expect to take place is likely to have an equally serious impact on the Good Samaritan's place in our society. At present, religious institutions remain the primary arenas in which people learn about the Good Samaritan.[18] Those who attend religious services regularly hear sermons preached about it. In the survey, for example, among those who attended church weekly, 88 percent had heard a sermon on loving their neighbors within the past year, compared with only 40 percent of those who attended less than once a month. Moreover, by a margin of 61 percent to 30 percent, those who said they had heard a sermon on loving their neighbors were more likely than those who had not heard a sermon to say they could tell the story of the Good Samaritan.

Not only do regular churchgoers hear sermons on loving

their neighbors more often, but these sermons also play a stronger role in the listeners' ability to recall the story of the Good Samaritan than they do among people who do not attend religious services regularly. Specifically: in the weekly church-going category, 79 percent of those who had heard a sermon on loving their neighbors said they could recall the story of the Good Samaritan, compared with only 48 percent of those who had not heard a sermon on loving their neighbors—a thirty-one-point spread. But among those who attended church less than once a month, only 45 percent of those who had heard a sermon on love within the past year could recall the Good Samaritan story, compared with 30 percent of those who had not—a fifteen-point spread.[19] In other words, going to church has an effect (makes one more likely to know the story), hearing sermons has an effect, and the joint effect of both is stronger than either effect singly. If fewer and fewer people participate regularly in religious organizations, then, the impact of the Good Samaritan story is bound to diminish.[20]

It will diminish, if for no other reason, as a result of people not knowing the story. They may think they know it, but their ability to remember it is likely to be impaired. They may recall only the bare outline or even get the story wrong. Compare the way Elmer Benson tells the story with the way Janet Russo tells it. Elmer Benson attends church every week. His rendition of the story covers all the main points: "A guy's on the road going from point A to point B, and he's set upon by bandits who attack him, beat him, and leave him for dead. Along come three people. One is a Pharisee or a high priest and he stays on the opposite side of the road. The second one looks at him too and goes on. And the Samaritan, who has the lowest social standing in the story, is the one who stops, binds up the fellow's wounds, takes him to a local inn, says to the innkeeper, 'Get some oil and pour it on this man's wounds, take care of him, here's some money, I'll be back if you need any more, I'll pay for it.' And Jesus says, 'Now who among these. . . .' Or, at least the lesson is drawn, who among these is loving and caring. Well, it's obvious that the person who binds up the wounds is, rather than the person who says my religion won't let me touch somebody." Janet Russo has not attended church since she was a child. She claims to know the story of the Good Samaritan too. But her story is a brief paraphrase. "It is," she

178

says, "about a gentleman who finds someone by the side of the road and is injured or hurt in some way and he goes to help him and ends up getting injured himself." Not only is it a brief paraphrase; it misses the main point.

· 12 ·

If the Good Samaritan story were to drop out of our culture, something vital would be lost. Even without the richness of its historic religious connotations, it speaks vitally to the social conditions we experience. It may be colored deeply by individualism, but it still conjures up an image of social relations. The story is, as I say, highly adaptable. We are able to make it relevant to the transient society in which we live. Despite its simplicity, and even apart from its religious connotations, it provides a framework that helps us define—and therefore see—the possibilities for compassion in our own world. Perhaps it does not spell out in detail how we should behave, but the very fact that it does not may be its strength. As W. H. Auden once observed, "You cannot tell people what to do, you can only tell them parables."[21]

It is significant that the story takes place along the road. Being in transit, on a journey, literally or metaphorically, has always symbolized a time of danger, a moment of uncertainty when ordinary social relations cannot be relied on for security. Times like these impose on us what anthropologists call a state of liminality. We are, as it were, betwixt and between. Dawn and dusk have always represented such times. Disrupted periods in a society's history, such as revolutions, wars, and holidays, have too. Similarly, being on a journey is to be neither here nor there. The journey takes place between the established realms of security our lives provide. At such times, we ourselves may be literally transformed, as in the case of a young tribesman who undergoes a rite of passage that transforms him into a warrior. The transition to a new social position is a transformative journey. In the process, our identities are ambiguous. Hence we call the adolescent years a journey. We are neither children nor adults. In the Good Samaritan story the liminal status of the injured man is clearly indicated by the fact that he is left "half-dead"—somewhere between life and death. The nature of the Samaritan is also ambiguous. He is a foreigner, someone about whom we know nothing. We have no clear expectations of him because he is not from our culture. In the course of the journey he turns out to be a friend. The story is thus a context in which interesting and dangerous changes in us and in our social relations can be envisioned.

It is the imagery of being on a journey, of being between places, of literally being in transit that still surfaces prominently in our understandings of compassion. Indeed, much of our caring takes place metaphorically in the context of journeys. Like hospitals of old that were really inns along the road, our charitable institutions are often built for those on a journey of some kind. Alcoholics Anonymous is an organization for those on the road to recovery. Soup kitchens and shelters are for those temporarily without food and housing. We expect them to seek jobs and regain their status as ordinary citizens sometime in the future. Increasingly, we have also come to view caring itself as a journey. It is something we learn gradually and accomplish slowly as part of the way we live. Caring becomes an unfolding experience, like faith or recovery from illness, and it is in the context of religion and therapy that we hear it described in these terms. Marge Detweiler, for example, had through her involvement in Alcoholics Anonymous come to understand caring in this way. As she remarked, "Part of the journey of caring is to let that person go down the road and do the same thing and share it again and carry it on."

In a deeper, but still metaphoric, way, our experiences of caring and being cared for along the road often stand out in our memories because they involved change and uncertainty in our lives. For Debbie Carson, it was the image of her friend in Alabama standing in the road waving goodbye that brought tears to her eyes. For Ted Garvey, the time that stood out most clearly in his memory of being cared for also occurred on the road. It was one of those storybook encounters between two cultures that creates a culturally transcendent space. He recalled that he had been ill with malaria while he was in the Peace Corps but had decided to make a pilgrimage through the mountains anyway. "I was in the Himalayas and my sandals had given out so I was walking barefoot. And I was going down with malaria again. I met some nice sheep herders who took me into their hut and gave me tea and biscuits and dried fruit. I recovered and had a wonderful experience. If I'd been healthy, I wouldn't have met them. When I was in trouble, there were people there." It was the kind of experience that rejuvenated his faith as well as his body. "It doesn't matter how bad a situation you're in," he reflected, "people will take up the slack for you."

The stories rescue-squad workers tell are particularly replete with the imagery of roads. Their work often brings them directly into contact with people who have been injured along the road. They are the contemporary embodiments of the Good Samaritan. But their stories sometimes take unexpected turns. Jack Casey, for example, once found himself the recipient rather than the giver of care. As he related the incident, I was struck by the force of its location. It dramatized the uncertainty of one's position when one is on the road. It involved a displacement of roles. It was in this state of ambiguity, moreover, that new insight into the nature of compassion became evident: "Several years ago I was involved in a house fire. It was in the basement, which is always very dangerous, and it was very hot outside that day. We'd heard there were victims inside the house so we were making a big push to get inside. I was standing in a doorway and we were hitting the fire with a stream of water. When that happens it can scald you pretty easily. Somehow I passed out and they dragged me out of the house. They put me in the street. I had heat exhaustion and smoke inhalation. I couldn't move but I could hear everything going on. So an ambulance came up and it was my best friend driving it. They took one look at me and said, 'Oh my God.' And they called another crew because they couldn't stand working on me since they knew me. Eventually they got me into an ambulance. I couldn't hang on, and it was the worst ride I've ever had. They weren't really going very fast, but to me it seemed like they were driving like maniacs. So being a patient like that really helped me understand what it's like. And later I had them drive me around again so I could see what the problems were. I'm better now at talking to patients and making sure they are secure and okay."

There are, to be sure, limitations to understanding compassion in this way. It can make caring little more than a passing gesture to a stranger along the highway. Rather than becoming more intimately involved, or developing a personal relationship with the stranger, or even thinking about larger programs that may be necessary, we simply offer a helping hand and then ride off into the sunset, like the Lone Ranger, with good feelings in our chests. After thinking for a long time about how he helped people in his everyday life, for example, one man resorted to the hypothetical image he had tucked away in his memory somewhere of the good Boy Scout doing his deed for the day out along the highway: "Say, for example, I'm at an intersection and there's a blind person trying to cross. I could just keep on going. Most people could probably do that and not feel guilty about it at all. But what I'll do personally if I see that situation, or if somebody is on the side of the road fixing a tire, I'll stop, I'll help that person across the road. And then I'll leave." To help someone along the road, like this, can be compassion without commitment. That is its most serious limitation. We care for a stranger and never see that person again. But in another sense this is the kind of society in which we live.

For us, the story of the Good Samaritan is fundamentally about the possibility of human kindness existing in a society of strangers. It speaks to us because we no longer live in intimate communities where the neighbors we are to love are people we already know well. As Elmer Benson notes, "I don't know my neighbors here very well. I've lived here for a year and a half and haven't had diddly squat to do with my neighbors. I ran into my neighbor in a restaurant the other day and didn't even recognize him until his wife introduced us." We do not feel close to neighbors like this. But the story of the Good Samaritan tells us that some basic element of our humanity can bridge the gap and create community even among strangers.

This understanding is clearly illustrated by the following quote from a school psychologist: "It's about a poor traveler who is waylaid alongside the road and some very upright people come past him. Then the person from Samaria came along and helped him. He didn't even know him or anything about him." Struggling for a moment to think of how the story might apply to a contemporary setting, she added: "Society has gotten so mobile anymore that people just aren't as group-bound as they used to be. So I guess the story is really just about one stranger helping another."

At the heart of the story lies an encounter between two human beings. The one is a Samaritan, the other a Jew. But their ethnic differences fade as the one helps the other. They relate to each other simply as humans. The story of the Good Samaritan is in this respect like some of the stories I reported in chapter 4. People said they experienced fulfillment because they were able to relate to someone else in a moment of vulnerability. Barriers were stripped away, allowing them to experience the common bond of being human. This was the lesson a number of people drew from the story of the Good Samaritan. One woman, for example, said she had come to recognize the Good Samaritan parable as a story about being human. "You recognize your own humanness and you recognize it in other people as well. It sort of helps me know what to expect from people." Another woman put a similar idea in these words: "Whether we believe in God or not or whether our political beliefs are similar or completely opposed to each other, the one common denominator that we do have is our humanity. We do belong to each other whether we like it or not."

The stripping away of barriers is itself an important feature of the story. It is this stripping away that allows a common human identity to emerge. A middle-aged woman who did volunteer work at her church, for example, summarized her understanding of the story in precisely these terms: "It's an invitation to get out of your own skin and get into the skin of other people who live in your world—to break down that barrier. The ultimate barrier is always between the person who lives inside you and people who live outside you." In the story itself, this stripping away is not only symbolized by the two men transcending their ethnic barriers; it is stressed forcefully by the act of stripping itself. The injured man is stripped of his clothes and robbed of his possessions. There is, as it were, nothing left of him but his basic humanity. And it is that humanity that moves the Samaritan to help him.

· 13 ·

It is also a story that reveals our diversity as a society—the divisions that ordinarily separate rich and poor, black and white, male and female, citizen and alien—and yet it shows that these divisions can be overcome. Debbie Carson believes the Bible teaches us to love our neighbors because God's love is universal. Nobody is better than anybody else. In her view, this is what the Good Samaritan story is trying to communicate. The people who pass by the injured man represent the established religious ethic of the day. They think they are better than everyone else. The Samaritan is an outcast, but we learn from his example the higher virtue of universal love. If she were to put the story in the context of our own society, she would tell it like this: "A black man was going down the road in his car, an old, beat-up car, and maybe it broke down, and he's sitting there trying to figure out what to do. Some other cars come by. The pastor of the established church in town comes by and he's on his way to an important meeting, so he doesn't have time to stop. Then a white government person was also coming by, somebody who's going to a committee to talk about the needs of the black community, and that person was too busy and kept going. Then a woman who was Puerto Rican with a whole bunch of kids in the car came along and she saw his need and stopped to help him."

People who know the story understand that the Samaritan is a social outcast and yet he is the one who shows compassion. It is not about us, the privileged, showing kindness to the downtrodden. It is about them showing kindness to us. It is not a story about handouts for the poor, not even a story about welfare for the disadvantaged. It is a story about reconciliation, about the healing of social wounds, about wholeness in the organism of society.

We hear this message of reconciliation when we recognize who the outcasts are today who play the role of the Good Samaritan. For Elmer Benson, a white middle-class Protestant, it is a story about racial and ethnic minorities: "A black man or woman, or whoever the most downtrodden group is, such as a Mexican person along the southern border of the United States who has twelve children." He says the story is meant to disabuse us of our stereotypes about who is most likely to show compassion. We should not make the Good Samaritan out to be some guilty white liberal with a background in the social sciences or turn the person who passes by on the other side of the road into a materialistic Wall Street banker. "The person who helps," he points out, "is somebody you don't expect to give aid."

Susan Robbins, the pediatric cardiologist, echoes Elmer Benson's remarks. In her view the important feature of the story is that the Samaritans "were thought of as an inferior people." And yet it was the Samaritan who helped the traveler in distress. She thought the Samaritan nowadays would be a person who everyone thought was really obnoxious, like somebody with AIDS. For her, the story shows that even somebody who is not "in" can make a contribution to society. It shows that what you do is more important than your location in the world.

In today's world the parable of the Good Samaritan is also about compassion that extends beyond national borders. The Samaritan, after all, is really a member of another society. He is a foreigner. And his compassion challenges the empty religious teachings of the domestic establishment. He is the voice of the poor that challenges the rich, the spirit of the Third World that calls into question the values of the affluent West.

For some, the story of compassion along the Jericho road has evoked a powerful shift in their own values. It has provided a base from which to rearrange their priorities. If the Good Samaritan is the outcast, then the values and life-styles of the groups we ordinarily look down on may need to be rethought. Carlos Sanchez, a young man I met in Texas, was one such case. A man in his late twenties of mixed parentage, he was combining graduate work in theology and the social sciences in the hope of contributing in some way to the betterment of the Latino community. For him, the story of the Good Samaritan had always been powerful. "What I notice," he said, "is that the Samaritan is the atheist, or in our context, the socialist, who has been doing what Christians should have been doing but weren't." He went on to point out that the story revealed Jesus' sensitivity to cultural differences and drew the conclusion that we too should be sensitive to our relations with Latin America.

The story of the Good Samaritan had become powerful for Carlos Sanchez, as for so many others, not simply by being read but by being acted out in real life. For Carlos, slain Archbishop Romero of El Salvador most clearly exemplified the life of the Good Samaritan. Standing by Romero's grave one day, Carlos experienced an epiphany. "Suddenly, I realized that I was part of his resurrection," he reflected. "I was just overwhelmed."

· 14 ·

Despite all the sermons and all the personal testimonies people can think of that remind them of the Good Samaritan, though, the power of a story like the parable of the Good Samaritan is probably shown best when it is done unwittingly. Frank Stevens is an elderly man with little formal education. He sometimes speaks in broken English. Occasionally he feels such deep emotion that he can hardly speak at all. For several years he has driven elderly people from a remote rural village into the city where they can receive the medical treatment they need. He is white; many of the people he has helped in this way are black. His life has become deeply intertwined with theirs. Like the Good Samaritan, he has encountered a basic humanness stronger than racial and ethnic boundaries. He told a story that, without his fully realizing it, also captured the light, the hope, the vision that can be experienced along the road.

The story was about the death of an elderly black woman. Miss Carrie, as her friends called her, was a wiry little woman who weighed less than a hundred pounds. She lived by herself well into her seventies and was known by her neighbors for making long treks down the dusty country roads to visit them when they were in need. When she died, her family asked Frank to say a few words at her funeral. "We all got to the funeral," he recalled, "and kind of a nice thing happened.

"Lilly Mae, her nearest relative, had asked me to say a few words. The minister spoke first, from the Scriptures I think, as though he had no real knowledge of her. And I could see down the front row all the family who'd come to be there. So when they called me up I just told it the way I remembered it. I told them how she used to love to get out to see her friends. I told them how she liked to tell about the time she'd walked twenty miles to town.

"Anyway, the feeling of speaking from *their* pulpit—I just felt very privileged to be speaking in this little black church telling these people what I had seen in Miss Carrie. She was known as the quilt lady, very creative, did some wood carving too. She had struggled to keep her lawn mowed and her porch painted and her vegetable garden in shape. So I was able to give them my picture of her, and it was a very moving experience for me.

"Then, after we left the church, they took her up to what they called the old cemetery." His words broke off momentarily as he tried to choke back the tears. "It was right beside the road where we go everyday. So we joined around the graveside. We had a big cross there. There were the headstones from her family nearby. And the last thing they put out—[there was a long pause as he cried softly]—were these two little bouquets of flowers. They were wildflowers I had brought." Choking with emotion, he cried again. "I was very gratified when they laid those down there, and we just said our last goodbyes to Miss Carrie. And now when I drive by, it's very rewarding because from there there's a marvelous view. You can look up the valley toward the mountains. I thought it was very appropriate that she should be buried right there."

PART IV

THE LIMITS OF CARING

Bounded Love

F<small>ROM</small> 6 <small>TO</small> 8 <small>A.M.</small>, Carla worked at a day-care center. From 8:30 <small>A.M.</small> to 12:30 <small>P.M.</small>, she taught grade school. From 2 to 6 <small>P.M.</small>, she taught at an after-school latchkey program.

"To save a woman from being sent to a nursing home, Carla had moved in with an Alzheimer's victim. So at 12:30, Carla rushed home to make lunch for her roommate. At supper time, Carla rushed home again to make supper for her roommate.

"Several years earlier, while working at the state prison, Carla had befriended, then fallen in love with, an inmate. . . . After washing the supper dishes, Carla hurried to the prison to visit him. At 9 <small>P.M.</small>, Carla dashed home to put her roommate to bed.

"In her spare time, Carla volunteered forty hours each month to the county mental health center. And she taught Sunday school."[1]

Carla sounds like many of the volunteers we have met in previous chapters: dedicated, caring, involved in the lives of others. The text from which her story is taken, however, is designed to show us that something is wrong. The emphasis is on schedules—the long hours Carla puts in. Unlike the stories we have heard from volunteers themselves, this one hardly notices the individuals Carla is trying to help. Neither the Alzheimer's victim nor the friend in prison has a name, let alone a personality. Carla herself never speaks in the story, never explains her motives, never describes her feelings. She only rushes home, washes dishes, hurries out, and dashes home again.

As the story proceeds, a truly unbelievable sequence of misfortunes overtakes Carla: "Within days, the furnace went out, the sewer pipe collapsed, the basement flooded, and gophers chewed through the gas line and the house almost blew up." To cap it off: "A neighbor selling his property used the wrong land description and instead sold Carla's house, and a pheasant flew through the bay window, decapitated itself, and ran through the house like a dead chicken."[2]

Doing good, it seems, brings its own punishment. In case we failed to see it, the author of the story draws a direct parallel between Carla and the decapitated pheasant: both running around like dead chickens. Poor Carla winds up drinking two quarts of vodka a day, wishing she could die.

Until—until she meets a therapist who explains how crazy she has been acting and gets her started on a recovery program. Gradually Carla is healed of her obsession with being compassionate. She learns to "stick up for herself and her rights, instead of fighting only for the rights of others." She discovers how to "set boundaries," how to "demand her birthright," how to say "enough is enough." She starts eating out and buying herself attractive new clothes instead of wearing hand-me-downs.[3]

What about it? Are the caring Carlas of the world self-destructive neurotics? Was Jack Casey revealing something vital about himself when he alluded to his fear of not being able to save someone he loved from dying and his compulsive need to help his friends? Are those who try to be like Mother Teresa actually living out some personal pathology?

· 2 ·

In California a series of intriguing studies has recently been conducted among AIDS patients. Researchers there believe that one's attitudes toward oneself and toward others have a great deal to do with one's capacity for survival under extreme circumstances. Earlier studies suggested that people who were compliant and self-sacrificing were *more* susceptible to cancer than people who were less compliant and less self-sacrificing. This pattern led researchers to hypothesize a connection between an individual's attitudes and the functioning of his or her immune system.

To test this hypothesis, AIDS patients have been asked batteries of questions to tap their basic orientations toward life. One of the questions is whether they would do a favor for a friend who needed it even though they might not feel like doing it. Of all the questions asked, this was the best predictor of AIDS patients' long-term survival. Those who said they would help someone died *sooner* than average; those who said they would not help lived longer. Compassion, it seems, brings its own punishment.[4]

· 3 ·

The point of these two examples is that our culture is sending us some very strong signals about the limits of caring. Set boundaries around it or you are likely to self-destruct.

How well do we do this? Do we successfully limit our caring so that it does not get in the way of our own needs? Or do we let our caring for others become obsessive to the point that we feel like Carla—a disoriented pheasant running around with its head cut off?

The answer to this question is of enormous practical importance to the millions of Americans who try to show compassion to their neighbors. Seeing how some people place boundaries around their caring can be a valuable lesson for us all.

It is easy to conclude from stories like Carla's or the studies of AIDS patients that it is safer just to look out for Number One. But the easiest conclusion is not always the best. We do not need to give up caring for others entirely in order to take care of ourselves. Millions of Americans, as we have already seen, provide useful services to the needy *and* gain a sense of personal enrichment and fulfillment from it. The trick is to develop skills that allow us to show compassion and at the same time take care of our own needs.

But there is another reason—besides its practical importance—for exploring the ways in which compassionate people in our society set boundaries around their caring behavior. By exploring these boundaries, we gain a better understanding of ourselves and the culture in which we live. Specifically, we learn more about how our culture shapes the definition of compassion. Like Jane Addams on her return from visiting Tolstoy, we learn that compassion is not simply an instinct that all people express in the same way: it may be an instinct, but our culture tells us how to express it. Some acts may strike us as examples of compassion beyond the shadow of a doubt; other activities may also be ways of showing compassion, but they are scarcely recognized as such. Our culture puts blinders on our eyes. By removing these blinders momentarily we may see that compassion is more—or less—than we sometimes think.

We also learn more of what it means to be an individual in our society. When people say they need to limit their caring in order to take care of themselves, they have a distinct notion of who that self is and what its needs are. Carla's therapist, for example, has a rather different view of how a healthy individual should function than Mother Teresa does. By listening to caring individuals' comments about the limits of their compassion, we can gain insight into the way our culture shapes our definition of individuality itself. As I have pointed out before, caring lies at the intersection of ourselves and our responsibilities toward others. To explore the boundary between the two is to clarify our understanding of both.

· 4 ·

The most effective mechanism we use to limit our compassion is to create a distinction between our *roles* and our *selves*. A role is a cluster of distinct and related activities defined by a set of specialized norms and expectations. Some of the roles we play might include mother, tennis player, computer programmer, newspaper reader, and church member. A self, in contrast, is a basic definition of who we are. It may consist of, and be exhausted by, all the roles we play. In many cases, it also appears to include something more fundamental. People often argue that even if all their roles were stripped away, something would be left: their selves consist not only of the things they do, but of the traits that define their beings, and perhaps some overarching sense of their biographies, characters, spirits, or souls. Some of our roles may be so large or time-consuming or central to our lives that they go a long way toward defining our selves. For example, the role of mother might compose a very vital part of a person's identity, whereas the role of newspaper reader probably would not. But a role is always bounded, whereas a self is not. I can take a vacation from my roles; I cannot take a vacation from myself.

We use the distinction between roles and selves to limit our compassion. We do this by associating our caring activities with specific roles, rather than identifying them with our entire selves. If compassion is part of a role, we can escape it. Caring becomes one of the many aspects of our lives. We can keep it in its place. Carla's problem was that caring was her whole life. It occupied her from morning to night. She had no time left over for herself. For most of us, associating caring with one delimited role allows us more easily to keep it in bounds.

The importance of this distinction between our roles and our selves was made particularly vivid to me one day by a young woman who was serving as the volunteer pastor of an inner-city church while she finished her seminary training. During the course of a wide-ranging discussion, she described an incredibly busy schedule that involved staying up nights to help at the church's shelter for the homeless, preparing sermons on Saturdays and giving them on Sundays, rushing to class each morning, running back to the church every evening to help with the soup kitchen, and taking afternoons to participate in community organizing. Her schedule sounded a lot like Carla's. Finally I asked her if she experienced a lot of stress, particularly at times when she had to minister to some especially difficult situation, such as calling on a parishioner who was dying in the hospital. "No," she replied. "I've been trained to do that; I know what to expect." Without hesitating, she went on: "You know what really stresses me out? Going to a cocktail party! That's not just a role, that's me!"

This woman had learned to draw a sharp distinction between her role as a care giver and her self. The one was manageable because it was restricted. As much as she cared for her parishioners, her efforts to help them did not really touch the exposed nerves of her personality in the same way going to a cocktail party did. She had been taught what to expect. The role defined how she should behave. When she visited people in the hospital, there was a script for her to follow. She might feel their pain, or feel rewarded for having visited them, but she could fall back on a specified set of norms and expectations. The cocktail party was different. In that situation, she was just supposed to be herself.

195

One might quibble by pointing out that "cocktail-party goer" is just as much a role as "hospital visitor." This woman was in a sense arbitrarily defining one as a role and the other as a situation involving her real self. But that is the point. What we place in one category or the other is to some extent arbitrary. It is up to us—or at least it depends on the way things in our culture are defined. Besides learning the activities and scripts that make up a role, we learn that certain activities and scripts *are roles*. We set them apart and refer to them as different from our basic selves.

Most of us have a wide range of discretion in choosing our roles. We can decide whether we want to play the role of pastor or computer programmer or hospital visitor. But we do not for the most part choose whether these roles are defined as roles. They are already identified as such by the society in which we live.

Selecting roles is somewhat like choosing groceries at the supermarket. We walk along the aisle and choose—a can of beans, a loaf of bread, a sack of potatoes. But these items were already there. We did not have to look at something and say, hmm, I think I'll call that a sack of potatoes.

Giving care operates the same way. We can choose to give care at all—like deciding to go to the supermarket in the first place. And then we can choose to behave in certain ways that are defined as care-giving roles—volunteering for the rescue squad, helping an illiterate person read, donating time at a battered women's shelter. We choose which care-giving role to play, but we do not define it; we do not look at an activity and say to ourselves that we will call this a care-giving role. It is already defined for us. As sociologists would say, the role is *institutionalized*. It is an established part of our society. We do not have to create it; it is already there.

· 5 ·

What this little lesson in elementary sociology provides is a new way of understanding the importance of the so-called voluntary sector in our society. Voluntary associations are not important just because they provide services to the needy. They

196

are important because they define certain activities as roles. Without rescue squads there would be no role of rescue-squad member. Without soup kitchens, the role of soup-kitchen helper could not exist. Thinking of something as a role is contingent on having organizations that institutionalize these roles.

Voluntary organizations are in fact enormously influential in defining what we consider compassionate behavior in our society. What we think of as caring is often an activity that takes place within the context of a voluntary association. In one of the recent national studies I mentioned in chapter 1, for example, three-quarters of the activities people mentioned that involved giving of their time to help others were linked to various organizations such as charities, churches, service clubs, health organizations, and neighborhood centers. Only a quarter of the activities mentioned were done informally and individually. The same is true in studies of financial giving. We read reports about money donated to philanthropy because statistics can be obtained from the recipient organizations. It is much harder to know how much money is given informally to individual relatives, friends, neighbors, or strangers. The picture of a well-dressed couple attending a charity ball sponsored by some voluntary organization makes the newspaper, defining our public sense of what compassion is, not the picture never taken of an elderly woman sitting up all night with her neighbor whose husband has just died.

Just how much we associate caring and compassion with institutionalized roles was particularly evident in the way people we interviewed talked about their activities. As we have seen, people talked fluently and at great length about the roles they played in volunteer organizations. They told stories of how they had first started doing volunteer work, of how they had gotten involved with their current volunteer activities, of the hours they spent and the people they saw, and of the gratifications they received. Often these stories seemed to be well-rehearsed, as if they had been told many times before to friends and acquaintances.

Doing volunteer work provided people with clear, definable contexts in which to talk about their caring activities. The compassion individuals tried to show outside these contexts, as reflections of their basic selves, was harder to describe. When these same people were asked to say what else they did, just in their everyday lives, to show compassion, they often fumbled for words and had little to say.

Debbie Carson, for example, was highly articulate and able to speak at great length about her involvement with international women at her church and in her community, but she was uncharacteristically brief in saying how she showed compassion in her everyday life. "I just try to be aware if there's a need I can help with," she responded. As clarification she added: "Just with my children, whatever their needs might be, or my husband. Friends. If they have a need, I try to make time for them."

Janet Russo, as we saw, talked easily about her volunteer work at the women's center, but when asked how she showed compassion in her daily life, she tried to sidestep the question with a joke. She said she guessed not honking at people on the highway was what she did, laughed, and then told a long story about a recent incident. When pressed on the issue, she finally suggested that she tried to be a good person and not carouse around, as she did when she was younger. Ted Garvey was another who had trouble saying how he showed compassion in everyday life. Although he spoke at length about his years in the Peace Corps, all he could say about daily life was that he "tried to relate to everyone I meet."

People also fumbled for words because they were embarrassed about sounding too altruistic in their daily lives. As I suggested in chapter 3, the stories we tell about our motivations are partly designed to show that we really are not just bleeding hearts. When our caring activities are linked to some volunteer effort, we can excuse ourselves from being do-gooders by talking about some unusual circumstance that caused us to become involved. That kind of involvement is also less troublesome because it is simply one of the many roles we play. Someone can talk about volunteering, but then show what a normal person he or she is by telling a story about his or her family or job or latest escapade at the casino. But everyday life is closer to the real self. If you admit that you do good deeds as part of your normal routine, you may well sound like an insufferable do-gooder. Consequently, you may downplay your caring activities or provide some excuse for them that ultimately makes them seem more self-serving than altruistic.

Elgin Perry, for instance, acknowledged that he tries to be caring in his everyday life by cleaning the hall and the laundry room in the apartment building where he lives. Having acknowledged he does this, though, he immediately tried to explain it away. He does it, he said, because he does not want to track dirt back into his own apartment. "It helps me know that my surroundings are clean. I'm a neat person and I don't like to see things being dirty." He stopped, acting a bit embarrassed, as if he wished he had not mentioned anything at all.

Another person recognized explicitly why she found it difficult to talk about the caring she did in her everyday life, apart from the formal volunteer work she did at a day-care center: "Those are the kinds of things you don't talk about," she noted. "It's almost embarrassing for me to tell you the kinds of things I've done, because I haven't done them to get recognition."

· 6 ·

The problem is not that people actually fail to be compassionate in their everyday lives. Their comments reveal that people do show compassion in many ways and want to think of themselves as compassionate in their everyday lives. They spend time listening to their friends and neighbors, do small favors, and try not to cause trouble. The survey evidence also reveals that compassion extends well beyond the activities of voluntary organizations. One indication of this broader, less-visible layer of compassion in our society, for example, is the large number of people who engage in caring behavior of one kind or another and yet are not involved in any volunteer organization. Consider:

Sixty-seven percent of the people who gave money to a beggar within the past year did NOT donate time to a volunteer organization.

Sixty-four percent of the people who visited someone in the hospital during the past year did NOT donate time to a volunteer organization.

Sixty-two percent of the people who loaned someone one hundred dollars or more within the past year did NOT donate time to a volunteer organization.

Sixty-one percent of the people who stopped to help someone having car trouble in the past year did NOT donate time to a volunteer organization.

Fifty-eight percent of the people who had cared for someone who was very sick within the past year did NOT donate time to a volunteer organization.

Fifty-eight percent of the people who tried to help someone stop using drugs or alcohol in the past year did NOT donate time to a volunteer organization.

Fifty-eight percent of the people who helped someone through a personal crisis in the past year did NOT donate time to a volunteer organization.

Fifty-seven percent of the people who took care of elderly relatives in their homes within the past year did NOT donate time to a volunteer organization.

In other words, a substantial majority of all these kinds of caring behavior is done by people who are not involved in volunteer agencies. They simply show compassion in small ways as part of their everyday lives.

It is important to recognize that compassion in our society is in fact something far greater than the care giving that goes on in nonprofit organizations. Sometimes we may feel that we are really not contributing if we fail to help out with the local pancake breakfast, fire fighters' benefit, or United Way campaign. But informal favors done for family and friends are the milk of human kindness that nourishes social relationships. Nonprofit organizations are the more visible manifestations of compassion because they have the wherewithal to advertise, solicit donations, and make their presence felt in the community. Yet much of the kindness shown on a day-to-day basis occurs invisibly, informally, without fanfare. The problem is only that people have a harder time talking about acts of kindness done informally than about care giving performed in an institutionalized role.

Coming back to the question of how we limit compassion, then, it is apparent that voluntary organizations not only facilitate care giving but also help us restrict our care giving to manageable roles. Psychologically, it becomes possible to tell ourselves that we are compassionate because we spend an afternoon a month, say, visiting convicts at a local prison. This activity gives us something specific to focus on, to talk about. The stories we can tell others about our activity provide stories that we can also tell ourselves. We do not have to be on guard all the time for ways to show compassion. In truth, we may also be compassionate in our daily lives, but at least having this specific activity to point to helps us know that we are compassionate some of the time. Voluntary organizations, therefore, help us set limits around the care giving we provide.

This is a psychological consequence of focusing our compassion on specific roles. It is made possible by associating ourselves with specific voluntary organizations. But the result is not simply a trick we play on ourselves. We can detach in good conscience, even if we have done relatively little ourselves, because we know there are other people and other voluntary organizations pitching in to help. The little we do still counts because the responsibility is being shared.

Debbie Carson says she never finds herself overwhelmed by the people she tries to help. "The stress comes from thinking about so many people all at once with so many different needs and trying myself to take on too much responsibility. There have been times when I've felt that I'd just taken on too much." When this happens, she simply cuts back on her commitments. She tells herself that the problem is "not finding enough people to share the burden." It comforts her knowing that other people in a whole variety of voluntary organizations are there to help out.

Jack Casey recalled how he used to feel totally responsible for people who had lost their homes when he first began helping out at the volunteer fire company. He felt very sorry for the victims of fires because all their worldly possessions had gone up in smoke. One time, he even told a couple of people they could stay at the fire station for a few days. He felt guilty and wanted to help in any way he could. But the more seasoned volunteers at the fire station made him see that he should limit his involvement. They told him, "You just can't let yourself feel guilty. Granted, it's a very unfortunate and tragic thing. But there are other organizations that will take care of them. We did our job. Yes, you have to feel some compassion toward them. You direct them where to go. But if you bring them back to the station, pretty soon everybody will be living there. We'd be a crutch to those people; they need to get back on their own feet. So we just direct them to the Red Cross or Salvation Army."

After they explained it to him that way, Jack recalls, he did not feel so bad. What his colleagues had done was give him a reasonable argument for limiting his commitment. Responding to a fire was enough. It was not only a role he could decide to play, rather than having to extend compassion to fire victims in his personal life; it was also a responsibility that needed to be limited in order for the fire company itself to do its job. Jack could feel better about the limited part he played because his organization was just one of many. There were other organizations, like the Red Cross and the Salvation Army, to pick up where the fire company left off.

As this example suggests, voluntary organizations also limit the extent of our involvement with needy people by restricting the frequency and duration of our contacts with them. In his work for the volunteer fire company and the rescue squad, Jack Casey seldom sees people for more than a few minutes. Once the fire is out or the patients are taken to the hospital, he forgets about them. He may get thank-you cards from them later or see them on the street, but that is the extent of it. The women Janet Russo sees at the crisis center are the same way. She may help them for as much as an hour or two. But she finds it awkward to say hello if she happens to see them in other settings. Martin Barnes has deliberately stayed on the same route with his Meals on Wheels deliveries because he enjoys seeing familiar faces. But even in his case the contact is always brief and most of the elderly people who require his services die within a few years. Susan Robbins makes a habit of calling on bereaved parents several months after her initial contact with them, but after that she seldom sees them. In fact, Debbie Carson and Marge Detweiler were among the few who listed any lasting relationships that had developed as part of their volunteer work. Many volunteers had become friends with other volunteers, but few had made friends with the people they served.

Partly it is in the nature of volunteer organizations to divide up the client load and structure the relations between volunteers and clients so that lasting relationships are almost out of the question. But our attitude toward these organizations also reinforces the casualness of these relationships. For many of us, volunteer agencies are like brands of cereal. We get bored easily, and so we change our loyalties frequently. Bran flakes one day, granola the next. Volunteering, after all, is something we do mainly for the enjoyment. It enriches us by catering to our interests of the moment. When we feel bored, we move on.

"I try to change volunteer duties at least two or three times a year. For a while I did volunteer work at the Lonely Joes, which is a shelter for the homeless. But after while I thought to myself, I'm burned out, this is too heavy for me. So I stopped and began helping put out a newsletter for another organization. I keep changing. I change a lot. Like this thing I'm doing now, it's a new thing. I'll spend some time on it. It involves sending out fliers for different agencies. I can do it at home. I really enjoy it. Someday I'll probably drop it."

In these ways, then, the existence of voluntary organizations in our society helps us limit our commitment to the needs of others. To be sure, these organizations are in business to serve the needy. But, ironically, they are also in business to restrict our individual obligations to the needy. They create roles that we can play, as just one or several of the many roles that make up our lives. In playing these roles, we can associate our compassion with a specific part of our lives, rather than having to be compassionate in all our lives or as part of our basic selves. The organizations bring us into contact with the needy for limited time periods and to perform limited tasks. In dividing up the labor, they also make it possible for us to justify the limited roles we play because other organizations are playing complementary roles.

· 8 ·

Even if we think of compassion as a basic characteristic of our selves, rather than just a role, it is easier to keep our care giving within bounds when it is part of an institutionalized role than when it pervades our entire lives. In this respect, we may admire a Mother Teresa, whose compassion consumes her entire life, but we also have reservations about her because she sacrifices so much. We feel more comfortable with a Janet Russo who expresses her love for others by spending two hours a week at a women's center.

But well-institutionalized roles can still get the best of us. Carla's story reveals the dangers. Someone who wants to help others in need can fill up his or her entire life playing one role after another: day care in the mornings, prison visits in the evenings, mental health work and Sunday school teaching on weekends. Even one role can become an obsession, whether it involves inviting an Alzheimer's victim to share one's apartment or just letting the two hours we spend at the women's center expand to the point that volunteering becomes a full-time job.

Institutionalized roles are in this respect a two-edged sword. On the one hand, they allow us to restrict our involvement by helping us separate our selves from our roles. On the other hand, they maintain themselves by asking more and more of us. Voluntary organizations are of course notoriously greedy. Because they depend on voluntary contributions of time and money, they often devote a great deal of their effort to soliciting such contributions. Many of the people we spoke to in fact talked about the time they spent recruiting other volunteers and staging benefits to raise money. Many others talked about feeling pressured to give more of their time and money.

The fact that voluntary organizations can consume more time and energy than many people have to give necessitates a second mechanism for limiting our involvement. We not only distinguish our roles from our selves, but we also detach psychologically and emotionally from these roles. We do not commit our whole lives to helping the needy, as Mother Teresa does.

Most of us do not even display the compulsiveness of Carla. We do not run ourselves ragged taking personal responsibility for the downtrodden in our communities. Instead, we cut ourselves loose when the emotional burdens or the time commitments become too consuming. We tell ourselves that we can be of little help to anyone else if we let ourselves become too involved. We learn when to say when.

Marge Detweiler, as I noted in chapter 2, sets strict limits around the edges of her caring relationships. When she becomes frustrated sponsoring someone in AA or finds the person she sponsors taking too much from her, she breaks off the relationship. In fact, part of the philosophy she has learned in AA is to make people take responsibility for themselves, rather than letting them become dependent on her. "I can only give them any wisdom I've learned about how to live the program of AA. And when I give them that and they keep saying yeh-but, which is usually yeh-but I'm different, it brings me to the point that I'm drained and I'm frustrated and I'm angry." Marge takes these feelings as the cue to extricate herself. "A beautiful part about the whole sponsorship relationship is that I then end it. I tell them I'm sorry, but I know what I have to give and they don't want it." She tries not to be cruel about it, but she takes a firm stand. She simply tells them: "If you want it a week from now or a month from now, I'll be here for you. But I don't have anything to give you now." Cold realism, she explains, is not being coldhearted. But it does require setting strict limits: "It's not that I dump them after the first yeh-but. I've been known to hang in there for about a month or a month and a half. It's not easy to terminate it. But I know that until she's ready I don't have anything to give her."

The lessons Marge has learned in AA about detachment are echoed loudly by individuals with expertise in therapeutic relationships. Ellen Steinberg, for example, says she has learned as a practicing psychologist that you have to know how to deal with people in pain without letting your emotions interfere with your ability to help. In her view, there is nothing new about detachment. Citing Maimonides, she argues for the importance of seeing the person who is suffering, not just the suffering. "To care about the individual is one thing; to overidentify with their pain doesn't help them a bit." Donna Frylinger has been taught the same thing in her social-work courses. She recognizes the importance of empathizing with people in pain, such as the abused women she counsels. "You need to establish rapport with the people who are being victimized as quickly as you can, and one way to do that is to try to put yourself in their situation. You need to think how you'd feel if you'd just been raped or if your husband had just beat you." But this empathy must be balanced by detachment. "You have to maintain a little bit of distance. You can't get sucked into it. Then you have two people who are so carried away by the problem that nobody can do anything." For both women, caring is a little easier because of the training they have received. Like the clergywoman I quoted, they have learned a role, and that role helps them protect the other parts of their lives from the emotional strain of caring for others. It is a set of activities from which they can divest their deepest, personal emotions and needs.

For compassionate people without specialized training, learning to set limits can often be a new and liberating experience. They have been taught that self-sacrifice not self-preservation, is the ideal. Like Carla, they have let their commitments to other people get out of hand. Technically speaking, they have become "codependent" on those they try to help. Too much of their own self-esteem comes from helping others. They need to learn how to detach.

In such instances, counseling or participation in self-help groups provides lessons in detachment. Care givers learn to think of their helping behavior as part of a role, rather than as a basic feature of their personalities. Marge Detweiler learned to set limits by participating in AA. For others who have not themselves suffered from alcoholism, different kinds of groups that operate on principles developed by AA provide the same kind of instruction. Among these are groups such as Codependents Anonymous and Adult Children of Alcoholics.

A woman in her early fifties described how participating in one of these groups had taught her to restrict her caring activities. She was invited by a friend who told her, "I think you will enjoy this group because you have always been a care giver and now it's time you learned to take better care of yourself."

At first she resisted going because the whole idea sounded very selfish, compared to the values she had always tried to emulate. But eventually she started going and discovered that she now feels less compulsive about helping people. "I used to be a pushover, but now I'm learning to define my boundaries. I'm learning to say no."

Others in very different types of caring roles also stress the importance of detachment. Jack Casey has actually risked his life several times to help others and, as I will explain in a moment, sometimes finds it impossible to detach from the trauma he experiences as a rescue-squad worker and a volunteer firefighter. But like the others, he believes firmly that you have to know your limits and take care of yourself. He has experienced several periods of burnout, so he knows the importance of detachment. He tries to take regular vacations, and if he feels himself becoming emotionally exhausted, he leaves town for a few days or calls in sick and stays home working on hobbies. If he fails to do this, he finds his effectiveness in helping others actually diminishes. One of the things that helps him stay detached is the advice of a friend on the squad: "Just think of the person you're helping as a car that's broken down; you try to fix it; you can't; no big deal; you take it to a better mechanic, a doctor who can; sometimes you can't fix them at all, some of them are too old and need to be replaced."

He also relies on humor to help him stay detached. "Black humor" was the term he used to describe it. "We tell jokes or make cracks to the new guys and it kind of helps them adjust to the stress. It's not intended to be cruel, but it's basically making jokes at the expense of the patients. Like, some guy comes in with his legs crushed and has to have them amputated, and we'll say something among ourselves about how this will probably end his basketball career. To an outsider, it seems horrendous. It's cruel and inhuman and disgusting. There's no way they can understand why we do it."

As he said this I thought back to that night he responded to the call for help at the mansion named after Tolstoy's estate. "What did you say that made your teammate grin so widely?" I asked. "Oh, I dunno," he replied. "I think I said it'd be better to let the sucker die than track crud in on their Persian carpet!"

· 9 ·

Detachment is relatively easy when the people one cares for are experiencing little pain or trauma themselves and when one's relationship with them is brief or highly structured. In other situations, the trauma is simply too acute. One may try to detach by suppressing one's feelings, but sooner or later those feelings have to be faced. It becomes necessary to acknowledge that your caring has affected you emotionally. Detachment then requires working through those feelings, rather than simply denying them.

Rescue-squad workers, like Jack Casey, and others who witness extreme trauma on a daily basis, such as doctors and combat soldiers, often detach from the pain they see by blocking it out. They simply harden themselves to the point that they feel little of the emotion others would normally experience under such conditions. Jack Casey, for example, observed that most of the people he knows on the rescue squad do not display emotion as readily as they once did. In his own case, he says he has seen so much human tragedy that he cannot remember the last time he cried. Most of the time he just suppresses his feelings. But even for someone as hardened as he, situations sometimes make it impossible to detach completely.

To illustrate, Jack recalled an airplane accident he had responded to about four years before. The plane, a small four-passenger craft, was starting its approach to the airport when the wings for some reason folded up. It dropped from an altitude of about three thousand feet onto a major highway, killing the family of four that was on board. Jack remembers arriving on the scene and finding an ambulance crew already there but unable to function. The crew members were just sitting there crying. "I asked what the problem was and they said we have four victims. So I turned and looked out toward where the debris was and I could see a shoe sticking up out of the ground. And then I walked around and started to find body parts. We stayed on the scene about four hours. And finally when we were able to leave, my roommate started crying and was pretty sad for two or three days. The old-timers on the squad were saying you have to be a man about it and suppress the feelings and not let it show. But I felt a lot of hurt that I needed to vent. So we got together and went to a bar and drank ourselves drunk. And I went home and suppressed it."

But suppression simply drove the feelings underground that needed to surface and be dealt with for true detachment to occur. Jack remembers that three or four months later he started seeing problems among the squad members, including himself. "We were having a lot of bad moods and our patient-care declined because we really didn't give a damn. Then everybody started not caring about themselves. I just didn't care about anything at all. One day I came home and just kicked my dog as hard as I could. I became very withdrawn and broke up with my girlfriend. I sat at home and just drank. I didn't realize what was happening to me."

Eventually one of Jack's friends pointed out to him how much he had changed. He realized his friend was right and decided to seek help. At the local hospital he found some meetings called critical-incident debriefings. Attending these gave him an opportunity to talk through his feelings and get them out in the open. "I vented a lot. It took about a year and a half. But eventually I got back into the swing of things. So the big lesson for me was that if you are involved in an episode like that you really need to vent your feelings. If you want to cry, cry; there's nothing wrong with it."

· 10 ·

Most volunteers are shielded from having to deal with trauma this extreme. Indeed, it is often easier for volunteers to remain detached from the people they serve than it is for those who just try to be helpful in their everyday lives. Making care giving a formal role helps restrict it to manageable proportions. You can detach because the person you see in pain is neither a loved one nor someone for whom you share a major responsibility. You can do your bit and then leave. If you feel uncomfortable being around pain, you can serve in some other way— perhaps by chairing a committee. This is the virtue of volunteer work. It is indeed voluntary, a kind of minimal commitment, if you wish, quite different from the obligations that are imposed on you by the natural rhythms of life among family and friends. People, in fact, speak quite differently about these obligations. They find it harder to detach when the relationships are not structured by voluntary associations.

Elmer Benson, the retired broadcaster who works as a volunteer for Recording for the Blind, drew a suggestive contrast between the ease with which volunteers can detach and the difficulties associated with detaching from family and friends. Asked if his volunteer work ever leaves him feeling drained, he said no. It does not because he takes control of any volunteer activity in which he becomes involved. What he meant was that he offers to help but only for a limited time and to accomplish some specific task. "Like once I was on a steering committee to get something started, and when it got started, my job was through. I was on the steering committee to get a community Christmas tree project organized, but once that was done, it moved out of my way." Being able to restrict his obligations was one of the things he liked best about volunteer work. "Before you get worn out on a project, you can get away from it. You just plan to give so much time and then move on to something else. I don't get burned out because I try to put a definite limit on things."

It took him a lot more effort and much more patience to deal with family members and personal friends. He still tried to detach from them, but it was impossible to do so simply by terminating his involvement. Some of them had interminable needs. All he could do was keep his distance geographically, and when that was impossible, laugh about it.

Elmer's cousin Sarah was one of those relatives with interminable needs. Drawing on a well-practiced stock of puns and metaphors, Elmer described her as a hypochondriac who had managed to grieve the death of one of her children for the past twenty-two years. "She came to visit us a few years ago and talked for four days straight! I was glad to get her on the train again by the time she left. She's so wrapped up in herself. It's very difficult to be patient and loving and caring. But boy, she really needs that love. I'll invite her down again sometime. And I'll drive her down to the cemetery where she can see the graves of her family. She'll bend my ear the whole time she's here. It won't be easy, but I'll do it because she really needs it."

210

Yes, he mused, "I'll invite her down again sometime—but not real soon."

In a more sobering way, Frank Stevens, the man who told about Miss Carrie's funeral, noted that being able to divide up the labor makes the task of caring so much easier in volunteer organizations than in personal life. "You realize it takes a team effort to help people," he observed. It is much harder to detach and take care of yourself when you are responsible for a loved one over a long period of time. "I think people who are under the most pressure are those who live with someone who is in chronic depression. My sister's had to do that; it's terribly draining." He said he had seen a lot of elderly people who could not detach or limit their obligations if they wanted to. "There's one lady for instance who's in her late seventies and has an invalid husband who's in his eighties. She's been caring for people for the last twenty years. She's at home and people just expect it because she knows how to do nursing care. Now she's seventy-eight. She should have someone caring for her. And she has to be home all day, sometimes for days on end. She can't get out at all."

· 11 ·

To be sure, there are people who can neither detach from the people they try to help in any situation nor work through the emotions that may result. Like Carla, they become obsessive about the needs of others. They have trouble expressing their own feelings, and because of some deep insecurity in their own lives, they hope to save themselves by helping others. Jack Casey, as we saw, has some of these traits. He compulsively runs errands for people in the middle of the night when they would be better off learning to take care of themselves. He relishes the idea of being a hero and, except in extreme cases like the airplane crash, is more likely to suppress his feelings, playing the iceman role or drowning his emotions in alcohol, than really confronting them. But people like Jack Casey and Carla are definitely in the minority. Contrary to the impression that has been given by the results of some clinical studies, compulsive desires to help others and a refusal to detach from their

211

needs do not characterize the majority of Americans. And these compulsive traits are no more common among active care givers than they are in the public at large.

One indication of the American public's readiness to detach and set limits on their commitments to the needy is the fact that 63 percent agree with the statement "to really help people, you have to detach and not get too involved with their problems," compared with only 36 percent who disagree. Among persons currently involved in charitable or social-service activities, the same percentage agree as in the general public.

Besides agreeing that detachment is important, the majority of the American public also stress the importance of taking care of themselves first and the value of letting people work out their problems in their own ways. Two-thirds of the public, as we saw earlier, agree with the statement "You have to take care of yourself first, and if you have any energy left over, then help others" (62 percent of those involved in charitable work agree). And 80 percent of the public agrees that "you can listen to someone's problems, but they pretty much have to come up with their own solutions" (81 percent agree among those involved in charitable work).

The results of other studies also suggest that care givers on the whole are somewhat more likely to manifest the traits of persons who take care of themselves than of persons like Carla who function from emotional deficits that lead them to act compulsively. A comparison of those in one national study who gave time to help the poor and needy with those who did not give time showed that care givers were more likely than nongivers to describe their moods as cheerful rather than depressed. And care givers were no more likely than nongivers to describe their moods as tense, to say they had trouble dealing with their feelings, or to depict themselves as having low energy levels. In the same study respondents who said they were satisfied with their efforts to help others were more likely than respondents who were less satisfied with these efforts to say they were able to express their feelings, were able to control their tempers, and had high energy levels.[5]

Although these findings do not address questions of causality, they are at least consistent with the comments that most of the individuals we have met made about themselves. Care givers by and large seem to restrict their charitable behavior rather than letting it worry them, leave them depressed, or sap their emotional energy.

At the same time, the minority of care givers who donate time and yet feel dissatisfied with their efforts confirm the potential problems identified in the therapeutic literature. This minority does appear to register lower levels of emotional health. Nevertheless, it is a relatively small minority of all care givers. The percentages in fact indicate that patterns of unhealthy and obsessive helping behavior are probably not so high among care givers as some of the literature has suggested. For example, among those who had given time within the past year to help the needy or disadvantaged, only 9 percent said they were dissatisfied with their efforts to help others, 10 percent described themselves as depressed, and 20 percent said they had trouble dealing with their feelings.[6]

· 12 ·

I said earlier that roles generally have well-defined expectations attached to them and that care giving in our society is often associated with voluntary organizations. But there is an opposite side to the coin that also helps us rein in compassion before it gets out of hand. Ours is in many ways a very tolerant society. We may think of compassion as giving one's time to help the voluntary organization of one's choice. Our tolerance is shown in the clause "of one's choice"—and the thousands of different organizations available to us make it possible to find a way of caring that expresses our individual talents and interests. But our tolerance is shown more deeply as well. When pressed, most of us are willing to see almost anything as compassion.

People who do volunteer work, for example, are often quite proud of the work they do, and the leaders of volunteer agencies are sometimes very critical of people who spend all their time looking after their own families, rather than becoming involved in volunteer work. But volunteers in our society are for the most part quite tolerant of people who care only for their own families. They do not argue that compassion must extend

beyond the home to be genuine. Indeed, they often invent extreme scenarios to justify people limiting their compassion.

When asked if someone who showed compassion only to his
or her own family was truly compassionate, Donna Frylinger
immediately turned the question around. Sidestepping the
broader issue, she asked whether or not someone could really
be compassionate and *not* love his or her family. "I've seen so
many parents who are not compassionate to their kids," she
observed. "So if you can find a parent who really cares enough
about their kids to sit down and talk with them, listen to them,
and try to work things out with them, instead of just yelling at
them, then they are doing a very great thing."

Ted Garvey also focused on the extreme case: "Some people
have extremely difficult lives just dealing with their family
members, but they're still compassionate." Then, as if to plead
more loudly his reticence to judge anyone else, he added, "If a
person like that doesn't have time for people outside their family, I'd understand it completely."

Volunteers do recognize the dilemma they face in defining
compassion this way. In saying compassion is just as good
even though it never reaches beyond a person's front door,
they undercut many of their own arguments about the value of
caring for the wider community. One person thought about it
for a while and then said she wished she had a dictionary. She
suspected that the dictionary would say compassion somehow
involved the wider community. But it was more common for
volunteers simply to hedge their arguments in some way—
again relying on the subtleties of language to express their personal reservations without sounding judgmental. For instance,
Elgin Perry remarked: "For me, it seems a little bit closed, but
there are people who care and just tend to avoid contact with
strangers." He wanted people to see the importance of doing
volunteer work. And yet all he could do was to personalize his
remark, prefacing it with "for me."

Debbie Carson had struggled for a long time with the question of whether compassion could reasonably be limited to
one's own immediate family. As a mother of two children, she
saw the danger of letting outside commitments take too much
of her time. "I think there is a tendency for a lot of people to
think of compassion as being something outside your own fam-

ily. Like the minister or the doctor who cares for everyone else, but his own family is home sick in bed and he doesn't look out for them. If a lot of your life is filled with that kind of work or with volunteerism, it's easy to take your own family for granted and to just assume they are covered. You go out and do this great thing for the world. Personally, I don't think that's good. I think there's something wrong if you can't be compassionate first with your family. That has to be where it starts. You start with the people you're most related to and work out from there."

But she also felt uncomfortable thinking that someone could really be compassionate just by caring for his or her own family. She did not want to limit compassion this much. The idea of a mother who is great with her own kids, but does nothing else, for example, bothered her. "The problem is that those people don't think of their world extending beyond their own family. They need to ask, what if my child were outside this immediate circle and needed help. They have a kind of tribalistic mentality that's concerned with just me and mine. They need to take that mentality and see that the whole world is their family. If we don't try to take care of the whole world, then our immediate family is going to suffer." She also recognized that a family focus can actually be quite self-centered because "a lot of people think of their children as extensions of themselves."

Her solution to the problem has been to invite international women into her home, in a sense making them part of her family. She is still able to spend time with her children. Indeed, acquainting her children with people from other societies broadens their horizons. They have come to realize that their own welfare is related to the wider world. In this respect, her own notion of compassion is quite inclusive.

And yet Debbie Carson's arguments provide ample basis for taking a more restricted view of compassion. Doing something to help others outside one's family is not a must. It is only a desirable option. Individuals must decide for themselves whether to exercise this option. It depends on their circumstances. Someone like Debbie's husband, who leads a demanding life as a physician, may have no time to think of anything but his job. Other people may have so much trouble caring for their own children that little more can be expected of them. Ultimately, the important thing is one's attitude. Taking care of one's family can be done with a narrow, self-centered, tribal mentality, or it can be done with a notion of the wider world in mind.

Most volunteers are willing to limit their views of compassion in one way or another. Their emphasis on individual circumstances works the same way as their beliefs about detachment. Both arguments assert, in effect, that you can only be expected to do so much. If you as an individual decide to focus your compassion on your family, then so be it. If you decide to do more, then make sure you have the time and energy to invest without betraying your own needs. Whether it is done for the community or restricted to your own family, love must be kept within bounds.

· 13 ·

What, then, is compassion in our culture? It clearly carries the connotation given it by the many volunteer agencies that clamor for our attention. Its public face is defined by the millions of Americans who devote long hours to these agencies in genuine service to those less fortunate than themselves. But it is bounded love, rather than the all-embracing commitment of a Mother Teresa. As she herself has said, compassion without suffering is "social work, very good and helpful," but not the deeper commitment to which she aspires.[7]

Compassion is possible in an individualistic society like ours because we limit it to what we can handle and still maintain our own individual needs and life-styles. Our volunteer agencies allow us to divide up the work—a little helping here and there, and when we get tired we go home, have a beer, and relax. We hope people will do their share for the community, but we understand if they cannot. Compassion at home is still an acceptable mode of caring.

In the final analysis, we regard compassion in much the same way that we regard all our commitments, whether to our work, our families, our hobbies, or ourselves. The important thing is not so much what we do but the spirit in which we do it. "If you're sincere in your motivation, then it can be compassion," is the way a therapist explained it. "The feeling is what counts," Janet Russo observed. Compassion is basically, as one woman put it, "a very warm emotion." In Debbie Carson's words, "compassion is a feeling type of thing."

You really cannot tell if someone else is compassionate or not because the essential quality is interior. As Elgin Perry argued, "All people are caring to a certain extent; it just may not show in some cases." In his view, "some people seem to exude humanitarianism and caring and love. Others just feel they don't have to be that overt."

Volunteer work is a way of making our feelings more objective, giving us something to talk about. But volunteer work comes in so many different forms that we still find it difficult to decide whether volunteers are more compassionate than anyone else. As Elgin Perry again remarked: "If you see somebody with a tear in his eye and say, oh, what happened, that's volunteer work as well."

As a people, we take the ambiguity in the verb "to care" quite seriously, using it to broaden the meaning of the word until it encompasses the actions of virtually everyone who tries hard to be a good, dedicated, conscientious member of society. To care can mean pulling someone from a burning automobile. It can also mean taking one's responsibilities seriously. In this respect, taking care of someone is not much different from taking care to do one's work well, whatever that may be.

· 14 ·

Just how far people were willing to stretch the concept of compassion was evident when they were asked about various kinds of careers. Some, like Elgin Perry, thought compassion just "goes along with all jobs." Giving a customer a cup of coffee, or coming in to work a half hour early, he said, demonstrated compassion. Most people thought some jobs were more likely to involve compassion than others. And yet they were willing to define compassion in such broad terms that nearly anyone could be regarded as caring as long as his or her job was done responsibly.

It did not stretch many people's imaginations to see that a research scientist might well be showing compassion, even though he or she never helped anyone on an individual basis. For some, it was the possibility that the scientist might discover a cure for cancer or some other solution to some of the world's problems that allowed them to consider the scientist compassionate. For others, it was just the idea that science is valuable in its own right. "Sure," one woman exclaimed, "what he's doing is worthwhile."

The thought that a Wall Street broker might claim to be compassionate because he tried to help his clients make lots of money gave people more difficulty. Some had trouble stretching the idea of compassion this far. No, said one, a broker is really just helping himself because he makes more money when his clients make money. Others reacted negatively to the idea because making money seemed less worthwhile than something like science.

And yet others found ways to see that even this could be compassion. One woman laughed for a moment, amused by the irony of a Wall Street broker being compassionate. But the more she thought about it, the more she warmed to the idea that compassion probably could be bent to fit this situation. For a stockbroker to be compassionate, she ventured, he or she would have to "have the best interests of his or her clients at heart and give the best he or she can to deliver the best product possible." Not showing compassion would involve "goofing off and shortchanging your clients." Ultimately, she reduced compassion to "quality of service in business" and "concern for the people who are buying your product." The term became little more than an antonym for "hard-nosed" and "evil." Compassion basically meant "producing the best possible product with pride."

As with other kinds of caring, people were willing to say that those who sincerely did their jobs well and had the right feelings were indeed compassionate as long as they said they were. Debbie Carson, for example, observed that for her personally, helping people make money would not be compassionate because she did not see money as a basic need. But this way of looking at it also forced her to acknowledge that someone else with different goals and values might think of compassion as making money. "I can see that it might make sense, given a Wall Street frame of mind," she noted, "because it kind of depends on what your goals are. If your goals involve making a lot of money, and somebody feels a real need for that, then you might be able to show compassion by helping them meet that need."

Saying that compassion depends on what your goals are is a poignant commentary on our culture. Conservative Christian that she is, Debbie Carson is willing to say what she herself believes. Helping someone make a lot of money would not be her way of showing compassion: "With my values, I would have a hard time putting myself in that kind of situation and saying it's a real need." But it might be someone else's way. In other words, compassion is in the eye of the beholder, or more accurately, in the eye of the doer. If you think some goal is worth pursuing, then pursuing it—and helping others pursue it—is compassion.

We make compassion culturally contingent. It ceases being an absolute and becomes relative to our values. In a society that doles out good deeds in small doses through volunteer agencies, voluntarism becomes compassion. In a society that values making money on the stock market, good brokerage may also be compassion.

· 15 ·

And what more do we learn about our individuality? It is, as I have argued throughout, a possession we cherish deeply. We believe it possible to guard our individuality even as we help others. We see no conflict between the two: individuality is a prerequisite for genuine caring, and genuine caring helps one attain one's individual potential. But this way of thinking is possible only because we understand compassion in a way that seriously restricts our obligations.

We do not believe in self-sacrifice; we do not even believe in sharing too deeply in the suffering of others. Our individual autonomy is too important. If caring for others becomes too demanding, we get out. We call it an obsession. We tell ourselves that we can serve more effectively if we detach and take care of ourselves. Compassion is something each one of us must define in his or her own way. We expect each person to set his or her own limits. And this of course requires self-awareness—knowing what we want, pursuing it, and shifting to something else when we feel the need. For many people the call to help others is still heard loudly enough, and the rewards of service are still sufficiently great, to cause them to participate in volunteer work. But we also relativize our view of compassion to the extent that caring only for our families or just doing our jobs well can be legitimate.

In doing all this we have created the conditions that make necessary the very voluntary organizations we look to for solutions to our problems. We cannot maintain our individual freedom in the way the logic of detachment requires if we take on the all-consuming commitments of Carla the headless pheasant or Mother Teresa the social misfit. We need to share the responsibility. So we look to our voluntary organizations to create roles that we can more easily fulfill.

In the process, these roles take on a reality of their own. They become different from our basic self-concepts. They reinforce a certain definition of compassion. They lead us along paths of limited commitment. And their diversity and limitations remind us that compassion is after all difficult to define. We hope people will participate in the valuable work of these organizations, but we happily find other ways to credit with their own forms of compassion those who do not. Some of the work—the work that can be divided into limited commitments—is accomplished. Much of it remains undone.

CHAPTER EIGHT

The Tarnished Image

T HE 1940 FILM VERSION of Steinbeck's *Grapes of Wrath* ends on a hopeful note. After Jim Casey decoys the police to prevent them from finding Tom Joad, and is brutally murdered, Tom (played by Henry Fonda) decides to become a volunteer, a man devoted to the needs of all poor and exploited travelers along life's highway. He tells Ma of his plan: "You know what I been thinkin' about, about Casey, what he said, what he done, about how he died, and I remember all of it." Tom explains his desire to be like Casey: "Maybe I can do somethin', maybe I can just find out somethin', just scrounge around and maybe find out what it is that's wrong and then see if somethin' can't be done about it."

Looking off into the distance, Tom paints a picture of how Casey's compassionate spirit will live on in him and others. "I'll be all around in the dark. I'll be everywhere. Wherever there's a fight so hungry people can eat, I'll be there. Wherever there's a cop beatin' up a guy, I'll be there. I'll be in the way guys yell when they're in need. I'll be in the way kids laugh when they know supper's ready. And when people's eatin' the stuff they raise and livin' in the houses they build, I'll be there too."

After Tom's departure, the Joads load up the truck and head for Fresno where twenty days of good picking lie waiting. Along the road, the movie comes to an end with Ma looking ahead through the windshield of the battered truck and articulating her vision to Pa: "We keep a comin'. We're the people that live. They can't wipe us out. They can't lick us. We go on forever, Pa, 'cause we're the people."[1]

· 2 ·

Compassion like Jim Casey's and Tom Joad's always inspires hope. It makes us think of a better day, a better society, and it gives us confidence that such visions can become realities. Seeing the kindness of a Mother Teresa has a healing effect. Just knowing there are people like her reminds us that the world is not entirely composed of greed and selfish ambition. Even if suffering is never eliminated, the struggle against it symbolizes our capacity to pull together and exercise our human dignity collectively. Something proud wells up inside all of us after a national disaster, such as a flood or an earthquake, when the president exclaims "Thank God for the volunteers."

But what is it about compassion that gives us hope? Is it just the possibility that goodness can in some way stand up against evil? Does compassion inspire hope the same way a fine painting or a great athlete does—through vicarious identification with the human potential achieved by another individual? Or does Ma Joad speak more than she realizes when she says, "We're the people that live"?

· 3 ·

In the rabbinic tradition there is a story about a man on a journey through the desert. Along the way he comes upon another man who has been robbed, beaten, and left without water. The first man has just enough water to make it through the desert by himself. He is thus faced with a deep ethical dilemma: if he keeps all the water for himself, the man who has been beaten and robbed will die; if he gives his water to the man, he himself will die; and if he shares the water, both will die.

The great rabbis have debated the ethical dilemma posed by this story for centuries. Some have argued that self-interest should always take precedence when there is no chance that an act of compassion will yield beneficial results. Some have argued that compassion for a fellow human being in need should always take precedence, even if it means sacrificing one's own life. Others, albeit a minority, have argued that the two strangers should share the water.

When confronted with this story, Ellen Steinberg sided with the rabbis who favored self-interest in place of an ineffective act of sacrifice. In her view the question had been settled by the rabbis themselves: it may seem cruel, but self-preservation is the answer in this case. Jack Casey explained that keeping the water for yourself also squared best with what he had been taught on the rescue squad. "You see that kind of situation time and time again here. The most prudent thing would be to keep the water yourself and continue on. You'll probably find everyone saying they'd share the water. But this would be a great question for me to ask someone who wanted to join this organization. If they said they'd keep the water and continue on to seek help, I'd make them an officer. He's looking at it from a realistic point of view. He's probably doing the best thing. If he said he'd give the water to the other man, we don't need that kind of person on the rescue squad, because the other guy may not make it out of the situation. Most people would probably feel very guilty about keeping the water for themselves. But if you step into my shoes and put yourself in a life-and-death situation, you've got to make that kind of decision, and it's stressful, but that's what you've got to do."

Martin Barnes took the opposite view. He said he hoped he would be unselfish enough to give the water away. But he also admitted he could not say for sure without actually being in the situation. Debbie Carson, noting that she had recently read about some boat people in a similar situation, thought at first that she might share the water and risk both people dying. But the more she thought about it, the more her conscience bothered her. Sharing the water, she concluded, "probably wouldn't be the greater thing to do." The most principled response, in her view, would be "me giving up the water and dying." On reflection, she thought she just might take that option: "I'm kind of the type who might end up doing that." And then she added: "Maybe I'm too much that way."

The most common view, however, was the third alternative posed by the rabbis: share the water and take your chances. Elmer Benson agonized over the story for a long time, kicking himself for having gotten in the desert in the first place; then, after a long silence, he finally said simply: "I would probably share the water and pray." Susan Robbins arrived (somewhat more quickly) at the same conclusion: she said she would "share it in the hopes that something will come along." Janet Russo said the same thing. Elgin Perry elaborated: "If they share it, they both might actually make it. There is always hope if they share it. If one guy keeps it, he may open it and faint and let all the water run out on the ground, and then neither one will make it. But if they share it, there's a better chance that at least one of them will make it out."

The responses to this story illustrate how closely compassion and hope are intertwined in our society. We find it difficult to take the view that someone should just look out for himself or herself, especially if it means another person will die. That view seems not only callous, but also overly cautious. It risks nothing, takes no chances, and therefore requires no faith. Freddie Jackson Taylor, for example, said he would share the water rather than keeping it all for himself simply because he is a person who takes risks: "I would definitely share it. I'm a gambler. I don't mean I go to Las Vegas and gamble. I mean I do take chances. I take risks and I take chances. And I always seem to land on my feet."

We also find it difficult to say we would sacrifice our own lives for the welfare of a complete stranger. We know better. We realize our instinct for self-preservation is strong. But we also figure this option is too shortsighted. Suppose we sacrifice our lives by giving the stranger all our water and he turns out to be too weak to make it through the desert anyway. Or suppose he comes to an oasis just after we have breathed our last.

Sharing the water and taking our chances is the option most of us prefer because it keeps hope alive. It forecloses none of the possibilities. We do not take the storyteller at his word when he says both of us will die. Instead we believe we can rewrite the story to have a new ending. Perhaps some other travelers will come along and rescue us both. By pooling our resources we at least buy time. Maybe we will think of something before the water runs out. Indeed, sharing forces us to plan ahead. As Donna Frylinger observed, "I couldn't just walk on and not give him any, so I would probably share it, and then I'd try to come up with some kind of plan that would help both of us get across the desert before we ran out of water."

Sharing necessitates having hope. It forces us to have faith, both in the possibilities of circumstances working out for the best and in our own ability to think of something. One person noted that it might rain. Another person staked her hope in human willpower. "I'm a trusting and hopeful person," she said, "so I would make an attempt to share—and then try like *crazy* to make it." In either case, hope is the essential element. Frank Stevens put it this way: "Hope is a very important ingredient in life. So I'd say share it and hope that something happens before we run out together."

It is in this sense that helping others becomes associated with hope. Each conjures up the other. Sharing makes sense because we have faith in the future. And our faith in the future is heightened by our capacity to share. We feel stronger because we are joining forces with other human beings. Helping them lets us know we are not alone. Perhaps they will return the favor. As long as we can stay alive, our compassion may even be rewarded in some way we cannot foresee.

· 4 ·

The long tradition of myths and fables that is embedded in our history tells us that good deeds may result in unexpected rewards. The fairy tale is at first glance an inauspicious genre in which to find lessons about compassion. It is more common to think of fairy tales as the literature of childhood fantasy, of courage or foolishness, or even as disguised political statements. Compassion, however, is one of the traits that sets many fairy-tale heroes apart from their peers. Although they may be extraordinarily simple or inept in other ways, they distinguish themselves in story after story with acts of kindness. As one authority on the subject has observed, "Even before the simpleton embarks on a journey to foreign kingdoms or undertakes diverse tasks to liberate a princess, he must prove himself worthy of assistance from nature or from supernatural powers by displaying compassion."[2] She goes on to suggest that an act of compassion somehow earns the hero good favor so that he can do no wrong thereafter, and indeed, gains allies who help him accomplish the tasks that lie ahead. In this sense, fairy tales are stories that illustrate the potential rewards of showing compassion.

Students of folklore have observed that a common theme in a wide variety of fables and fairy tales is indeed the miraculous good fortune that comes to those who show compassion. Someone happens to be walking along minding his or her own business, in the typical story, and suddenly sees some poor creature in trouble. Without stopping to think, the person stops and engages in some small act of kindness—and suddenly the poor creature turns out to be the good fairy. Kindness in these stories does not bring its own punishment, as it did for poor Carla; it produces marvelous rewards. If only inadvertently, then, the lore of fables connects kindness with hope for a better day.

In American culture one of the tales that best illustrates this motif is the story of the wonderful pump.[3] First appearing in print in 1901 as part of a syndicated weekly series that appeared in many of the nation's leading newspapers, the tale is thought to have been told orally in a variety of versions for many decades before. It is about a New England farm couple who symbolize all that is good and wholesome in American life: "sober, honest people, working hard from early morning until dark to enable them to secure a scanty living from their poor land."[4] As the narrative begins, the wife (who always "meekly and faithfully performed her duties") is making the long, difficult, tedious journey down from the house to the brook to fetch water. Like the Good Samaritan, she is traveling (as it were) along the road when she spies a creature in need. The creature is a large beetle lying on its back and struggling ineffectively to turn itself upright. On seeing the beetle, the woman—"who had a kind heart"—gently turned the beetle over so it could scamper down the path.

The next day, the woman is surprised to see the beetle lying in the same position. Again she sets it on its feet. But this time the beetle speaks. Indeed, it voices a lengthy soliloquy on the great deed of kindness the woman has performed: "You saved my life—saved me from my enemies. . . . And this is the second time you have come to my assistance, so I owe you a debt of gratitude. Bugs value their lives as much as human beings, and I am a more important creature than you, in your ignorance, may suppose."[5] The bug then discusses the woman's water situation with her and suggests she go home and encourage her husband to try again digging a well beside the house.

The upshot of the story is that neither the woman nor her husband has enough hope at first to dig the well and install the pump, but after more encouragement from the beetle they do so. Through the miraculous bug's intervention the pump in fact produces not water but five-dollar gold pieces. The woman's kindness is indeed rewarded magnificently. That is the main lesson of the story.

But then the story goes on to reinforce this lesson by negative example. Realizing their treasure, the man and woman decide they would like to extend their generosity and give the poor parson something the following Sunday at church. Pure kindness, however, is suddenly overcome by pride as the man and his wife make a show of dropping their coins loudly into the offering plate. After this, like a cancer, their pride grows to the point that they tell everyone in town of their good fortune. And the bad men in town, hearing the news, raid their house and rob them of all their coins. The tale ends with the beetle admonishing the woman to work hard, to continue showing kindness to those in need, and to be more humble about the rewards that come her way.

In one form or another, stories of this kind have been prevalent throughout history and remain so even in contemporary settings. One common motif is the beggar who imparts blessings. He is in a sense the animus of modern life—the simple beggar who has chosen poverty or suffered some tragic fate, but who still knows more than we. He is the keeper of sacred wisdom. By helping him, we gain privileged access to his mysterious knowledge. In his *Confessions*, for example, Augustine tells of meeting a beggar, pondering the joy on his face, and from him learning a higher truth than he had found previously in all his searching.[6] Almost the same theme has been echoed by a popular contemporary lecturer who tells of leaving a scholarly conference disgusted with its pedantry and meeting a beggar in the park who reveals to him the secret of a happy life.[7]

Most of us of course do not expect the beggar we meet on the street suddenly to impart deep truths or become a fairy godmother. But we sometimes, in effect, tell similar tales when we romanticize the poor. A Harvard professor makes a trip to rural Alabama in search of the American spirit, and suddenly (in a surprisingly fluent Cambridge dialect) a poor black sharecropper reveals the secret serenity of his impoverished existence. Or a busload of tired teenagers returning to the comfort of their affluent church in an upper-middle-class white suburb in the

Northeast report glowingly of a week spent helping poor people in Appalachia: what impresses them most is that these people really do not want better houses, or shoes to wear, or cars to drive; they have found a more peaceful and happy existence living without the burdens of affluence.

The tales of hope—of deep insights about life that cannot be found in our own affluent culture—are often not this crass. They at least benefit from an attitude of openness to being instructed by the poor, rather than the view that those of us who have more material resources also have all the answers to life and are merely here to help the less fortunate. But the line between learning what we can from the poor and romanticizing their poverty is always thin.

Even a person as sophisticated and articulate as Debbie Carson, for example, had difficulty selecting the right words to tell her story of insight and hope derived from encountering the poor. Her trip to Kenya had inspired her to be more compassionate, she said. The people there seemed to be more natural in their caring than she had been able to be. In this sense, she had been instructed by them. But it was also clear that they provided her with an animus to modern life, especially to the materialism she detests in American society: "Going over there and assuming we're so fortunate here, and thinking we're trying to help them be more like us—well, what impressed me was that I'd never want them, never want them to be like us. They're so free in their ability to love life and enjoy life, to enjoy their children, to enjoy each other—they have an ability to just be in touch with life in a way that we've lost. It was just so attractive to me. They've had to deal with the raw part of life and they know how to do that. The only real thing you want for them is that they could have health care and food and clean water. After that, it's like you wouldn't want to give them one more thing. They're so happy and content. And their children are just amazing. They have no toys but they were just the happiest kids. You didn't see a lot of fighting and bickering. It was a quality that I wish we could regain.

"They were extremely caring people. There's no orphanages. They just take care of each other. They don't have old folks' homes. Living in a community that way, if someone's husband or wife dies, they aren't alone. They're still part of a caring community. You're needed. They don't think of things as volunteer work, like here, where we have all these labels, like 'this is volunteer work,' but they're all helping. This one little eight-year-old girl was taking care of her four-year-old brother and a little neighbor kid. That's just part of their life. They don't think of it as doing a great service. They have to, of course, but I think it does show what human nature can be like."

The moral of such tales, whether from storybooks or real life, is that an encounter with the needy may turn out to be the doorway to a better future. There may be hidden blessings—not perhaps material riches, but a chance to recover values we have lost or to find truths we have been seeking. One should always be prepared to help out because an act of kindness may cause the door to spring open. The logic is similar to the ancient custom of setting an extra place at the table in case a stranger should suddenly appear at the door and turn out to be the Messiah. Hospitality to the lowly may result, as it is said, in entertaining angels unaware. The goodness that results may not accrue just to the one who shows kindness; the blessing received may be an epiphany, a revelation. The care giver must not, above all, show kindness in order to receive a blessing, and must not turn the blessing received to selfish purposes. But the message of hope is clear: even the smallest act of kindness may result in a better life.

· 5 ·

As a society, we still believe that collective compassion may result in the gods smiling on us. At least this is what many people think about having a strong voluntary sector. The words of Tocqueville are echoed again and again: the strength of our voluntary associations will ensure the viability of our society. No disaster can destroy our spirits as long as we pull each other out of the rubble and pay due respect to the brave volunteers who arise in our midst. The goodness shown by our volunteers will somehow make up for the scandals that gnaw away at our moral fiber. If enough of us pitch in and help the needy, we can forestall the slide into economic and political chaos. These are the slogans we hear repeatedly voiced in the media.

It is perhaps the belief that our volunteer efforts will save us that causes so many of us to feel so strongly about the virtues of volunteer organizations. For many of us, these organizations can do no wrong. Indeed, to suggest criticisms is to raise suspicion about one's own commitment to the needs served by these organizations. During the course of an interview, for example, one volunteer became quite upset with a series of questions that asked simply whether she agreed or disagreed with various criticisms that had been voiced about volunteer work. "I don't like the tone of these questions," she objected; "they're divisive!" Another person felt that people who expressed criticisms of volunteer organizations probably were doing so in order to excuse themselves from doing anything to help the needy. "Until you get involved," he said, "you're just blaming the organizations instead of looking at your own responsibility."

Some studies of the public's views of the voluntary sector have documented an exceptionally wide base of support for and confidence in these organizations. Ninety-two percent of a representative sample of the public in one study, for example, agreed that "charities play a very significant role in our society." In the same study, 82 percent thought the need for charities was increasing.[8]

Although people vary in the degree of confidence they are willing to place in any public institution, voluntary organizations also tend to receive more favorable reactions than most other sectors of American society. For example, 46 percent of the public say they have a great deal or a lot of confidence in "charities providing health or social services," compared with only 21 percent who say the same for business, 28 percent who say this about the United States Congress, and 22 percent who feel as much confidence in organized labor. At the other extreme, fewer than one person in twelve registers "very little" confidence in charities, compared with as many as one person in three for these other institutions.[9]

When asked specifically about various ways to make America a better society, the public's faith in volunteer activities is particularly apparent. One person in two (47 percent) believes that "getting everyone who could to donate five hours a week to volunteer organizations" would help a lot; another 38 percent feel this would help a little, while only 14 percent believe it would not help. By comparison, the public has much less confidence in the ability of government programs to improve our society. For example, only one person in five (21 percent) thinks that "spending more money on government welfare programs" would help a lot, while 42 percent of the public think it would not help at all. Faced directly with the comparison between voluntary organizations and government programs, moreover, 72 percent of the public said they agreed with the statement "Private charities are generally more effective than government programs."[10]

Symptomatic of the faith most Americans place in the voluntary sector is the fact that many people not only look to it to provide services to the needy but also want it to play a larger role in shaping our nation's goals and values. Only one person in ten, for example, thinks the nonprofit sector has too much influence in shaping our goals and values, whereas one person in three thinks it has too little influence. In other words, those who would like to see nonprofit organizations exercising greater influence outnumber by a ratio of three to one those who would like to see this influence curtailed. By comparison, our view of the influence of politicians and business leaders is quite different. Seven people in ten think politicians have too much influence; only one person in ten thinks they have too little influence. For business leaders, one person in two says they have too much influence, while one person in seven thinks they have too little.

· 6 ·

Individual volunteers were quick to provide reasons why they pin high hopes on voluntary organizations. Part of their logic is that it is better to do something to help others, however little it may be, than to sit around and complain. The fact that their stories of caring, as we have seen in previous chapters, so often focus on particular individuals helps make this argument plausible. The one individual who receives help becomes a demonstration case, a symbol of hope, an irrefutable piece of evidence showing that compassion did indeed make a difference, even if it did not entirely eradicate the problem. The executive director of a large volunteer agency explained it this way: people sometimes criticize voluntarism (she referred to a recent article she had read) because it only helps a few individuals rather than developing national programs. But in her view, a volunteer who may teach just one child how to read is performing a vital service, whether or not a national program ever gets started. "It may be all that volunteer can handle, but it may be enough to get that child over a hump." She also recognized that helping one child can have a demonstration effect, especially if many volunteers can be mobilized. "It demonstrates and continues to demonstrate the need for children to read. If you have an impact—and if you have a million of these examples on the national level—you are saying, yes, we really do need to teach our children to read and here's what we need to make it happen."

Another argument that is frequently voiced about the positive effects of volunteer work takes its cue from the old saying, "But for the grace of God, there go I." This adage identifies the helper with the person needing help. It not only expresses thankfulness for one's good fortune by recognizing that bad fortune could just as well have struck; it also expresses faith in the goodness of people in need. If they are like me, and I (surely) am good and decent, then they are too. They deserve my help. One can, therefore, take a positive attitude toward volunteer work because one figures the people being helped are not just exploiting the system.

A social worker who had helped a number of poor people in the inner city articulated an argument of this kind in explaining why she did not believe some of the criticisms she had heard voiced about volunteer organizations. "A portion of the population learns how to use the system and where to get free goodies," she admitted. As an example, she mentioned a man who phoned her one time to find out how to obtain rent assistance, and when she told him how, he said, "That's too much trouble. I might as well go out and get a job!" But people like this, she believed, were rare exceptions. Most of the people helped by volunteers are, in her view, "truly needy." "Maybe their whole life has been rough; they never have a chance to get out of the hole they're in." And then there are people, too, who are in need just because they "had a terrible tragedy strike them." In either case, she felt volunteer services were making a positive contribution.

The interesting thing about these arguments is that volunteers are not naive. They do not believe, as some of their critics suggest, that acts of compassion toward needy individuals will actually solve society's problems. They do not even believe that all the millions of hours devoted to the thousands of voluntary organizations that exist in our society can solve our problems. The social worker I just quoted, for example, admitted she often felt that volunteer work was just a Band-Aid, a temporary solution, and that broader changes in the structure of American society would be needed to eradicate the problems of inner-city poverty. Debbie Carson said much the same thing. Despite the fact that she is an evangelical Christian who believes deeply in the value of focusing her efforts at the individual level, she also felt volunteer work could only go so far. "I believe we need basic structural changes," she said. In her view, volunteer work can often do little more than bring large social problems to public attention; after that it takes government programs to deal with them effectively. Another person, a volunteer with extensive experience in the public schools, made a somewhat more complex argument about the effectiveness of volunteer work. She was unwilling to say voluntary agencies were ineffective, even though they seemed to have little impact on the overall problems of society. The reason they are still effective, she said, is simply that "there's value in one person helping another person."

The connection drawn between voluntarism and the gods smiling on us, then, is a subtle one that lies, like the story of the wonderful pump, in the realm of symbolism and myth. Volunteer work will not, like a vaccination against polio, save us from evil. We will not have a better society because all the homeless people will eventually be housed and all the illiterate people taught to read. No. Volunteer work will save us because it implies hope. It gives us a sense of efficacy, of being able to make a difference. It inspires confidence in the human condition, in the goodness of those who are truly needy and deserve our help. To participate in voluntary organizations means we are making a choice for the better, siding with the good, doing something, rather than sitting idly by while the specter of chaos and corruption advances.

This, as I say, is a hope that lies in the realm of symbolism and myth. But it is no different than many of our other dreams as a society. The hope that science and technology, or more specifically nuclear energy and a cure for cancer, will save us is, after all, one that also lies in the realm of symbolism and myth. Every such technological dream has proven to create as many new problems as it solves. It is not really the belief that a cure for cancer will give us eternal life that inspires our hope. It is the image of people like us struggling against the odds that inspires us. We believe life may eventually be extended for many people, but the hope connoted by the quest for a cure is associated with the quest, not with the cure itself.

So it is with volunteer work. Helping others may not lead to a better society, but it allows us to *envision* a better society. The one person who learns to read may in the larger scheme of things make very little difference to the overall health of our society, especially when the public-school system is increasingly falling into disarray. But teaching that one person to read does have a demonstration effect. It reminds us—those who hear about it—of the importance of reading. In this sense it reaffirms a specific value that we cherish deeply as a people. It also reinforces a more general belief in the possibility of goodness. As Debbie Carson put it, "even the small things provide something for people to look at, something to raise people's values. It's a reminder that life is more than just self-seeking endeavors." Volunteer work reinforces hope because it necessitates hope. To participate in volunteer activities is to dramatize the essential faith, as Ma Joad says, that we are the people that live.

· 7 ·

There is, however, a less positive and less hopeful side to the picture of American voluntarism. The seeming hypocrisy of some philanthropists has been part of the problem. Images such as John D. Rockefeller handing out shiny new dimes to people whose jobs have been lost as a result of his own cutthroat business policies do not fade easily from the public mind. Another part of the problem has been the apparent hypocrisy, if not outright mishandling of funds, by the leaders of some voluntary organizations. More recent images, such as the spectacle of television preachers raising donations from widows and orphans in order to pay themselves huge salaries, have cast a long shadow across the voluntary sphere. At the local level, cases of graft and fraud in volunteer organizations have also been publicized.

Such cases are undoubtedly the exception rather than the rule, and yet they have clouded the public's perception of the voluntary sector as a whole. In the survey, for example, 75 percent of the public expressed agreement with the statement "Many charities fatten the pockets of their administrators instead of really helping the needy." Nearly as many (70 percent) agreed that "a lot of the money given to charity is really given for tax reasons."

Other features of the voluntary sector that have tarnished its image include the misuse of compassion for political gain and for personal prestige alike. Candidates for office have seldom missed the importance of photo opportunities provided by visits to local shelters for the homeless or inspection tours of natural-disaster sites. "Nancy Reagan stands up with some woman who has been working her butt off in the ghetto trying to keep kids off drugs" was the example one volunteer gave. This sort of thing disgusted her, not only because the government was trying to take credit for what was being done, but also because it turned caring into something partisan.

At the personal level, individuals know the value of cultivating their standing in the community, at work, or among friends by getting their pictures in the newspaper for public service. As Elmer Benson noted, "It's a status symbol. Doing volunteer work is better than almost anything else you can mention." Cranfield Holmes offered the same observation, noting how shallow some forms of giving are as a result: "In a society like ours, a lot of people do volunteer work in order to get a good feeling. For example, many charitable organizations believe they have to hold cocktail parties to raise money. So people go away feeling they've done something good, and they have of course, because they've contributed money, but they've contributed very little of *themselves*."

The emphasis that has been placed on gaining fulfillment

and good feelings from volunteer work, such as the advertisement I discussed in chapter 4, seems to have resulted in some discoloring of the voluntary sector's image in the public at large. In the survey, for example, 62 percent of the public agreed that "giving to charities is a way of making yourself feel good without really getting involved." Martin Barnes illustrated this sentiment when he brought to mind an image "of rich socialites standing under tents with fine bonnets, rich people worth millions of dollars, saying we're donating a thousand dollars to the heart center." This kind of compassion filled him with revulsion: "It's a superficial way of giving back to the community and making themselves feel great for having done it." A young woman involved in the peace movement said she thought volunteer work sometimes was just a way in which middle-class people made themselves feel better: "I think that can happen in some situations where someone helps out only to make themselves feel good. There probably are people like that—like the man in the Bible who had a large amount of money and just gave a little bit of it to the poor."

Volunteers are often torn, as these comments suggest, by the participation of the rich and powerful in their efforts. On the one hand, volunteer agencies depend on philanthropy, posh benefit dinners, and political sponsorship. On the other hand, those who dirty their hands daily in the trenches of these organizations express annoyance at the casual and seemingly superficial assistance they receive from the wealthy and powerful, especially when this assistance is all that the public sees. Debbie Carson, for example, recalled the year she had spent after college as a volunteer for a program in the inner city: "It is easy for wealthy people to feel like they're doing something good. When I worked in the inner city we were under a board of directors, and it was mostly wealthy people who lived out in the suburbs, and they felt they were doing something good by being on the board, but they would never actually come and even have a meeting where we lived. They were afraid to death that their car might get smashed. So those type of people do have a guilt complex about what's happened, and they want to do something. What they do may be helpful in one sense, but they weren't willing to go beyond that and really get involved."

· 8 ·

The voluntary sector has also been plagued increasingly with questions about its effectiveness in dealing with complex social problems. Americans are a pragmatic people, as are the citizens of most advanced industrial societies. We want things to work; indeed, we often judge their value in terms of their effectiveness. An automobile may be pleasing to the eye, but we want it to get us to our destination. Higher education may be a fine place in which to seek knowledge for its own sake, but the parents and taxpayers who foot the bill for college tuition want it to get their children good jobs and a high standard of living. Many of us take the same attitude toward volunteer work. Compassion is a fine ideal, we say, but it may be better to create new jobs, promote business, and launch large-scale efforts that will really improve the society.

I noted already that many volunteers are unwilling to judge their organizations strictly in terms of effectiveness in solving social problems. And yet in the public at large there is a widespread perception that voluntary associations are merely a stopgap measure—perhaps necessary, but not really effective in coping with the major issues of modern life. By a margin of 57 percent to 39 percent, for example, the American public agrees that "charities provide 'Band-Aids' instead of really solving our problems."

In some cases, volunteers have also been criticized for inefficiency and lack of training. For instance, Susan Robbins noted seeing statistics on some volunteer organizations in the health field showing that little of the money raised actually went to their clients, compared to the huge amounts devoted to administrative overhead. Freddie Jackson Taylor talked about similar problems in the organizations he had worked for in caring for the homeless. In some volunteer agencies, he noted, the homeless actually wound up being exploited because of red tape and inefficiency. He remembered "seeing a lot of things" at a shelter for the chronically mentally ill homeless, for example. "I saw these people treated so unfairly by other agencies, not that these agencies were cruel, but they didn't know how to deal with these people, so they just threw them out. You know, they threw them out of the hotel, threw them out of the shelter, told them they didn't want to see them again. They didn't give them their medication because they were dirty. They'd make them go get cleaned up before they could come back." In addition to the problems of ignorance and prejudice, he also felt these agencies were ineffective because they lacked money. "There have to be more facilities," he said, "not institutions, but facilities where these people can shower and spend the night. It's going to take money, and I don't see that happening."

More calls have also been voiced for paid professionals to replace volunteers, as has largely taken place in fields such as nursing, teaching, social work, and counseling. Ted Garvey, for example, said he thought the shift from unpaid volunteers to paid professionals was both inevitable and desirable. In his view, the United States is undergoing a healthy transition from being "an uncaring capitalistic society" to becoming "a more caring society in which helping is institutionalized." As an illustration, he pointed to the growth of social work as a profession—"it's kind of society's success story." "Hopefully in years to come that will be followed by more success stories. I hope volunteers are eventually phased out and we have more professionals taking care of these problems." In other cases, even those who believe strongly in the continuing value of volunteer work question whether these efforts can withstand the social and economic pressures working against them.

Donna Frylinger, for example, decries the decline of volunteer efforts in the fields of social work and counseling. She thinks voluntary helping cannot keep pace. "The need always seems to outweigh the resources. You can have unlimited volunteers and there are still more problems than you can deal with." She also worries that volunteer agencies sometimes do not perform their tasks well enough to gain the respect of the community: "A lot of them kind of have lousy reputations in the community, which makes it hard to get funding and volunteers."

Jack Casey also decries the fact that voluntarism, in his experience, seems to be on the decline. Rescue squads and volunteer fire companies suffer from shortages of workers and from transience among volunteers. Often it takes more time to train a new volunteer than that person's contribution to the organization is worth. Jack Casey sees the day coming when rescue work and fire fighting will all be done by paid professionals. And he fears that something vital in our tradition will have been lost.

Ironically, part of the decline Jack Casey fears in the voluntary sector is associated with a proliferation of specialized organizations promoting specialized causes. "What really bothers me," he explains, "is that there are so many causes. Everybody has a cause, and they all run together: Save the Whales; Save the Gay Whales, prolife, prochoice—I can never keep them straight. I like the T-shirt that says nuke the gay unborn bay whales! It really bugs me when people put all these silly issues above humanity. Sure, it's okay to want to save an animal, but I'm tired of scraping people off the pavement because they didn't want to hit a squirrel. It's a squirrel, for God's sake. It has a nice happy existence, but why are you plastering yourself into a tree to save a poor innocent squirrel? And I think there's a lot of organizations like that." He says it often makes him cynical when he thinks about voluntary organizations because they all want money and volunteers, and yet few of them seem to be getting anything done. The hope he associates with volunteer efforts has been badly tarnished.

· 9 ·

Aside from the problems that people see within the volunteer sector itself, there is also the realization that many of our society's problems are larger than volunteer agencies alone can handle. This is not to say that individual efforts to help others are entirely ineffective. But many problems require huge expenditures of public money or legislative action or the coercive powers of government in addition to simple acts of kindness. One woman explained: "Volunteer work is very necessary— there are always benefits. At the same time, I think it does cause people to think they are making a bigger contribution than they really are. If that same amount of energy were put into making changes in the society itself, a lot of those volunteer efforts wouldn't even be needed. In fact, it would be much better if people didn't need help from volunteers because it's degrading for people to accept their services."

Increasingly, the problems of society are seen as systemic, going beyond the misfortunes of particular individuals. As a result, people who are themselves committed to doing volunteer work are increasingly worried about its limitations. It makes them feel proud when national leaders exclaim, "Thank God for the volunteers," but it also makes them fearful that such statements may be a smoke screen aimed at hiding a reluctance to commit public resources. As the head of one volunteer agency observed, "We *always* need volunteers, but sometimes when the government calls for volunteers to do things it may be a cop-out in terms of not being willing to raise taxes or to tax the very wealthy in this country at a higher rate." One of the social workers interviewed was more pointedly critical: "President Reagan always stressed the need for churches to do more, and I just felt like, wait a minute, he's just trying to get rid of his responsibility and put it on the backs of other people."

It is particularly in areas such as crime, homelessness, and inner-city problems that volunteers express doubts about the effectiveness of the voluntary sector alone in bringing about a better society. The hope they associate with individual care for the needy is sometimes overwhelmed by their feelings of despair at the enormity of the problem. Especially when volunteers are themselves in the same situation as their clients, the sense of being up against invincible odds can be overwhelming. This was the case, for example, with a woman in her midfifties whose volunteer efforts focused on helping other women her age, most of them divorced, begin a new and economically productive life. She felt that the women she was trying to help were being discriminated against, as she was. "We're getting older every day, and we live in a youth culture, a throwaway society, and there's no way to turn that around. It's so frustrating. I don't get angry very often, but this makes me very angry." When asked what could be done to solve the problem, she said members of her voluntary organization were still trying to figure that out, but were mostly just frustrated: "It's bigger than us. Everything is stacked in favor of corporations. It seems like there's nothing we can do. I mean, we write letters to our representatives, but there's only one who's interested. I don't know what it's going to take. I don't give up easily, but. . . ."

Faced with an intransigent system that gives token respect to volunteers but little material or political support for their efforts, volunteers find their prevailing optimism difficult to sustain. Frustration results in burnout and burnout results in a sense of futility. Volunteers begin to wonder if their efforts really make any difference at all. Despair may follow. And if despair is not the dominant feeling, the volunteers at least want a more active partnership between voluntary agencies and other sectors of the society.

Margaret Cook is a woman in her early forties who has been active for the past several years as a volunteer for Mothers Against Drunk Driving (MADD). Like other volunteers, she gives time generously and finds personal rewards in counseling people who have lost loved ones as a result of drunk driving. Her hopes for a better society revolve around her dream of someday seeing the scourge of such accidents diminish. Doing a little herself each week as a volunteer helps keep those hopes alive. But she also pins her dreams on programs and actions that MADD alone cannot bring about.

She explains: "I would like to see more jail space so that persons who are sentenced for drunk driving could actually serve their sentences instead of being turned loose to go back on the streets. I think we also need programs monitored by the criminal-justice system for offenders: drug programs, alcohol programs, treatment programs. Those programs need to be monitored to make sure they are effective and to make sure people stay in them. We don't need people thumbing their nose at society and saying, okay, so you paid a thousand dollars to put me through this program, but it isn't going to do me any good." For Margaret Cook, MADD can help raise public consciousness about the need for such laws and programs. But ultimately she knows the government will have to do its part as well. "With jail space and treatment programs, you have your rights, so it requires a court system that works and it obviously requires government programs."

· 10 ·

Like Margaret Cook, many volunteers pointed to areas of legislation and funding for social services in which the work of volunteer agencies needed to be supplemented by the government. Fewer mentioned areas in which the nonprofit sector's work needed to be supplemented by for-profit firms. But in the survey it was evident that a large share of the public does believe the present limitations of the voluntary sector could be alleviated if the corporate world became more actively involved. Nearly two-thirds (63 percent) of the American public, for example, feel that "corporations doing more to help the needy" would help a lot to make our society better, and nearly everyone (another 30 percent) thinks this would help at least a little. A very high proportion of the public (83 percent) favor "corporations playing a more active role in promoting the work of volunteer organizations." And an equally high proportion (84 percent) favor "tax incentives for corporations to hire and train disadvantaged workers."

Janet Russo summed up the attitude that apparently lies behind many of these survey responses when she suggested that volunteer organizations can make people more aware of social problems, but when the problems are large, as they often are, the basic changes have to come from other sources, particularly government and corporations. "Corporations especially," she thought, "need to start giving back more things to the community."

Judging again from survey responses, corporations could indeed do much more than they currently are doing. Despite the fact that a growing number of corporations have launched highly visible advertising campaigns to create an image of compassion and community spirit, these efforts remain limited to a fraction of the corporate world and are often more visible in image than they are devoted in practice. When persons employed full-time or part-time were asked about their companies' activities, only a minority indicated that their companies were currently doing anything to assist the work of voluntary agencies or to help the needy directly: 46 percent said their companies donated money to some nonprofit, charitable, or philanthropic organization; 35 percent said their companies sponsored community-improvement projects; and 22 percent said their companies gave employees time off or other incentives for doing volunteer work.

· 11 ·

While we continue to have faith in the value of volunteer agencies and allow ourselves to be inspired by the hopes that caring and compassion conjure up, we are nevertheless confronted with perplexing questions about how realistic these hopes may be. It is still possible to think of volunteer work as an effective means of helping individuals when we restrict our vision to the individual level. Telling stories about particular volunteers and particular recipients of care helps, as we have seen, to sustain our conviction that such efforts are worthwhile. But our vision of what to do about problems on a societal—or even global—scale is less clear. For well over a century, at least since the great debates about social reform that swept across western Europe in the 1830s and 1840s, the value of private charity and individual compassion has been questioned. Social programs, government reforms, economic progress, and even revolution have all been looked to with greater hope than the modest efforts of individual volunteers. Yet the United States has not participated directly in the movements that inspired some of those broader political dreams. It has been more able, perhaps because of its affluence, to sustain the belief that progress alone would solve most of our problems, and that those left unresolved could best be alleviated by charitable activity. Particularly in the wake of government programs that have left many doubtful about their effectiveness, hope has again been placed squarely on the voluntary sector.

But the experience of nearly an entire century of economic upswings and downswings, increasingly complex problems associated with large cities and diverse population groups, and an ever more interdependent world economy has left volunteers themselves and the public at large more cautious about the role of voluntary organizations. They still inspire hope, but the residue of that hope Tocqueville expressed a century and a half ago rests less on concrete programs and more on the symbol of mutual aid. It is a hope that shines brightly at the individual level, less brightly on the larger issues that beset our nation as a whole. Helping others requires us to be optimistic about the future. It reaffirms the goodness of our fellow human beings. It may even spark again the mythic hopes buried in legends and tales about a miraculous reward of riches and insight. But these hopes shine at best through a cloudy sky. Their light, whether manifest in a thousand or a million rays of good deeds, is increasingly in danger of being overshadowed by the limitations we know are present in even the most effective of volunteer agencies.

· 12 ·

John Steinbeck did not end his novel about the travails of the Joad family the way Hollywood concluded the film. After Tom leaves and the family sets off to Fresno, Ma does express a brief hope for the future: "We ain't gonna die out. People is goin' on—changin' a little, maybe, but goin' right on."[11] These words, however, appear forty pages before the book actually ends.

When the Joads arrive in Fresno, their hope for twenty days of good picking is dashed. All the cotton is picked in a single day. Before nightfall, rain begins. It rains for days and days. Many of the migrants living in makeshift shacks and camping out in ravines lose their lives in the high water. Many of those lucky enough to escape the flood become ill from malnutrition and starve to death. Eventually the Joads find themselves trapped in an abandoned barn with no food, no money, their truck stuck in the mud, and floodwater rising on every side.

The last scene of the book occurs in the barn. Soaked to the skin and facing certain death, the surviving Joads discover a man lying in the straw so near death that the only nourishment he might be able to take is a little milk. In an act of supreme kindness Rose of Sharon, the Joad daughter, offers this stranger her breast. "'There!' she said. 'There.' Her hand moved behind his head and supported it. Her fingers moved gently in his hair. She looked up and across the barn, and her lips came together and smiled mysteriously."[12]

Steinbeck's imagery is scarcely the triumphant hope of people surviving against hardship simply because they are the people. His imagery is drawn from the ancient legend of Cimon and Pero. An aged man, Cimon lies in prison awaiting execution. He has been denied food by the jailer. But the jailer's daughter, Pero, secretly keeps him alive by giving him her breast.

The story is a legend of hope. But it is also a story of oppression and injustice. An evil system keeps Cimon imprisoned, just as an evil system forces the Joads off their land in Oklahoma and leads them to certain death in California. The warm nourishment from a female breast stands only to emphasize the harsh, masculine cruelty of a society that pursues nothing other than power and wealth. Jim Casey's death is in vain unless people like Tom Joad rise up before it is too late to combat the evils of this system. They must be more than compassionate. They must also work for social justice.

PART V
THE WIDER CONTEXT

CHAPTER NINE

Envisioning a Better Society

Jane Addams's decision to become a volunteer also forced her
to become an advocate of social justice. The girl from rural Illinois moved to Chicago with the hope of helping disadvantaged individuals. She quickly discovered that caring for individuals could go only so far. To improve the conditions of
poor people in Chicago would take the help of city hall and
eventually even the federal government. With the help of labor
unions and social-reform organizations, she was able to institute juvenile-court laws, the first "mother's pension" law, tene-
ment-house regulations, an eight-hour workday law for
women, factory-inspection laws, and workers' compensation.
The reason she could not follow Tolstoy's example of bread
labor was not simply that she was busy organizing tea parties
for her neighbors in the slums. She was busy lobbying for social justice.

Jane Addams's contemporary, Margaret Sanger, experienced
a similar transformation. Like many of the people whose stories we have heard in previous chapters, she experienced a personal crisis—and witnessed being cared for—in a way that
made her resolve to help the needy. Two years after she was
married, and only a few months after the birth of her first child,
her recurring struggle with tuberculosis worsened to the point
that she gave up all interest in living. Preparations were made
for a lingering illness that would terminate in death. Only the
friendly encouragement of a young doctor stood in the way.
"Do something," he admonished. "Want something! You'll
never get well if you keep on this way."[1] With determination,
she followed his advice, pulled herself out of invalidism, and
went on to become the great leader of the modern birth-control
movement.

At first, she was moved primarily to serve as a volunteer,
helping individuals in need. Like many volunteers, she was
motivated by seeing the plight of particular individuals, not by
an abstract view of the impoverished masses. As she explained

in her autobiography: "These were not merely 'unfortunate conditions among the poor' such as we read about. I knew the women personally. They were living, breathing, human beings, with hopes, fears, and aspirations like my own, yet their weary, misshapen bodies, 'always ailing, never failing,' were destined to be thrown on the scrap heap before they were thirty-five."[2] But these individuals also forged in her a resolve to do something more, to seek out the root cause of the evil she saw resulting in miseries "vast as the sky."[3]

· 2 ·

In our time Dr. Martin Luther King, Jr., is the person who comes most readily to mind as an advocate of social justice. Many volunteers identify with him. They remember him as a fellow volunteer. But he was clearly more than that. Although he did show compassion to many specific individuals, his efforts were devoted more to bringing about social reform. He was interested in eradicating the root cause of racial injustice, in working for justice and equality through broad economic, social, and legislative reforms. Like Margaret Sanger, he came early to a recognition that the miseries of his people were as vast as the sky.

It was principally this awareness of the enormous scope of the problems with which he was dealing that, in the minds of many volunteers, set Martin Luther King apart from other compassionate individuals. "He had a clear sense that it was government and society that were causing the problems," said Ted Garvey. "There was so much prejudice and injustice that helping a few individuals wasn't going to make much difference," noted Susan Robbins. "It's like working for peace: as an individual you can't do much unless you get other individuals involved as well." Debbie Carson explained, "he just realized that you can work with individuals all you want but there needed to be structural changes too."

Besides seeing a bigger picture—besides working for structural change instead of helping a few individuals one at a time—Martin Luther King had a keen sense of the importance of justice. Compassion was not so much giving people a helping hand as it was respecting their human dignity and helping make sure their basic rights were protected. He was able to speak out in favor of broad social reforms because he could see that people's rights were being violated. Legislation was needed to end these violations.

Some have argued that compassion and a concern for social justice are quite different. The compassionate person, in this view, must be willing to give up his or her rights. Compassion requires a focus on relationships, on what two individuals together can accomplish. Justice, in contrast, is intensely concerned with the rights of individuals. It focuses less on the happy merging and blending of two individuals, and more on each jealously standing up for the dignity and autonomy of the other. In this perspective, compassion is a more "feminine" virtue, colored with mercy and self-sacrifice, like the caring of Mother Teresa, while justice is a more "masculine" concept, like Dr. King's orientation, emphasizing competition, struggle, and the harsh love that may mean sticking up for another person even when that person does not realize a need or feel inclined to cooperate.[4]

But the testimony about compassion that we have examined thus far belies this distinction. It suggests that compassion in our society is also rooted in a respect for individual rights and an unwillingness to engage in self-sacrificial acts. If this argument is carried to its logical conclusion, it also holds that one's compassion implies a strong sense of the rights and needs of others. Ted Garvey, for example, suggested that compassion always depends on one's sense of justice. "If you scratch the surface of compassion," he noted, "you get someone's idea of what it means to be just. Compassion comes from what you think is just."

The argument can also be turned around: justice without compassion is empty. A focus on rights must be tempered by an awareness of individuals in their full humanity. We may feel there are different styles of compassion evident in Martin Luther King and in Mother Teresa, but we insist for the most part on finding a healthy balance between compassion at the personal level and a broader sense of justice for the whole society. Cranfield Holmes expressed it most simply: "True justice has mercy attached to it, and mercy lies at the heart of compassion;

so the two go hand in hand; the just society is a society that is also compassionate, and a compassionate society is one that elevates justice."

Debbie Carson provided a helpful illustration of how the balance between compassion and justice can be achieved. She recognized an important difference between the two: "With some it's more a focus on the principles and what's right; they can stir up people and get them thinking; with others, they're just good interpersonally, so they do what they can." She also observed that many people, including herself, may prefer to work with individuals or feel their talents lie there, rather than in dealing with the masses, as Dr. King did. But that, in her view, need not deter someone from combining compassion with a commitment to social justice.

The example she gave was that of a friend of her husband's family. The man had become a millionaire while he was still in his twenties. "He had all this money, but he began to have family problems. His wife was going to leave him because he was so into his money and lush life-style. So he decided he was going to give all his money away and help needy people. It was just incredible! He started working at a black university, but then he quit that too and started the organization that Jimmy Carter's been involved in called Habitat for Humanity. His idea is not to work with government but with volunteers. People give what they can to help people repair a home. It's not just charity. They kind of survey an area for housing. And what they do is, like there'll be a poor family living in a house that's run-down and rat-infested and they're paying $250 a month for it, so they build a house for the same amount that the rent was and people can buy their own house then, so it's kind of a no-interest thing. Anyway, he started this and it's now all over the world."

Debbie Carson said she was impressed by this man's ability to do something on a large scale, using his business talents to help bring about social reforms in a compassionate way. But she was equally impressed with the fact that he lived out these values in his own life. She recounted going to visit him one time. "He was living in a very simple house, not poverty or anything, he didn't go to that extreme, but he had an old, beat-up, secondhand car. He could have been living like a millionaire, but he had had it, and he knew what that kind of life led to, and of course a lot of it had to do with his Christian beliefs. But he just gave all that over, and now he lives a very happy and fulfilled life. He's using his ability to make money to help the poor. It's a great work, it's one that works. And he had the ability to work on that level."

· 3 ·

Some volunteers in our society have been forced to turn toward broader questions of justice and exploitation. At first their efforts have been directed more to specific individuals in need. But as they become involved with volunteer work, their vision expands. Like Margaret Sanger, they realize that individual suffering is rooted in larger social arrangements. Ted Garvey, for instance, noted that many of his experiences as a volunteer had exposed him to situations of injustice. As an example, he recalled: "I once worked helping a person whose mother had died in an auto accident, so he was now an orphan in a society that doesn't look well on orphans, and his educational future went from secure to very doubtful. He needs money and someone to take care of him too. He gets a little help from me and from his grandparents, but that's about all. It's a constant reminder to me of what money really should mean and be used for." Freddie Jackson Taylor said he had seen plenty of injustices, working in the civil-rights movement, campaigning against segregated housing, and more recently trying to help migrant workers. Not long before, he had engaged in civil disobedience in a protest for justice and had spent six days in jail as a result. Another person had come to feel strongly about injustice as a result of doing volunteer work with the mentally ill. "I've seen how unfair it is for the state legislature to tell us how to run a treatment center and then not provide sufficient resources; everybody gets shortchanged," she charged.

Serving as volunteers at least put these people in a position to see injustices to which they otherwise might not have been exposed in the course of their ordinary middle-class lives. This had clearly been the case in Debbie Carson's experience, for example. Asked if her volunteer activities had ever exposed her to situations of injustice, she recalled: "When I did jail work, it was in Mississippi; we would go visit these people in the jails. It was mostly women, and there were children, small children in these jails, and at that point I really didn't know how to get involved in what was going on, but obviously these children had no place to go. That was in the 1960s in Mississippi, so yes, there was lots of oppression going on. Then when I worked in the inner city in Newark, it was right after a lot of the riots; of course the black ghetto is obviously a situation of oppression."

For Jack Casey, serving on the rescue squad took him into all kinds of neighborhoods, exposing him directly to the enormous contrasts present in American society. "Being on the rescue squad, I've gotten a better picture of reality than before," was how he put it. "I saw something that I knew most of my friends at school really didn't have a grip on, especially all the nice middle-class boys who'd spent their whole lives going to school in New Hampshire. You get a lot of calls down in the ghetto; it's a really high-density area, a lot of people are smashed together there in those row houses; to go and see these people, and then at the same time to take a call at the mansion I told you about—within a quarter of a mile of the ghetto you can go to these million-dollar houses. You see 'em both, and you see everything in between."

He went on: "I was raised in white-bread suburbia, and there you really don't see the whole spread. It's kind of a cliché, I suppose, to say that everyone is the same, but you begin to understand that. Sometimes it gives you a real sense of hope and sometimes it gives you a sense of frustration. You see dramatic differences, and that's reality, that's the people." Then musing, sounding older and wiser than his age, he concluded: "I've been in all the houses, I've been on all the streets, I've seen them all in the hospital; it's given me a better sense of what I define as reality."

· 4 ·

But many of the volunteers we spoke with remained shielded from deeper injustices. Their compassion had focused too much on people like themselves, or they saw the people they helped only as individuals, not as symptoms of some larger problem in American society. When they thought about injustice, the notion was therefore more distant, less charged with emotion, like a concept they had read about but not experienced directly. Marge Detweiler, for example, said she simply has not been exposed personally to any situations in which she thought people were being treated unfairly. From broader knowledge, she said she knew that recovering alcoholics and drug addicts sometimes were not treated fairly by insurance companies. She also thought gays and blacks probably were subject to injustices, but said she knew of no instances personally.

Especially for volunteers whose time was spent with organizations like the Girl Scouts or the local PTA, or helping out with community bazaars, injustice was largely a secondhand concept. One older woman's comment was typical: "No, no, I guess I really haven't been exposed to anything in particular; I mean, I hear about things of course, like there was this incident I read about in New York of some guy getting hauled in by the police who'd just been trying to help, but no, I guess I don't think of anything."

They remained shielded, as these comments suggest, or they simply defined social problems in some other way than as evidence of social injustice. This was especially true of economic inequality. Volunteers recognized huge disparities in the economic well-being of Americans. Some of them even thought efforts should be made to reduce these disparities. But few were willing to define economic inequality as an outright injustice that should, therefore, become the focus of legislation or litigation.

Susan Robbins provides a particularly instructive case. She is, as we have seen, an intelligent and highly educated woman who has risen from humble rural origins to a position of wealth, power, and prestige as a pediatric cardiologist. Politically, she considers herself a liberal, and she defines that perspective primarily as a belief in equality and social reform—a belief she came to through firsthand acquaintance with poverty and racism as a child in the rural Midwest and later by working as an intern in an inner-city hospital in the Northeast. She was deeply moved by Martin Luther King and the civil-rights movement. Yet her views of social justice stop short of any drastic measures that might seriously alter the distribution of wealth and poverty.

Susan Robbins feels she has seen injustice on many occasions. She says there are often times in her practice when a poor patient does not receive adequate treatment because of some arbitrary rule. Racism, she believes, is also a persistent source of injustice. But the raw edge of these concerns is tempered by her feeling that life is always like this. As she explains, "injustice is just life." Or, as she says of gross economic inequality, "It's not fair, but it's just part of life."

Because injustice is in her view inevitable, the best thing a caring person can do is "make people feel better about themselves." When volunteers do this, she believes, "it just snowballs and those people are able to treat others better too." The reason she feels this way is her belief that people basically—within limits—control their own destinies. The system may be unjust, but life is like that, so a person is most likely to triumph over the system by developing a healthy attitude. She recalls coming to this conclusion as an intern in Syracuse: "Eighty percent of the children we treated as patients were from welfare families. And it seemed like the people had just sort of given up. They didn't own anything. They saw no hope for life getting any better. So they weren't contributing anything to society either. They weren't even trying anymore. Maybe there's a certain type of person who's never going to want to contribute. But I had the feeling that a lot of these people would have tried to better themselves if they hadn't been in the depths of despair."

What to do? Susan Robbins is a firm believer in legislation to end blatant discrimination. But she feels our system is already basically about as equitable as one can expect. She opposes more active efforts to promote social justice through welfare programs, reverse discrimination, or tax reforms. It is not clear that she has thought through all her reasons for opposing these policies, but she does associate them with giving people handouts. And that she resists because handouts in her view make people "feel worthless" about themselves.

Susan Robbins is nevertheless unwilling to put the entire burden of social justice back on the heads of the victims. What she favors most are selective programs that provide *opportunities*—chances for those special individuals with talent and drive (presumably individuals like herself) to pull themselves up. If she is reluctant to accept the language of social justice and social reform, she is comfortable with an emphasis on such opportunities. She believes strongly, for example, in the importance of education, in providing poor children with good schools and giving them role models. She is especially interested in volunteer efforts that might help make such opportunities available. The problem with government-mandated programs, she feels, is that they treat everyone the same way and are therefore wasteful. Volunteer organizations, in contrast, can spot the few who have talent and the desire to work hard. This, then, is where her views about compassion essentially part company with what others might describe as an emphasis on justice. For her, compassion is tailored to the individual. It recognizes personal differences and the inevitable inequities that result from personal differences. Justice, in contrast, focuses on the individual rights of an entire group of people. As such, it evokes programs that treat everyone the same way. That, in her view, is acceptable only so long as these programs emphasize opportunity. After that, it is up to the individual to sink or swim.

· 5 ·

It is clear from comments such as these that volunteers' individualism can have a marked effect on their views about larger social questions. Believing in the worth and efficacy of the individual may not conflict with their willingness to care for the needy on a one-to-one basis, but it did conflict with their ability to see social problems as something more than the fault of individuals. The volunteers' compassion was tempered by the view that victims are often suffering because of their own decisions. To help out, therefore, is mainly a way of alleviating pain, not a means of preventing pain from occurring in the first place.

The arguments volunteers use to excuse themselves for not becoming involved personally in larger social-reform programs are similar to the ones they use to excuse people for not giving time to volunteer organizations. Their individualism leads them to define caring very broadly, to point out that a complex society like ours needs all kinds of people, and to suggest that individuals should pick and choose depending on their various gifts and interests. Donna Frylinger, for example, was well aware because of her training in social work that, as she put it, "there's the age-old debate about whether you keep it on a clinical level or go out and do Jane Addams's type of community organizing." For her, the choice was largely a matter of preference: "I tend to be a more individually focused person. But I think there is a place for both." Another person explained that he identified with Dr. King's emphasis on social justice, but was himself more of an introvert; thus, "it was a good thing for him to do, but isn't the path I'm going to choose." As Debbie Carson put it, different people have different abilities.

To those who may believe that large-scale social reform is the only effective means to a better society, such arguments may appear to be dishearteningly predictable. Volunteers are deeply individualistic after all; their individualism focuses their attention so close to home—or at least on needy individuals in their immediate vicinity—that they cannot think clearly or speak fluently about the needs and interests of the larger society. But that is not the case.

Many of the volunteers we have heard speak in previous chapters are also quite articulate in voicing concerns about the wider society. They believe social reforms, community organizing, and efforts to promote social justice are all needed. They simply do not believe these programs are a panacea. Indeed, many of them have been well schooled in the hard knocks, disappointments, and failures of the social programs begun during the 1960s. They are representatives of a postwelfare generation.

A woman in her early thirties with a master's degree in public administration seemed to sum up the view of many of her contemporaries in the postwelfare generation when she remarked, "we talk about having a free-market economy, but it's not; we talk about America being a land of opportunity, but it's not; and we've tinkered with things to the point that we have a kind of blend between democracy and socialism; but neither one is working very well; so there's some basic rethinking that needs to be done." Like many others we spoke to, she was not quite sure what to recommend for American society. The problem was not that she was uninterested in improving the society; it was more that she was all too aware of the failures of the simple solutions tried in the past. She could not latch onto easy political rhetoric in responding to questions.

For this woman and others like her, some combination of public concern and individual initiative seemed best. In their view, helping individuals through volunteer work is not a cop-out. The real cop-out is talking endlessly about a revolution that will never come and would probably not work if it did. Showing compassion on an individual and daily basis is, in their view, at least a way of doing something to alleviate the pain and suffering that presently exists. In this woman's view, "government has to be responsible to work out the basic changes; volunteer groups should bring the need for change to the attention of the government, should work to support and press for change, and should help people in need in the meantime." In the eloquent words of another woman, "sometimes I get pessimistic; I think everything is a lost cause, and I ask why I'm wasting my time; but then I think, these problems are never going to be eradicated completely, but it's important for people who are aware of them to speak up and hold others accountable—hold themselves accountable—and make whatever changes we can."

Ted Garvey had seen plenty of injustice, both in the Peace Corps and in working with the homeless. He was not only living a life-style consistent with his concern for the poor but was also spending an ample share of his time on political causes and other social-reform efforts. He saw the systemic sources of social problems and, for this reason, asserted emphatically that "we do need basic changes in the society." Unlike many other volunteers (as we shall see), he thought government could actually play a positive role in bringing about social reform: "It's the role of government to be the conscience of society. The government should lead as well as just be a caretaker of day-to-day activities. It has to lead in these social areas. It has to have more foresight than just the average individual citizen." He was even optimistic that changes for the better were taking place and would continue to take place. He nevertheless believed strongly in the continuing value of volunteer work: "We can't do without volunteer agencies while we wait for change to happen. You're not likely to bring about all the changes we need all at once. So if you change ten things, you're still going to have a whole bunch of other problems. You'll always need volunteer agencies to take care of those problems unless you somehow have a perfect society."

Ellen Steinberg also represents the thinking of the postwelfare generation. Unlike Ted Garvey, she is old enough to have lived through the civil-rights movement, the Great Society, and the peace movement of the 1960s. In fact, she remembers fondly the days when she considered herself a radical and participated actively in all these movements. She believes they helped her see more clearly the extent of social problems in America. Few of these problems, she believes, have gone away. She claims she sees injustices almost daily, both in her work as a therapist and in the things she reads and hears about her community. "The poor are being unmercifully persecuted," she remarks, "especially single mothers with children." She also thinks the elderly are often subjected to severe injustices. Like the sixties liberal she once was, she still believes military expenditures are too high and social-welfare programs are being neglected. She thinks more attention needs to be focused on education. She even retains her view that government is ultimately the only agent that can bring about these changes. But Ellen Steinberg at age fifty-six is far less confident that government will actually respond than she was at age twenty-six. "I find myself feeling very depressed about this because I feel we're just going to continue on," she says with emotion. Scandals, waste, and corruption, not to mention indifference, have in her view dampened her earlier faith in social reform through governmental initiative. She now feels there is much stronger reason to place one's efforts in the voluntary sector. At least volunteers can serve as "spokespeople to the larger society."

· 6 ·

What volunteers do reveal is a firm conviction that our society can be better than it is. Even if their faith in government-initiated or government-sponsored reform programs has diminished with time, volunteers are for the most part concerned about the wider society and committed to the view that it can be improved. Their volunteer work is in this sense not exclusively directed toward individuals in need but is symptomatic of their concern for the good of society.

In many cases their visions of a better society focus on specific problems that need solutions. The first thing Marge Detweiler mentioned was a reform of the justice system. She said her divorce had convinced her of this. Frank Stevens said the main thing to work on was curbing the defense budget. The school psychologist we spoke to thought we needed to raise the minimum wage. Another person moaned, "Shoot the president!"

The volunteers' vision of a better society, though, primarily meant one in which compassion itself was a more prevailing orientation. Ted Garvey, for example, thought America would be a better society if people simply became aware of the suffering in their midst. "I think there has to be more awareness across the different levels of society of how the others live, of how bad it is, and what makes it that way," he remarked. "You need to speed up the changing awareness that bums aren't just bums because it was their choice and they're some kind of deviants, but they're people who worked for thirty years and then lost their jobs making cars in Flint, Michigan, and are unemployed now." In his view, volunteers could help bring about a better society just by contributing to the public's awareness. "Society's in a vicious cycle. We don't have paid positions to take care of some of these problems because we aren't aware of them, and we aren't aware of them because we don't have people in paid positions to make us aware of them. Volunteers kind of get in there and break up that vicious cycle."

Marge Detweiler was also able to move easily between talking about the kinds of problems she saw on a personal level in Alcoholics Anonymous and her vision of a better society. She did not compartmentalize the two; indeed, the same diagnosis applied to both. Like Ted Garvey, she emphasized an expanded awareness, a retreat from denial and from blaming the victim. "One of the symptoms of a drinking alcoholic is denial, and that makes it very difficult to treat it. Another symptom is absolutely insane decisions and not being able to face the consequences of those decisions. So everyone around them has trouble dealing with this person because they can't make sense of them. I happen to believe right now that America is behaving like a drinking alcoholic. One of America's biggest problems is denial of the problems that are here. One way we're feeding that denial system is getting involved in Central America and Latin America and Africa. We're telling all those countries what they're doing wrong. Well, as long as we can continue to do that, we don't have to focus on what's wrong here. Some of the decisions we're making are made to feed that denial system. Some of the decisions about money and how it's spent in this country are just insane. So I'd like to see some changes. But we didn't get in that state overnight, and we're not going to get out of it overnight."

Marge Detweiler feels she is wiser now that she is older. Like Ellen Steinberg, she no longer hopes for instant improvement in the social fiber. But she does still have hope. "I like this country and I like being an American," she admits, "so my bottom line is I have hope. If I didn't have hope I would certainly be worried as a mother and a grandmother. It would not be a nice position to be in. I don't happen to trust any politicians, so I could get very depressed. But I have to have hope. As to how they're going to do it, I don't know. The only thing I can do is vote. And I can work for local politicians who I believe in. At least you feel, I worked hard, I did what I could, and if you make some change in the system, great."

· 7 ·

It is often easier for volunteers, like the rest of us, to express their visions of a better society negatively than positively. They decry certain trends in our society that seem to be threatening the good life. They do not believe naively that these trends can necessarily be stopped. But they are concerned with slowing these developments, and with rethinking their goals and values, at least to the point that they can make intelligent choices about the future.

One trend that many volunteers—and indeed many Americans in general—are particularly concerned about is the expansion of government bureaucracy. Jack Casey described it as an inevitable trend, useful in some respects, but still disturbing because of its coercive nature. "Personally," he ventured, "I think government has its hands in too many situations. It regulates the food we eat. It regulates our water, the pollution that comes out of our cars." He thought this was not necessarily a bad thing, but felt that government could not be expected to do much about improving the society. "All it can do is come out with more laws and regulations. That would make people do what they don't want to do—that's what a law is, basically. It's a regulation of sorts."

Susan Robbins also seized on the growth of bureaucracy as one of the negative factors keeping us from realizing a better society. She was opposed to a number of specific government programs, especially welfare programs that seemed to perpetuate poverty and dependence rather than helping poor people stand on their own feet economically. It was as much bureaucracy itself, though, that bothered her as it was an instinctive distaste for the welfare system. When asked what would make the society a better place, she thought for a moment and then cited the American tax system as an example of a cumbersome bureaucracy weighed down with red tape. "Tax forms take a CPA or a lawyer to fill out," she noted. "That's ridiculous!" Part of the problem, she believed, was a complicated system of loopholes that served the interests of the rich. But perhaps because she was relatively wealthy herself, she did not place blame on the rich. Instead, she identified ever-increasing layers of bureaucracy as the basic problem. "There's far too many lawyers—and lawyers beget lawyers. The legal system has gotten so embroiled in its own bureaucracy that I don't know how anybody could change it."

For many people it was also clear that bureaucracy was an idea that stood for something they wanted in our society but found lacking: a sense of community and of greater individual involvement in the society. Bureaucracy was not just a problem because it prevented us from doing something about tax loopholes. It was a problem because it made us think someone else was going to solve things for us; it made us feel dependent, just as the poor feel dependent on welfare. We succumbed to apathy and despair because we no longer believed anything could be done to improve our society.

In the public at large, concern about the threat of bureaucracy—government and otherwise—to American life is very much in evidence. When asked about the seriousness of various problems in our society, for example, 84 percent of the public agreed that "big bureaucracies" were a serious problem (41 percent said they were an extremely serious problem). And 68 percent said "government regulations" were a serious problem (24 percent said they were an extremely serious problem).[5]

At the same time, it is apparent that on this issue, as on many others, the public is not entirely consistent in its views. Specifically, we are a nation that dislikes government bureaucracy, Yet we believe government should at least in principle be responsible for helping those who cannot help themselves. For example, in one recent national study 76 percent of the public agreed that "Government should guarantee that every citizen has enough to eat and a place to live," and 77 percent agreed with the statement "Government has a basic responsibility to take care of people who can't take care of themselves."[6] Somehow, though, we expect government to do this without a large bureaucracy and without increasing expenditures on programs to help the poor.

Our concern about the growth of bureaucracy, therefore, is the kind of fear that arises from ambivalence. We know bureaucracy is inevitable, at least if we are serious about the tasks we expect government to handle. But we also worry about its costs—both its costs in tax dollars and its costs to our way of life. Bureaucracy becomes a reminder to be on guard, to worry about pursuing our goals without letting the means subvert the ends, to be vigilant lest the good life slip through our fingers just as we reach out to grasp it.

The other main trend that many volunteers—and many Americans in general—find particularly worrisome is the present emphasis on materialism. In the survey, for example, 84 percent of the public agreed that "too much emphasis on money" was a serious problem in our society (38 percent thought it was extremely serious). Related issues also evoked responses indicating widespread concern. For example, 86 percent of the public thought "economic pressures" were a serious problem and the same proportion thought "corruption in business" was a serious problem.

Debbie Carson explained: "I feel we're so fixated on things and have such fear of what might happen if we don't have nice things that we've lost our sense of relationships with people. Our jobs and our careers just tend to consume us." Susan Robbins was as concerned about placing our hope in more goods as she was about the threat of growing bureaucracy. "Producing more material goods isn't necessarily going to benefit anyone," she noted. "Most of us in America have more than we need already. And if we try to keep on producing more and more, it's just going to add to our environmental problems."

This may be the unique perspective of comfortable middle-class Americans who already have all the material possessions they need. Certainly it does not suggest that any substantial portion of the American public is ready to give up the quest for material success; in the same survey, 37 percent said "making a lot of money" was very important to them personally, another 38 percent said it was fairly important, and only 24 percent said it was not very important. And this emphasis on money was, if anything, stronger in the middle class than in the working class. In other words, people with money and the prospect of making more can perhaps pay lip service to the belief that money is also a problem.

But others with fewer toys also expressed a similar concern. They did so almost on cue, as if reciting a dictum tucked away in their memories from childhood: money will not make you happy. Ted Garvey put it in almost these words. Elmer Benson did too. Ellen Steinberg said those with money were not necessarily the lucky ones. Elgin Perry lamented, "society places too much emphasis on how much money you earn, how and where you spend it, what you wear, and what you look like. We're getting more and more of that as the years pass. I see this happening all over the United States and it's very disturbing. Where are we going to be twenty years from now?" And in the survey it was actually the working class rather than the middle class that felt most strongly about the dangers of our nation's obsession with money.[7]

Others stressed that it was not so much the money that mattered but how our system distributes money. For them, materialism meant greed. To pursue wealth single-mindedly was tantamount to exploiting the poor. As one young woman put it, "you can say that capitalism is what's made our society great, but I think you can also say there's some injustices in it; there's too many people making too much money at the top—and yes, I know, it's their hard work, and blah, blah, blah, and they deserve that, and we don't want to take anyone's motivation away from them, but it doesn't mean that the people at the bottom—the people cleaning the toilets in the hotels—they should be paid enough money that they can live decently."

And so, in expressing doubt about the trend toward materialism in our society, people who cared deeply about our nation's well-being were saying, in effect, we need to focus our attention elsewhere. Money will not bring happiness to the individual. It will be no more effective in bringing happiness to the society. Indeed, we are probably deluding ourselves if we think it will. While we waste our energy striving for greater prosperity, our nation may be losing its soul.

· 8 ·

Knowing that bureaucracy and materialism are two special concerns of many people in our society is helpful for better understanding the meaning of voluntarism. The caring that is most visibly expressed in our society through voluntary organizations clearly symbolizes something deep in the American spirit. To be sure, it is an expression of our compassion. But it is also an expression of our culture—of our aims and aspirations as a people. We see volunteer activities as a way of envisioning a better society. What these activities and organizations stand for is, in our perception, what a good society should be. And the threats that endanger the work of these organizations—that tarnish their image—tell us as much about the trends we find worrisome in our society as they do about voluntarism itself.

The volunteers with whom we spoke frequently articulated their visions of a better America through the hopes and fears they expressed about volunteer work. For them, and perhaps for us all, compassion becomes a symbol of the society we would like to have for ourselves and our children. The good we see in compassion stands for the good we would like to see in our society. And the threats that we fear endanger our efforts to help others symbolize the deeper threats we fear may be weakening our nation as a whole.

For many people, voluntarism symbolizes what has been good about America in the past—the free spirit, the lack of coercion, the camaraderie of the small town, the personal touch one experiences among friends. As Jack Casey put it, the rescue squad is "a very traditional organization—like other voluntary organizations." He thinks the people in these organizations are often quite devoted to traditional values and do not want to see change sometimes, even when it may be necessary. In his own view, being a volunteer is indeed one of the best traditions in our history. "If you look back to Ben Franklin's and George Washington's time, everything was volunteer—the fire companies, the rescue squads, everything. Everybody felt good about doing it that way because they felt good about doing it themselves for the community." That feeling, he observes, is still a vital part of the volunteer spirit in America.

Marge Detweiler resorted to an image of times past as well. For her, volunteer work symbolizes the kind of intimate community she knew as a child. "When I volunteer, I get a feeling of family. I end up with an extended family, whether it's a small group or a neighborhood. Some of my brightest memories as a child are when my community was in trouble, like when a tornado hit or when we got twenty-three inches of snow and everybody was home from work for two days, when everybody comes out and joins together to help—those have left lasting memories for me of real togetherness and family. So the gathering together on a volunteer basis gives me some of that."

The executive director in charge of coordinating volunteer services in a large city also spoke with nostalgia about the meaning of voluntarism. In the past, she noted, there was always the "proverbial housewife with her basket of goods." And that model still prevails in many settings: "Certainly in a church setting you see people tending the flock of whatever congregation and all those church members that go out with baskets of fruit or canned goods or take somebody to the doctor—those people are just doing what they can to help out." She recognized that large coordinating agencies, like her own, and hundreds of paid workers were often necessary to supplement the work of volunteers. But all of this, she felt, was merely an outgrowth of the volunteer spirit. "We really haven't lost the volunteer component," she argued.

In short, volunteer work stands for goodness and decency. It is colored with the heroism of well-known individuals, like Albert Schweitzer or Mother Teresa. It stands for courage, conviction, a willingness to go against the crowd, even freedom. But it also conjures up an image of the warm communities in which people must have lived in the past, the communities most of us no longer live in, but feel we would like to. We think of volunteer work, or of caring more generally, and we are able to visualize at least momentarily what a good society should be.

· 9 ·

Any such symbol of the good is precariously perched above a threatening abyss. What endangers it is as telling as the way we perceive it. The evils that beseige the good souls sheltered inside the fortress of voluntarism are themselves symbolic. They may in fact be undermining the fortress. But they also betoken the dangers we fear may be undermining our entire way of life. They express negatively what we think a better society should be.

The greatest danger facing volunteer agencies is, in many views, the same threat that we face as a society—the danger of ever-expanding bureaucracy. The free, personal, communal spirit symbolized by volunteer agencies is endangered by large, coercive, impersonal, bureaucratic organizations. And when people talk about big bureaucracy, they are often speaking euphemistically about government. What they see infringing most on the freedom of the voluntary sector is the coercive power of government.

This is not to say that people want voluntary organizations to do the work of government—or even that they want government to play a smaller role in caring for the needy. Opinion polls in fact show the contrary: most people want voluntary organizations *and* government both to play their parts.[8] But this also means that definitions of the role each should play become all the more important. People worry about keeping the voluntary sector strong, and fear the corrosive effects of expanding government bureaucracy.

The negative aspects of bureaucracy come out in sharp relief when people draw contrasts between voluntary agencies and government. What they like about volunteer work is the relative smallness of most volunteer agencies, and the freedom and flexibility that comes with smallness, as opposed to the layers of bureaucracy they associate with government. For Donna Frylinger this contrast made the voluntary sector particularly attractive. Being legally blind, she did not feel she could cope with government bureaucracy herself. But she also felt government agencies were simply less effective because of their size. "In the agencies I've been involved in, they've been small, and that's a big factor in them working as well as they do. I imagine if I went and worked for the welfare department there would be massive inefficiency."

The threat of bureaucracy, though, is clearly more pervasive than just its manifestations in government. People also worry about bureaucracy within the voluntary sector itself. They like voluntarism because it seems to be a safe haven in the sea of bureaucracy all around them. It stands for something more personal—caring in the first person, not the cold, impersonal bureaucracy that we fear may not care for us as individuals. And they then fear that something will be lost if the voluntary sector becomes too large and too heavily burdened with the weight of bureaucracy. One volunteer, for example, expressed her reservations about bureaucracy in the voluntary sector this way: "Too many layers of bureaucracy get piled on and get in the way of whatever service needs to be provided—I get very frustrated by that."

In the survey it was also clear that people prefer the small, delicate, more personal face of the voluntary sector, rather than some monolithic superagency that has become heavily bureaucratized. By a margin of 72 percent to 25 percent, people in the survey agreed that "small local charities are usually better than big national charities."

On the surface, this attitude seems to be inconsistent with the fears we examined in the last chapter about voluntarism being ineffective when faced with large social problems on a national scale. One would think that large problems would best be dealt with by large agencies, and therefore that people concerned with making the volunteer sector more effective would favor greater bureaucratization. Just the opposite, though, is in fact what they think. Seizing on the example of government, they believe large organizations are actually less effective than small organizations. Somehow a large organization becomes, in the public's understanding, layered with red tape and too cumbersome to meet individual needs. When asked if inefficiency were ever a problem in volunteer organizations, for example, Susan Robbins's thoughts automatically leaped to problems of scale. She thought of agencies that just perpetuate themselves, rather than meeting actual needs. "Sometimes," she noted, "the need decreases, but the bureaucracy doesn't ever decrease."

People probably would not say the same thing about a large corporation. There they would talk about economies of scale and better possibilities for marketing and delivering services. But in the human arena they worry about the ill effects of size. It does not occur to them that both the Red Cross and the United Way are large yet effective agencies in the voluntary sector. Instead, they think of the proverbial mom-and-pop store as the ideal medium for providing goods and services to the needy.

Why is the mom-and-pop approach better? Because we believe strongly that compassion should have a human face. We may think of caring, as we have seen, as a means of expressing ourselves as individuals. But our emphasis on the value of the individual in American society also extends to the people for whom we care. To supply them with goods and services may be a way of getting the job done, but we worry about losing sight of the person. Bureaucracy's woes remind us, by negative example, of one of the values we cherish most deeply.

A young black woman who worked as coordinator for disabled students on a large university campus provided an illustration that helped me understand more clearly what we in fact feel is problematic about bureaucracy in the context of caring. "Time and time again," she told me, "I hear disabled students say that they went to some agency with a very specific need, like a wheelchair or a leg brace or a request for large-print books." But what these students were given, she explained, went far beyond their specific requests. They were told, sometimes explicitly, that they really did not know what they needed. Instead of giving them what they had asked for, the agencies would subject them to all kinds of psychological tests, put them in counseling groups, send them to specialists for medical help, and so on. The recipients felt their individuality was being violated. They were being treated as members of a category, rather than being taken seriously as individuals. The charitable institutions, it seemed to them, were more interested in making use of the services they were there to provide than in tailoring these services to individual needs. It was also possible in some cases that the agencies were required by law to conduct numerous tests in order to determine whether the potential recipient qualified for their services. In either case, the person was being forced to fit a certain mold and to take on an identity simply as a representative of a broader social category.

I asked this woman if the disabled students she worked with would have felt better about their relations with these agencies if administrators were better able to demonstrate compassion. She responded negatively. "It isn't compassion that they want; it's understanding." And by understanding she meant an ability to pay attention to specific requests rather than subjecting people to a battery of tests they did not need or want.

· 10 ·

The other danger that many people worry about, in the realm of voluntarism no less than in the larger society, is variously expressed as materialism, greed, affluence, advertising, or simply the world of business. Voluntarism symbolizes a free space uncontaminated by these various financial concerns and orientations. And what we fear is threatening voluntarism from the business world symbolizes the larger evil we see spreading across our lives.

The idea that economic pressures are squeezing the lifeblood out of the voluntary sector was in fact a recurrent theme in the comments of many volunteers. An elderly man seemed to put it best when he said, "a lot of people who would probably like to do volunteer work bump into time problems because of having to work long hours for money to stay in their house or something. The sheer cost of things is driving people into extreme situations."

An idealistic attitude lies behind some of these comments. Volunteers worry about the threat of materialism to their own organizations because they fear the spread of materialism in our society in general. What they like about voluntarily caring for other people is that it removes them temporarily from the money economy. They enjoy not having to sell themselves in the marketplace the way they so often have to do in their jobs. So any sense of economic pressure from the outside is seen as a real threat to the volunteer's way of life.

But this is not always the case. Volunteers can be quite happy with the materialism of our society and still see it as a threat to showing compassion on a voluntary basis. Janet Russo, for example, seems to have made her peace with materialism a long time ago. She is proud of the fact that her husband earns a high salary. She does not exactly boast about her possessions, but she says she feels she and her husband are justified in having them. But she still worries about the effect of economic pressures on the world of voluntarism. When caring is turned over to paid professionals, in her view, something valuable is lost. But this, she feels, is an inevitable trend. "You'd never get people [to volunteer]," she says, "because everyone values how much they can make in a year." We might as well admit it, she observes: "Money is just such an important factor in our society that there's just no other way to do it."

In other cases, the threat of materialism is seen less as a function of broad, impersonal economic pressures and more as the result of rich people in particular not carrying their fair share of society's burdens. For volunteers who witness these burdens firsthand and make sacrifices themselves to help out, the thought that rich people could do more than they are doing is especially galling. We saw in the last chapter, for example, how Debbie Carson despised the rich who simply served on boards of ghetto programs but worried about even attending meetings because their hubcaps might be stolen. Ted Garvey was equally outspoken: "Rich people should at least have to give as much in taxes as poor people do. But they don't. They can take advantage of the tax code. According to the newspaper, rich people even give less to charities than poor people do. The same is true of volunteer work. Poor people will spend about five hours a week doing volunteer work, and among rich people it's not much at all. It's a fact, I think, that rich people aren't holding up their end."

In the survey people expressed concern about the threat of materialism to the voluntary sector in a variety of ways. They agreed in large numbers with the view that many people give money to charities just to escape paying taxes. They agreed in equally large numbers that much of the money given finds its way into the pockets of greedy administrators rather than helping the poor—which is another reason for their fears about large bureaucracies. And they think rich people should give away more of their money to help the poor.

"Materialism" is also a code word that some volunteers use to describe a shift in the way business is organized, a shift that endangers compassion because it makes caring in the workplace more difficult. It is the scale of modern business and its competitiveness that people worry about most. They find it hard to imagine caring as part of this context. The small business conjures up an image of personal relations, of genuine concern between an employer and a small group of employees, whereas the modern corporation suggests an impersonal, hierarchical climate in which turning out profits is the only goal.

Elmer Benson provided a vivid account of how the small-business environment seems to be supportive of caring—indeed, seems to embody the same values that volunteers cherish in voluntary organizations. For twenty-three years he ran a broadcasting company. It was a small firm, but one he started from scratch and ran successfully, after paying off the initial loan, without ever feeling severe competition or financial pressure. Because it was his own business, he felt he was able to do things that were of value to his employees and to the larger community. He took a kind of avuncular pride in his relations with his employees, sometimes treating them like children or favored nieces and nephews. Every year at Christmas, for example, he would take the profits from the Coke machine in the office and buy steaks and barbecue them in the parking lot and everyone would sit around in the lobby together and eat them.

At Christmas and for birthdays, he and all the employees also gave each other presents. He even denies that the employees thought of him as their boss. "I knew everybody. I always made it a point when I was passing out paychecks to say thank you, you did a good job. We had all worked to keep the business going, and here was their part of it for the week. Sometimes I hired people I shouldn't have because I wanted to see what I could do with them. Sometimes I didn't fire people because I was too chicken to do it. One woman had a lot of emotional problems, but I wanted to see if I could provide her with the tools to get along in life. Maybe I got too much involved in their personal lives. Every now and then one of them would come into my office crying and we'd sit there and cry together. But it was good because we all helped each other with our problems."

Martin Barnes, in contrast, provided an example of the pressures one may feel trying to show compassion in the context of a large corporation. He said it was possible to be compassionate at his company—something he obviously tries hard to be. "But you won't get promoted for being compassionate," he notes. Indeed, something about the business environment itself seems to strip away even the more basic human kindness people might ordinarily show: "Whenever we have a meeting, the mudslinging seems to start. I don't know why things can't be a little more civil—why we can't say to someone, oh, you missed that deadline, maybe you can try a little harder next time. Instead, the meetings are always witch-hunts. Some dilemma occurs, so we have a meeting, and everybody has their folder that shows they did what they were supposed to do, and then everyone is just looking around trying to find out who caused this problem. And then when you're pinned against the wall, you find you have to be a little aggressive, a little nasty, and say some harsh things, even though you may try hard not to. You just lower yourself to the mudslinging level."

Frank Stevens drew the moral explicitly: "Compassion takes a big loss in the normal office situation where you're all supposed to just line up and march in a column. It's a lot easier to be compassionate when you're out of that environment and can think as an individual again."

· 11 ·

For some people, then, bureaucracy is the main threat to the voluntary sector; for others, materialism is. In truth, the voluntary sector is perceived as an endangered species beseiged by temptations and pressures on each side. Frank Stevens put it clearly when he remarked, "in modern life we have to organize, and organization costs money. We go to existing public media to help us. Too many organizations have gotten suckered in this way. They've hired the big Madison Avenue approach that promises getting a return, the right technique, and you end up spending three-quarters of the gain just oiling the machinery."

But Frank Stevens was speaking dispassionately about trends he thought were merely nipping at the exposed edges of the voluntary sector. Others saw the issue as a matter of grave concern. To them, it was not just simply a question of whether voluntary associations were succumbing to the pressures of bureaucracy and a Madison Avenue approach to finances. It was rather a question of society itself going downhill. Voluntary associations were like a faint candle glowing in the darkness: at any moment their glow might be snuffed out by the evil winds of social change.

For one middle-aged woman who lived in a white, middle-class suburb, volunteer work was one of the few things that still seemed good about American society, and even it seemed like a faint voice for good in a sea of noisy and destructive societal forces. "Maybe I'm being a pessimist," she admitted, "but I see the way things are going in the United States and other places, like South Africa and the Middle East and even Ireland: it makes me think things are just getting worse." She said things would probably be worse than they are in the United States were it not for volunteer organizations. But, she worried, "the power of a volunteer organization to change something cannot compete with something as big and potentially as corrupt as government and big business in the United States."

Big and corrupt. Those were the words that seemed synonymous with bureaucracy in her mind. But materialism was the root problem. "Really, money is controlling most of what's going on here." Volunteer organizations were the exception; "they don't have a lot of money." But for precisely that reason, they were also powerless to fight the major problems of our time. "We're sacrificing the earth, polluting the earth, building up incredible piles of nuclear weapons that we really don't even know how to control. . . ." At this point she trailed off, laughing momentarily at the scene she was painting. And then she resumed, noting that the trouble with big business is that it is always driven by short-term profits, while the truly valuable programs and goals—for example, "child-care centers"—require long-term planning and support. "We just don't have the power," she concluded, "to make the radical changes that need to be made."

· 12 ·

The net result of people being fearful, on the one hand, of overweening government expansion, and on the other hand, expressing concerns about the spread of economic values, is that compassion is in effect relegated to a free zone somewhere in the middle. Terms that have become popular in recent years in academic circles, such as "independent sector" and "third sector," actually seem to correspond in some crude way with what the public thinks. In other societies, such as Japan or Sweden, the work of volunteer agencies might be closely linked with corporations or government bureaus, but in the United States we prefer to think of these agencies as an autonomous domain. We want them to retain some of their traditional purity and we hope they will somehow battle the forces that impinge on them from either side. We do not want them becoming sullied by participating directly in the activities of government and corporations. Nor do we want these other organizations dictating what voluntary agencies can do.

One woman expressed the contrasts among government, business, and the voluntary sector very clearly: "We live in a society where basically the government pays you to do things or industry pays you to do things," she observed. "If it's not being done by the government, and it doesn't make a profit, then it's critical for people to get involved and do things voluntarily."

· 13 ·

What are the consequences of thinking of compassion in this way, of locating it particularly in a separate sphere variously labeled as "independent," "third," or "voluntary"? The main virtue is that we identify a zone—perhaps more in our values than in the way our society is organized—in which goals, ideals, and collective values that may be different from those dominating the political and economic spheres can be expressed.

Indeed, closer analysis of the survey data reveals that the more people worry about the dangers of bureaucracy, materialism, and other threats to our society, the more strongly they feel about the importance of compassion. Conversely, the more important they think compassion is, the more they worry about these dangers. Caring for the needy, it seems, serves as a reminder—not just that there are people who need help, but that we as a society sit precariously on the slippery slope leading to destruction. Whether the small things we do to help the needy will actually save us from destruction is debatable. But at least the ideal of compassion—and its embodiment in the voluntary sector—invokes an awareness of the dangers at hand.[9]

From this perspective it is perhaps good that some people are able to limit the worrying they do about problems of effectiveness and efficiency within the voluntary sector. To be sure, these are legitimate concerns that worry many volunteers, as we saw in the previous chapter. But in another sense effectiveness and efficiency are not the only values by which human behavior can be judged. They are, after all, criteria particularly associated with the pragmatic worlds of business and government, worlds that increasingly impinge on the way we think about everything. One can easily come to judge volunteer efforts strictly in terms of cost-benefit calculations: how many people were helped, to what degree, and at what price? Much recent concern within the voluntary sector has been with pre-

277

cisely such calculations: how much labor is being devoted to volunteer agencies, what is the value of these worker-hours, how much goes for overhead, and so forth? It is important, though, to remember that voluntary organizations also express and embody other values.

One man who did volunteer work through his church admitted he did think of inefficiency sometimes in relation to volunteer work. But something troubled him about the question. Finally, he articulated his concern: "That's more of a term for the business world." For the world of voluntarism, he thought creativity and just the ability to care and to think of alternatives to what else is going on in society were the more important values. "For example, if we're talking about welfare functions of charitable organizations that supplement what the government is doing through its welfare activities, it's not efficiency that's the issue. It's . . . is there a genuine alternative? Is the situation somehow better for people because of the voluntary organizations' presence and activity?" As he tried to explain further, he seemed to say that care and compassion could be shown, and indeed should be demonstrated as values in themselves, even if the actual services provided were not always performed in the most efficient manner possible. One way to think about it might be in terms of quality. Another way might be the creativity or experimental nature of activities that could be fostered by volunteer agencies. As a footnote, he suggested that this was one reason for worrying more about appearances in the voluntary sector than in business or government. "I'm also very aware that there are certain charitable organizations which appear to be more the evil fulfillment of their staff heads. We've seen that with the problems of [television preachers] Jimmy Swaggart and the Bakkers. Situations like that are not particularly honorable or positively inspiring."

I could only agree with what he was saying. Words like "honorable" and "inspiring" are perhaps throwaways. To be sure, we want our business moguls and our government leaders to be honorable and inspiring too, but not in the same way that we want Mother Teresa to be honorable and inspiring. When Jimmy Swaggart gets caught with a prostitute, we feel more outrage, even if we are not his followers, than we would if Donald Trump did. We may expect a government bureaucrat to let greed get the best of him; we do not want to hear that the Red Cross has been lining its officials' pockets. The reason for the difference is simple, given what we have observed in the comments of volunteers themselves. The voluntary sector is indeed a protected zone, the last bastion of our highest hopes and aspirations, and so we want it to be more than just a deliverer of services; we want it to be pure, like motherhood and apple pie, as a reminder and a preserver of goodness and decency.

· 14 ·

But there is more to it even than this. Why do government bureaucracy and the materialistic ethos of business conjure up negative contrasts with compassion given voluntarily? Is it only that corruption and shortsightedness actually are problems that beset modern life and that threaten the traditional values of voluntarism? Or do we speak about corruption and shortsightedness because they help us express something else about our understanding of compassion?

To speak about corruption and shortsightedness is, I suspect, to employ a vocabulary that really allows us to express something deeper. Bureaucracy and business contrast with compassion because they structure our lives in preplanned, prepackaged ways. Both tell us what to do. Ideally, at least, they get things done by setting forth precise rules and expectations for us to follow. Corruption symbolizes the limits of those procedures. Someone who is corrupt learns the boundary between blindly following bureaucratic rules and exercising personal discretion in the application of those rules—but learns to exploit that boundary for personal gain. The shortsighted businessperson does the same thing. He or she learns how to bend the rules, how to exploit a system meant (under ideal market conditions) to benefit everyone, how to turn it to his or her own selfish purposes.

Compassion is different. To care deeply about anything is to go beyond the rules, to do more than is expected, to choose more than what the system tells one to do. "It's bending the rules," one woman said. It goes beyond a job description, Elgin

279

Perry noted: "because it is a personal thing, it comes from inside you." But it is the kind of doing more that serves other people, the society, or higher values, rather than selfish ends. It is, in this sense, precisely the opposite of corruption in government or shortsightedness in business. Jack Casey suggested as much, for example, when he described compassion as a teacher putting in a little extra effort to help students learn better or a stockbroker who says "Here, I'll give you some money out of my own pocket until you can get back on your feet." To care, he said, means "getting involved in people's lives." Martin Barnes described it simply as going the extra mile, no matter what you are doing. For both, this kind of caring was contagious. Seeing that you cared for them would cause people to strive harder to do their own parts more responsibly.

The essential contrast, therefore, is not strictly between doing something you want to do and doing something you have to do. Voluntarism contrasts with bureaucracy only in part as a symbol of personal freedom. The added contrast—the comparison evoked by our fears of corruption—is between two kinds of overcommitment. Corruption is a form of overcommitment just as compassion is. In a society like ours that values personal achievement, both are recurrent dangers. We are seldom content just to live within the institutionalized roles that tell us what to do. Indeed, the success of our system depends on people doing more than they are told, being creative, using discretion.

Talk about compassion is thus a cautionary tale about how to behave. It tells us of the fine line between caring and corruption. We often need to violate the expectations of bureaucratic institutions, but we need to make sure we do so in a caring way. Going beyond the call of duty to help others, to fulfill our responsibilities, and to make the society better constitutes caring. Going beyond the call of duty for personal gain, material reward, or mere longings for power and prestige constitutes corruption. The one guards us against the other. Or, as Elmer Benson put it when asked if he thought there would always be a need for volunteers: "I can't imagine what else people would do," he exclaimed, "except get into trouble!"

I can now add another dimension to what I said about bounded love in chapter 7. To be sure, we do for the most part limit our caring activities by confining them to institutionalized roles: we help out at the senior citizens' center one evening a week, rather than simply trying to be do-gooders in everything we do. But the fact that we define compassion in broader, even nebulous, ways is also important. By equating compassion with caring, and caring with going the extra mile in all we do, we let compassion spill out of those institutionalized roles. We make it an object lesson for all of life. Volunteering may be a role, but caring means doing any role with more than casual detachment. It means giving of ourselves.

· 15 ·

The negative side of all this is that these mythic qualities of the voluntary sector can get in the way of its ability to help those who need its services. The voluntary sector is, as I have argued, not merely the manifestation of our most compassionate impulses but also an expression of our individualism. It allows us to carve up our caring in little chunks that require only a level of giving that does not conflict with our needs and interests as individuals. It focuses our attention on individuals in need who sometimes mirror our own insecurities and often provide us with the immediate gratification of emotional fulfillment, rather than encouraging us to become actively concerned about larger questions of justice and social reform. And it sometimes provides us with real and mythic images of intimacy, warmth, personal freedom, and the nurturing womb of small communities even when these may not be the most effective or efficient ways of helping those truly in need.

These are the costs. They do not necessarily overshadow the importance of those less-tangible qualities of the voluntary sector. It is indeed critical to any society to have a free zone in which to envision a better life. For all our individualism, we do at least worry about what the good life should be—collectively. We act out in small ways the values we hold dear for our society, and we see glimpses of higher ideals and aspirations. Yet we need to strive continually for greater clarity about the meaning of our compassion. We need to keep on sorting through what it means, and indeed why we should value it at all.

The Case for Compassion

IMAGINE for a moment that our roles are reversed: you are the writer and I am the reader. Impossible, you say; it will not work; it is only some not-so-subtle trick you want to play. But see: you have already begun to speak. Perhaps there are interesting possibilities here after all. Ask yourself, before you say anything more, whether you believe compassion is a good thing. And if you believe it is a good thing, see if you can frame an argument that will convince me.

As you ponder the question, let me make it clear to you that I am prepared to accept whatever argument you want to make about the value of compassion. As you have seen, I am already basically convinced that compassion is a good thing. Like the majority of my fellow citizens I hold caring for the needy as a personal value, and it worries me to think that our society may be fundamentally selfish rather than compassionate. You have a genuine advantage in trying to persuade me that compassion is a good thing because I have already cleared away some of the objections with which some people might wish to confront you. For example, I presented evidence (chapter 7) that most care givers in our society are not suffering from some self-destructive pathology that robs them of their dignity and personhood when they care for others. Compassion, as I said there, can be beneficial to others without damaging our own personalities because we know how to set limits around it. I also made it easier for you to argue that compassion is a good thing by observing, as I did in the previous chapter, that compassion's value may not depend entirely on its being effective. You can even turn my observations about the way we define compassion in our society to your advantage. It does not have to be something narrow, like the compassion a volunteer fire fighter or a nurse might show. It can be defined broadly enough that any number of conceivable benefits might derive from it. So I am fundamentally predisposed to believe compassion is somehow of importance and value. I simply want to be convinced.

· 2 ·

You may, like the people who talked about their own motivations for being compassionate (chapter 3), recognize that various arguments can be made for compassion. You may believe personally that some of these arguments make more sense than others. But you may want to try several on me, for the sake of argument, just to see how I respond.

Let us say you begin by arguing that compassion is a good thing simply because it is an intrinsic value. You argue: Compassion is one of those things, like beauty and truth, that is simply an end worth pursuing in itself. All religions and most philosophical systems have recognized its inherent worth. The ancient prophets believed they spoke with divine authority when they told people to love their neighbors as themselves. Modern philosophers may not believe compassion is a divinely commanded obligation, but they do believe it is beneficial. Indeed, they argue that showing compassion is not something you should think about too much, at least not in the way you might think about getting a job in order to make money to buy the things you want. Compassion itself is the goal. One should be compassionate naturally, instinctively, because it is good.

Here is my response: I am not persuaded by this kind of talk. As far as religious arguments are concerned, I have seen that they do not really make a difference in mobilizing people to be compassionate unless those people happen to be involved in a religious community—which makes me think values are not absolute after all, but depend on which community you happen to be a part of. In any case, many people in our society are not involved actively in any religious community, so they are not likely to be persuaded by religious arguments. And you yourself say that modern philosophers no longer believe compassion is a divine obligation. You do suggest that modern philosophers believe compassion is beneficial. But you do not say why or to whom. You only say I should not ask so many questions. I suppose you mean it is better to show compassion than to talk about it. And I agree. But if we are going to make a case for it, we do need to discuss it. I want to know why compassion is an absolute value like beauty and truth. Are these not, as they say, in the eye of the beholder? Do we not have trouble defining them in any exact way? Does beauty not depend on the standards of aesthetic judgment that some community of experts proposes? Is truth not dependent to a large degree on the perspective one takes? And even if we agree on their value in the abstract, how do we prioritize these values? When, for example, is it best to pursue compassion rather than beauty? Or, for that matter, when is it better to pursue compassion rather than self-interest?

I am basically unconvinced by your argument that we should simply accept compassion as an absolute value because I have, for better or for worse, been reared entirely in the modern world. Although I want desperately to believe that compassion is just good for its own sake, I am suspicious of arguments about absolutes. I am not such a relativist that I am unwilling to make judgments between love and murder, between theft and generosity. But I find it hard to put my inclinations into words that can be defended as universal principles. The reason, I suppose, is that universal principles depend on some metaphysical system, on some philosophical outlook that makes logical connections among these principles and legitimates them in terms of some basic view of the world. I might be able to construct a system of this kind for myself if I tried hard enough. But it would still be my own system. I doubt that it would convince many other people. Beliefs and experiences in the modern world are too diverse. They have taught us to be more modest in our claims.

Let me add, though, that in responding this way I am not oblivious to all the compassion that has been shown in the name of religion, or suggesting that religious or other metaphysical arguments for compassion be silenced. I am aware that many people value compassion because they have been taught to in their churches, synagogues, fellowship halls, and meeting places. I am also aware that these organizations command valuable resources for mobilizing people, turning their good intentions into concrete actions, so that the needy are actually helped. What disturbs me is simply the fact that so few religious people seem to be able to recall any of the specific teachings they have heard about compassion. If they are moved by abstract theological arguments, they are certainly not amateur theologians themselves. They are able to recount the stories they have heard, such as the story of the Good Samaritan. And these stories probably have a power we need to rediscover and understand more fully. But the way most people understand the Good Samaritan leaves them with little more than the admonition "go and do likewise." The story reminds them of the importance of compassion but does not develop a case for it. In short, it seems likely that religious people are compassionate because they are part of a particular community of faith, a community that gives them opportunities to be caring, but not a community that actually convinces them of the worth of compassion by providing them with rational arguments.

I am not even suggesting that religious organizations or other entities that attempt to encourage compassion should try to enhance their work by developing better rational arguments. Motivation is, as we have seen, less a matter of responding to rational arguments and more a matter of having stories to tell ourselves that make sense of our behavior. Such stories develop and take form as people participate in churches, communities, and voluntary associations. But these stories also contain implicit arguments that cause us to understand compassion in certain ways. And most of us do not tell stories that begin: And the Lord said unto me. Nor do we tell stories that conclude: I have proven beyond the shadow of a doubt. Our stories do not defend compassion in such absolute terms. Instead, we make our stories more personal, more contingent, and we situationalize them in ways that evoke different arguments about the value of compassion.

· 3 ·

You were, as you said at the outset, not fundamentally wedded to arguing for compassion as an absolute principle yourself. You simply wanted to see if I thought there was merit to the argument. You are a product of the modern world yourself. You are in fact on much more solid ground, you believe, in arguing for compassion on the basis of its utilitarian value. You write: The best way to convince people to be compassionate toward others is to demonstrate to them that they themselves will benefit from this behavior. This argument may sound crass on the surface, but it makes sense because it works, and it works because it fits best with the prevailing characteristics of our culture. Ours is, after all, an intensely individualistic culture. We value success and the struggle for success. We believe in the importance of individual autonomy, wanting and expecting people to take responsibility for their own needs and desires, even when this means marching to a different drummer. In our society each individual must decide what he or she wants in life, and we will jealously guard each person's right to make these choices. We do not want people to sacrifice their own rights, needs, or interests to help others. That strikes us as pathological and ultimately self-defeating. We want people to show compassion toward the needy because they have chosen freely to do so, and have made this decision knowing that they themselves will benefit enough to make the investment worthwhile.

The first point that can be made in presenting a case for compassion, then, is that compassion does not conflict with the value we place on individualism. We might suppose naively that the two are fundamentally at odds with each other. We might even look to compassion as a corrective to our individualism. To help others, we might say, requires us to look beyond ourselves, to think about their needs instead of ours, to set limits to our selfish desires and recognize our fundamental interdependence with other people. But while that may be true in some abstract sense, life is more complex and adaptable at the practical level. Indeed, compassion itself is complex and adaptable. We have been able to define it in our culture so that it does not require the all-encompassing self-sacrifice of a Mother Teresa. We have institutionalized it in various roles—especially the role of volunteer—so that the time and energy we pour into it can be limited. We tell ourselves that we can really be of no use to anyone else unless we take care of ourselves. We take pride in the ability to detach from the emotional trauma someone else may be experiencing. Our individualism helps us do this. It tells us that other people essentially have to bear their own burdens and solve their own problems. We can help them and empathize with them, but ultimately the problems are theirs. Our compassion also reinforces our individualism. Spending time on the rescue squad makes us feel free again because nobody is telling us what to do. Our decision to join dramatizes our freedom to choose, and we can also quit if we choose. Showing compassion is also a way of setting ourselves off from the crowd, of showing our nonconformity, our commitment to doing our own thing.

The second point to be made about compassion is that it actually does benefit us individually. Helping the needy is a way of broadening our experience, of developing some of the skills and talents that may lie dormant in our careers or in our family lives. It is a way of rounding out our personalities, a way of making us feel more confident about our ability to work with people in diverse situations, maybe even a way of working up to positions of greater responsibility. Helping the needy can also provide us with prestige in the community, publicity, friends, and contacts valuable for our work, although we might be reluctant to say explicitly what all these benefits are.

As long as we are appropriately modest about it and not too blatantly calculating, we can expect being helpful to pay off. We do not have to be persuaded by the United Way or the latest direct-mail solicitation to believe this. We can draw on the long tradition of fables and myths in our culture and in cultures preceding it to see that people have always entertained hopes about the benefits of showing compassion. The stranger we invite in for dinner may turn out to be the Messiah. The beggar we give a coin to may be the bearer of deep insight or divine wisdom. The creature we help in some small way along our path may suddenly become our fairy godmother.

Of course we are too sophisticated nowadays to take such fables literally. We may still romanticize the beggar, hoping that he does have some deeper wisdom because of his alienation from the materialism of modern life, and we may glorify the simple virtues of poor sharecroppers or expect to learn from the needy of the underdeveloped world that small is beautiful and simple is better. We may even expect the ghetto welfare mother we help find a job to quit needing welfare assistance and therefore to keep our tax burden down. But we do not expect a pregnant teenager in the inner city to become our fairy godmother and reward us with untold riches.

No, the best case for compassion is not that we will benefit in some tangible or material way, but that we will reap personal fulfillment. The pregnant teenager we help at the volunteer center cannot repay us in kind, as in a transaction in the marketplace, but we can enter into a reciprocal exchange relation with her. We give her clothing and shelter, in return for which she gives us good feelings about ourselves. Americans crave feelings of satisfaction and self-esteem; this is part of the importance we attach to ourselves as individuals. And evidence shows that people who help the needy do receive feelings of fulfillment in return and say this is an important reason for being compassionate in the first place.

What is more, getting fulfillment from those we help fits very well with the anonymous, segmented society in which we live. It is the perfect arrangement for a society of strangers. I may never see the pregnant teenager again. What would happen if I said, as people might have in centuries gone by, I'll help you out of this jam and when you get back on your feet you can come work the debt off as a maid on my estate? Or what if I said, I will do this for you now because it will improve my image as a magnanimous leader of my village and all my serfs, including your parents, will therefore show me greater respect and work harder for me? Those kinds of obligations do not exist in our society. All I can expect from the stranger I help at the volunteer center is a sense of fulfillment. I can go on my way hoping for nothing more. But that is convenient. I would not want it any other way. I would not want this poor teenager showing up at my house a year later, baby in arms, offering to dust my living room. I want to remain anonymous. I want to remain a stranger.

So, all in all, there is a good case to be made for compassion in terms of the psychological gratification it provides. One does not have to resort to metaphysical arguments to see the value of showing compassion. To be sure, it may take a little effort to help someone in need, but probably not that much. You can always find a volunteer activity that suits your interests and your schedule. It may be a little scary at first to do something new. But take the risk, let yourself grow a little. You will experience rich emotional rewards as a result!

· 4 ·

This is how I respond: I find your argument quite compelling at one level. You have stated it very well. I agree that individualism in our society is unlikely to go away anytime soon. We might long with nostalgia in our hearts for some lost communal society that our ancestors presumably lived in and enjoyed. But that life is basically lost and, if truth were told, most of us probably would not adjust very well to it if it suddenly returned. We drive out to the country on weekends to see the little villages where everyone knows and cares for everyone else, but we hasten back to our anonymous lives in the city before nightfall. We do indeed want the freedom to make our own choices, to pursue our own stars, to be autonomous, and to take responsibility for ourselves. So any compassion that might hope to exist in our society is going to have to adjust to the reality of individualism.

I also agree with your argument because it seems to me that an individualistic society in which compassion flourishes as much as it does in ours cannot be all that bad. Apparently it is not just the warmhearted saints like Mother Teresa who can show compassion. Unrepentant individualists can too. They take care of themselves, set their limits, know their strengths and weaknesses—and still reach out to the needy in their communities. They do not live as islands of self-determination; they interact with other people, feel empathy for them, give up some of their precious time to help others, and feel good about themselves in return.

I even happen to believe you have made a better argument than you may realize when you identify fulfillment as the main benefit we receive from showing compassion. You are quite right in recognizing that more durable obligations between a recipient and a care giver would probably not work out in our society the way they did in centuries past. To be sure, some good-hearted souls would probably come around wanting to repay their debts. But most would go on about their business and we would never see them again. Fulfillment does indeed bring immediate closure to the transaction. But beyond that, it has at least two other advantages. One is that it is a legitimate form of payment. As we saw, care givers felt embarrassed to admit they made friends or received promotions or earned job skills from their volunteer work. They felt no embarrassment talking about the good feelings they received. Being intangible, the good feelings are apparently a useful commodity in this respect. The other advantage is that good feelings are not easy to measure. They are very much in the eye of the beholder. This means that the person receiving my help does not have to have the wherewithal to repay me, like a five-dollar gold piece to thrust in my palm. The recipient is somehow able to repay me with good feelings almost without doing a thing! For my part, fulfillment is whatever I define it to be. It is not subject to being disconfirmed in the same way that a monetary exchange might be—look, here is a five-dollar gold piece; oh, no, it is actually just a dollar. So fulfillment is indeed a good thing to receive in return for showing compassion.

My objection to your argument is this: You have not given me any special reason to be compassionate. All you have done is given me an argument to justify almost anything on which I might decide to spend my time. Fulfillment is the reward from giving—giving of oneself to anything, not just giving of oneself to a person in need. I can receive fulfillment from working in my garden or from making a lot of money in the real-estate market. I do not have to devote time to the needy to receive good feelings about myself.

That is debatable, you may respond. Surely there can be nothing as fulfilling as helping the needy. Maybe so, but that is not what the evidence we examined in chapter 4 demonstrated. Judging from what people themselves say (and since fulfillment is subjective, this is important), just about as many people receive a lot of fulfillment from things like their work, their leisure activities, and taking care of themselves as they do from helping others. More important, we also saw that the fulfillment people say they receive from helping others contributes little to their overall sense of happiness in life. Those who receive fulfillment from helping others are not demonstrably happier and do not have higher self-esteem, taking other things into account, than people who do not help others and who do not receive fulfillment from this source.

To be sure, people are always searching for happiness. So the promise that volunteer work or some other kind of caring behavior will make you happy can be tremendously alluring. It can be especially appealing for people who already have enough money, or who are frustrated in their jobs, or who (as is increasingly the case) find themselves without partners, children, or close friends for whom they can express love. But to hold out fulfillment as the main reason why it is good to be compassionate in our society simply does not persuade me. There are too many other ways to gain fulfillment.

I should also note that I find arguments about fulfillment—although not necessarily in the way you presented yours—troubling for another reason. Too often, it seems to me, we emphasize the good feelings we receive from helping other people while totally ignoring the costs that may be involved. Compassion is presented as a painless panacea. Come help at the volunteer center this week and feel richly rewarded. Yes, but then what happens when I discover that people who come to the volunteer center are really in pain? What happens when I go home feeling some of their pain? What happens when the volunteer center calls me next Saturday night to come in and I had been planning a night of excitement on the town? If the costs are not presented too, people will quickly discover that easy talk about fulfillment is a sham. And if the costs are presented, I question whether your argument about fulfillment remains as compelling as it seems on the surface. Helping the needy may be a cheaper way to find thrills than working my way through law school—as long as I think it costs me nothing and secures good feelings without the pain. But if I realize helping the needy is hard work, I may just as well opt for law school.

What troubles me most about your argument, though, is the suspicion that haunts me as a result of your image of how the recipient of my care pays me back. If I understand correctly, you are suggesting the exchange of help in return for fulfillment is like the giving and receiving of gifts: I give you something, you give me something in return. You are suggesting that the transaction is very much like giving a beggar a handout and receiving a blessing from him. Or that it is like helping a beetle on the road and having the beetle tell me how to retrieve gold pieces from a magic pump. Or that it is like doing a favor for a friend who sometime later does me a favor when I am in need. What troubles me about your analogy is that the recipient of my favor does not actually give me fulfillment. In fact, the recipient of my care does nothing. The recipient is simply passive. The good feelings I go away with come from within. They do not depend on receiving a warm thank you. They come from my telling myself "You did good, you should be proud of yourself, you are a great guy!"

The fulfillment I receive is thus a transaction with myself. It is indeed the perfect kind of relationship to cultivate in a society as individualistic as ours. It creates no real social relationships. It does not put me at risk in any way to the response of the person I help. I receive fulfillment whether or not he or she says "thank you." I do not have to wait until I am in need to be repaid. No lasting obligation or expectation develops between us. If I am concerned about the anonymity of our society, then this kind of transaction hardly helps at all. Compassion given for a feeling of immediate fulfillment does not promote solidarity; it only perpetuates individualism.

So ultimately I am not persuaded by your argument that compassion is good because it is fulfilling. I know this is a popular argument. But it troubles me nonetheless. Perhaps compassion can only be defended on some utilitarian ground, but for me at least this is not the best argument to make. It focuses too much on what the care giver gets out of showing compassion. If the care giver happens to value caring already, then the result may indeed be fulfillment. But if someone else values money or success or pleasure or simply navel gazing, then that person is likely to find fulfillment in other pursuits. The psychological reward can come from too many other sources. And the social reward that may come from engaging in a transaction with another human being is diminished because a genuine social relationship is not really a part of this argument.

292

· 5 ·

You have argued your case well, if not in my view persuasively. You may also have some other arguments you wish to make about compassion. For example, I suspect you might have tried out the idea (had I not interrupted you) that compassion is worthwhile simply because the needy benefit from it. You could surely have scored some points with that argument because it seems to focus more on the victims than on the care givers. But you probably would have become frustrated in pursuing it because it takes the same form as the old saw about necessity being the mother of invention. To be sure. But necessity has never prompted compassion automatically, and, as we have seen, compassion is much more than simply lending a helping hand. The eradication of needs can be accomplished, perhaps even more effectively, through a variety of other mechanisms—population policy, economic growth, professional services, government programs, to name a few. For these reasons, I would prefer to move on to a different sort of argument.

There is a saying that what goes around comes around. It is one of those trite pieces of folk wisdom, like "the buck stops here" or "a penny saved is a penny earned." People sometimes quote it in connection with their caring activities—and then turn quickly to another topic as if to avoid having to explain what it means. I would like to consider what it means, for it suggests a different way of making a case for compassion.

The notion of something going around and coming around is probably best illustrated by the gift exchanges most of us may have participated in as children, among our classmates, with friends, or perhaps among cousins. In the typical gift exchange each person's name is written on a slip of paper, the slips are tossed into a hat and mixed around, and then each person draws out one of the slips. You give a gift to that person and eventually, as the gifts are unwrapped, you receive a gift from someone else. What goes around comes around.[1]

An exchange of this kind works fairly well as long as the group is relatively small, as long as the rules are very clear, and as long as everyone takes his or her responsibility seriously. Failing any of those things, the exchange breaks down very rapidly—which may be why such exchanges generally exist only in the dim recesses of our childhood memories. When the exchange works well, it operates on utilitarian principles that in no way conflict with our sense of self-interest. I buy a five-dollar gift for the person whose name is on my slip, knowing that someone else in the group will spend five dollars on me. Still, there is a sense of giving. I try, for example, to select something for five dollars that I think my recipient will genuinely appreciate. Moreover, the game reinforces a genuine sense of community. Unlike the fulfillment I may receive from helping a stranger, I actually must depend on another person in the group to repay me, and collectively, the exchange dramatizes our common membership, cousinhood, or whatever. The only problem, as I say, is that the game is terribly vulnerable to all sorts of problems. Should one person decide to be overly generous and give a ten-dollar gift, everyone else will feel cheated. Should one person forget to bring a gift, someone will also feel cheated. And if the rules are not specific about who is included in the circle and how much to spend, pandemonium will be the only result.

A gift exchange provides a potentially powerful case for compassion. Why should one be compassionate—or, alternatively, why is compassion a good thing in a society? Because what goes around comes around. What does that mean? I show compassion to someone by, say, helping them learn to read. They show compassion to someone else by, say, helping them get a job. That person helps another person, who helps still another person, and so on. Eventually the kindness comes full circle. Perhaps I find myself in the hospital and the nurse who takes care of me was inspired to enter a caring profession because of someone who provided him or her with an example of caring, and this person, through some long series of transactions, had been part of the chain of compassion I initiated when I helped someone learn to read. The case for compassion in this scenario is twofold: my initial investment is worth it because eventually I will be repaid, not just in some intangible sense of fulfillment, but through some actual service provided me by another

human being; and the whole series of relationships demonstrates our dependence on one another, creating a sense of
common membership that at least tempers each individual's
fiction of being a purely autonomous creature.

Some of the people we talked to in fact saw their efforts to
help others in terms quite similar to this model of a large gift
exchange. Martin Barnes, for example, admitted this was one
of the reasons he donates time to the Meals on Wheels program. "It all comes home eventually," he remarked. "Maybe
someday I'll be the one standing there saying 'Thank you so
much for the meal.'" He was not suggesting that any of the
recipients on his route would actually be there to return the
kindness. But the Meals on Wheels program seemed to operate, in his way of thinking, like the hat children put their
names into for a gift exchange. He is putting his name into the
hat by giving time to the program. When he is old and alone,
some future volunteer will come along and draw his name out
and bring him a meal.

Debbie Carson put it in somewhat broader terms. The important thing about caring, she felt, is that we all exist not just as
givers but also as receivers. "There's times when we can give to
others, and then there'll be times when we'll be the needy
ones." She thought it was wrong for care givers to see their
activities as being one-sided: "Some people go at it thinking
they have everything to give and the people they're helping are
somewhat lower than they are. But I think it's mutual: I have
something to give, but these people do too. Someday I may be
more in the disadvantaged situation myself."

There was also some awareness, at least in the survey, that
compassion goes around and eventually spreads out until the
whole society is somehow better. In chapter 3, I reported people's responses to a number of statements offered to them as
reasons for trying to be people who are kind and caring.
Among the reasons people selected as providing the best arguments for being kind were statements that focused on the good
feelings one received as a result of caring, the personal growth
associated with caring, and the importance of identifying oneself as a caring person. These were all responses that highlighted what the individual giver receives from showing kind-

ness. In comparison, people were less likely to believe in any kind of direct return from the recipient or even from other people. That is, they did not think of some immediate or eventual return of their gift as an important reason for being kind. But they did believe that caring was somehow beneficial for the larger society. Indeed, the largest percentage responding favorably to any of the statements was the 75 percent who said that "the society is better off when we care for each other" was a major reason for trying to be a kind and caring person.

· 6 ·

In what way is the society better off? Most people, as I just noted, do not think it is a strong argument for compassion to go around expecting that you yourself will in some way be repaid. They do not like putting it that way—it seems too calculating and crass. But they do actually believe there is some truth to the idea that what goes around will eventually come around to their own benefit. For example, the survey also showed that 78 percent of the public agrees with the statement "If I help others, it is likely that someone will help me when I am in need." Despite the fact that we live in an impersonal society, we somehow remain convinced that acting graciously and generously toward our neighbors will make the society in which we live better for us personally.

The problem of course is that this belief makes much more sense in the context of our actual neighbors than it does in the larger community of strangers. Not acting like a bastard toward friends and family is indeed a good way of increasing the odds of receiving consideration from them when we suffer bereavement or find ourselves lying in the hospital. It is even possible to believe that our neighbors may help us out of a jam if they know we have given time to some community organization, such as a church or a program providing meals for the elderly. Our volunteering is a public way of making visible our goodness and decency. It is sometimes a way to put our neighbors in our debt: we help them out by responding to their call for volunteers, and then they feel compelled to help us when we are in need personally. It is much harder to believe that the elderly person in the ghetto who receives a meal from us is likely to be there for us when we need her.

The idea that compassion goes around until it comes around is not very compelling so long as it is taken so literally. Like the precarious gift exchange among children, it breaks down all too easily. In a large, impersonal society like ours there are too many links in the chain to make it work. It may be true, as "small world" researchers claim, that even in a large, impersonal society we are all linked to one another through no more than a few indirect friends of friends or acquaintances of acquaintances. But we do not know those people down the chain a few links from us personally, and they do not know us. It is quite unlikely, therefore, that my helping a stranger in need will result in that person helping another person in need and, after a few more iterations, some stranger helping me when I am in need. Just as in a chain-letter sequence, some person along the way is going to forget or is going to be a complete flake and never pass the kindness along. Someone in the system is going to become a "free rider," taking what he or she can get and paying nothing in return.

Even if there are no free riders, caring in the larger society does not work like a classroom gift exchange because there is too much diversity, too much inequality, and nobody to specify clearly what the rules should be. Efforts have been made (and are being made) to suggest such rules—for example, the idea of a tithe in the biblical tradition, or the current "Give Five" campaign which encourages everyone to give five hours a week to some volunteer organization. But these efforts are doomed to failure both because of the free-rider problem (no means of enforcing compliance) and because of disparities in available time and money. All they can hope to achieve is a truly minimal level of investment in caring activities. They are like the classroom gift exchange in this respect. Take a classroom in which some of the pupils are sons and daughters of millionaires and others come from homes close to the poverty line. A five-dollar gift exchange may be possible to organize, but a hundred-dollar exchange is not. The only possibility is to let each child give as large or as small a gift as he or she chooses. But then all the rest of the rules have to be made voluntary as well: one can choose not to give anything, and one can choose to whom to give one's gift, meaning that the neediest will not necessarily be served. Under such an arrangement, one certainly cannot make exact calculations, figuring that if one gives generously one will eventually receive something in kind that meets one's own needs.

· 7 ·

What we must do, therefore, is to modify the example provided by children's gift exchanges to make it a more compelling argument for the kind of compassion that can exist in a complex society like the one in which we live. What are the essential features of the gift exchange? Surely not the fact that everyone must receive a gift that is worth exactly as much as the one he or she put in. If that were the important point, everyone should simply buy a gift, bring it, and take the same gift home again. That way you could be sure of getting good value for your money. By leaving it up to the whim of someone else, you may receive a five-dollar gift, but one you cannot use or do not want. The gift exchange is also not really very likely, or even designed, to meet people's needs. The poor child who receives a pair of warm mittens may in fact be helped, but the mittens do not solve his or her poverty. At most, they can dramatize his or her need and make clear to everyone concerned that other gifts would be appropriate as well, and more important, that some larger efforts may be needed to ensure greater equality. The gift exchange serves other functions, whether or not it is effective economically. Furthermore, as long as strict economic utility is not its primary purpose, the gift exchange does not even have to involve the trading of equivalent commodities. It should not matter if one person gives a larger gift than someone else or if someone receives a smaller gift than another person.

The essential feature of the gift exchange is that it links the whole community. This is how it differs from gifts given between friends. Were there no gift exchange in the classroom, this pair of buddies might give each other gifts and that clique of friends might go out together to help each other with homework. But the gift exchange forges bonds across these smaller islands of intimate association. It forces some people, at least, to give to strangers. It does not require every individual to give something to every other individual. But it creates ripples that spread throughout the entire group.

Should the entire group become relatively large, no single individual is likely to know the exact chain of gifts that linked the person who received his or her gift to the person from whom he or she received a gift. You might even be unfortunate enough not to receive a gift—perhaps someone is sick or absent that day, or moves away. But the knowledge is still there that your own gift was part of a chain that connected a number of individuals and that other chains existed as well, connecting sets of friends with other sets of friends who nevertheless remained strangers. Elmer Benson put it in these words when asked how someone he had helped could pay him back: "I wouldn't expect him to. If he could turn around and provide something like that for somebody else, that would be fine. But I wouldn't be keeping in touch to find out what he had done."

By giving something, each person in the group has the satisfaction of knowing two things: that he or she did in fact make a contribution and by that act played a role as a member of the group, and that the group itself was a reality. To be a member of something not only constitutes one's identity as an individual, it also constructs the identity of the group. Simply by participating in the exchange of gifts, you recognize the existence of the group. Its authority, if you will, is dramatized because you submit to its rules and expectations. You demonstrate that you subscribe in some small way to the value of the group by deciding to contribute to it. And it is, indeed, the group to which you are contributing—the group in its entirety, not just the particular individual to whom you happen to give a gift, not just yourself, and not just your own small circle of friends.

What I am suggesting is that there is an important *sociological* case to be made for compassion. It is the psychological case ("It'll make you feel good") that we hear most often, and after that probably the economic case ("It'll keep your taxes down and help the needy more efficiently than government programs do.") Regrettably, the sociological case has not been voiced so often or so loudly. But it is perhaps the most compelling of all.

When someone shows compassion to a stranger, it does set in motion a series of relationships that spreads throughout the entire society. Even if the chain is broken at some point so that no direct benefits come back to us as individuals, the whole society is affected, just as an entire lake is affected when someone pours in a bucket of water. Despite the fact that we live in a society of strangers, we can still be aware of our contribution to others by understanding how compassion spreads out through the wider society. We do not have to reap the rewards personally to know that we are all better off. Elgin Perry explained it this way: "If somebody [I help] can advance to the point he can make his own life better, that's enough right there. Hopefully someday my student will be able to read better so he can get a better job or get the promotions he's missed in the past. That in itself is already a reward. It doesn't have to be for me. Maybe by the time he gets to the point where he reads as well as I do, I might be long gone, in another city, or dead. But if it can help him have a better life, to provide better for his family, or inspire his own children to do well, I think that's enough."

A large majority of the American public is involved in one kind of volunteer activity or another, and most of these people, as we have seen, have stories to tell about receiving care at some point in their own lives. They have, in this sense, passed the torch along that once lit their own path. Beyond the volunteers, moreover, virtually everyone shows small kindnesses to friends and family members, neighbors, and colleagues at work; virtually everyone recognizes the value of caring and compassion; and stories about people—famous men and women or intimate acquaintances—who have demonstrated compassion are abundant.

Acts of compassion are vitally important in the large, complex societies of which our contemporary world is made precisely because our individuality is so important. We no longer live in closed communities where needs and obligations are clearly defined by the group. But we do not live as isolated, fully self-sufficient individuals either. Most of us live in open networks of intimate associations and casual acquaintances.

We devote much of our time to our immediate friends and derive most of our personal fulfillment from those relationships. Indeed, it is easy to limit our horizons so that we see only those primary relationships. But we also interact with large numbers of people who come and go, passing quietly through the hallways of our lives or stopping only momentarily to converse. These are the diffuse webs of association that tie us together. The caring we may show toward persons other than our intimate friends and family demonstrates our commitment to these larger networks. These networks attach us to the wider society and world, just as we are attached through our work, our purchases, our political commitments, and the reading we do. But compassion symbolizes attachments of a different sort: a commitment to those who may not be able to reciprocate, an acknowledgment of our essential identities as human beings, and a devotion to the value of caring itself.

· 8 ·

I suggested in an earlier context (chapters 7 and 8) that compassion has a broad and ambiguous meaning in our culture. That is all to the good insofar as we wish to see the social significance of compassion. Individuals do in fact have different talents, different amounts of available time, different interests, and different levels of discretionary income. To define compassion narrowly—say, as active involvement in a volunteer agency— may be beneficial up to a point, insofar as it creates a specific role that assists people in limiting their compassion but that lets them be compassionate in some demonstrable way. But narrow definitions of compassion also restrict our vision of what it is, causing us to miss its larger possibilities and indeed its larger presence in our society.

Formal volunteer efforts are sufficiently widespread in the United States that they themselves connect many of us in networks of diffuse association. But informal caring extends well beyond these efforts and needs to be seen as an important part of the mechanism that ties us together as common members of American society and the human race. The parent who stays up all night nursing a sick child contributes to the gift exchange that binds us together as a people just as much as the person who gives a fifty-dollar donation to a national charity. As many of the individuals I have quoted insisted, compassion must begin at home, and it must be something that even a person with limited time and energy can express.

I would even go so far as to agree with those who recognize possibilities for demonstrating compassion in other, perhaps less personal ways. The researcher who works quietly in the lab to find solutions to medical problems may be showing compassion in his or her own way. The journalist who writes a story about Mother Teresa, thereby amplifying her work to the larger world, may be showing compassion. So may the person who is stuck working as a functionary in a large bureaucracy, but still finds a way to cultivate a climate of caring in that setting. These people may be showing compassion—or they may be thinking strictly of themselves, their career advancement, and their material interests. By caring for their clients, or readers, or the ultimate consumers of their work, and by doing their work with the interests of others at heart, they contribute in a small way to the vision and reality of a good society.

· 9 ·

The other modification that helps enormously in making a compelling case for the social value of compassion is to recognize its metaphoric qualities rather than focusing strictly on the literal characteristics of helping behavior. At one level, this is perhaps hardest to do in our society, for we live in an individually oriented and pragmatic culture. The stories we tell about giving (or receiving) care focus on the one individual who moved us, who motivated us, and the peculiar circumstances of our encounter with that person. We also like to think of compassion primarily as helping an individual, of actually alleviating pain and setting that person on the road to recovery. When we think in these ways, we limit compassion. We turn it into helping behavior, a social service, an experience located primarily in our private lives.

But we also saw that compassion is imbued with a rich layer of symbolism and that at least some of this symbolism concerns the larger society in which we live. The compassion of a Mother Teresa or a Jack Casey mirrors, in the sense of reflecting and amplifying, the intense, individualistic values on which our society is based. People who care are often depicted as individual heroes, rugged nonconformists who are willing to engage in some form of deviant behavior—namely, the deviance of caring for the needy. We may see these individuals as success stories: people acting out their special talents and interests and fulfilling their potential in the process. We certainly tend to characterize them as part of the free tradition, the individual freedom, the culture of individual discretion that we believe has made our society great. In all these ways, compassion is hardly the antidote for an individualistic society. Despite the fact that caring involves a relationship with other human beings, we minimize those relationships by asserting the importance of temporal and emotional detachment. We focus more on the individual care giver than on the relationships established. And, despite its individual focus, this image provides us with a portrait of our larger society—a society of individuals.

Were this the whole story, there would in my view be considerable reason for concern. In this account, compassion becomes cheap, overly psychological, utilitarian, focused on the needs and interests of the giver. Our individualism makes compassion of a certain kind possible, but also limits it. We do not for the most part view volunteer work as a way of cultivating lasting relationships with the people we serve. We treat them only as casual clients, strangers who walk in and out of our lives with exceeding rapidity. We also neglect the costs, the actual sacrifice of time, energy, and individual autonomy, that may be necessary for genuine compassion to occur.

But there is another aspect to the metaphoric dimension of compassion that does focus squarely on the larger society in which we live. The person we help along the road, in fable or in real life, may well be a stranger we relate to for only a few minutes, and yet the relationship is depicted in a way that reveals our common human identity, a way that deliberately (as in the Good Samaritan story) bridges the barriers of ethnicity, race, and social status. The life of compassion also symbolizes our fears of the impersonality of modern life and the corruption and exploitation that can occur in a bureaucratized society. It provides a way of expressing our concerns about materialism and its corrosive effects on human life. In this sense, compassion stands for something larger even than itself. It reminds us of our humanity and therefore of the deeper qualities that are essential to our common human existence.

Susan Robbins articulated this dimension of compassion with particular clarity. "Being interested in helping people," she argued, "makes you feel more a part of society." Society? She said she did not mean society in an economic sense, she meant "human society." To illustrate the difference, she drew a comparison between ancient and modern societies: "In older times with the extended family or the tribe, people felt they were part of the whole group. The tentmaker felt he was a part of that tribe." But nowadays, she observed, "people make tents in factories and it's too impersonal." So showing compassion was, for her, a way of regaining some of the traditional humanness of society and making herself feel more a part of it. "It makes me feel more human, like I'm more a part of the earth and society," she remarked. "Even if laws and money could make a utopia, it still wouldn't be very human. Caring for others gives us significance in this brief period we are on earth."

In thinking about compassion, we remember that not all of life depends on efficient, large-scale organization and a productive economy. If only by negative example, we create a space in which to think about our dependence on one another, the needs that can never be fulfilled by bureaucracies and material goods, and the joys that come from attending to those needs.[2] Above all, compassion gives us hope—both that the good society we envision is possible and that the very act of helping each other gives us strength and a common destiny. Part of the sociological case for compassion, therefore, is built into the fact that we already understand, through our metaphoric depictions of it, that compassion is a value that speaks not only to us as individuals but to our sense of living together in society.

· 10 ·

You are, I suspect, beginning to feel cheated. When you were the writer, you gave me a chance to respond to your arguments. Now you want to respond to mine. Very well. I know there are objections to the sociological case I have tried to present in defense of compassion. In fact, there are several important ones that you probably want to raise with me. First, you are, I am quite sure, troubled by the loose way in which I have defined compassion. You may be saying to yourself, if compassion can be defined as broadly as this, then we surely run into the same problems we did in talking about fulfillment: why compassion, after all, why not just any kind of activity? Second, I suspect you are troubled by the seemingly heartless attitude I have taken toward the needy in all this. Surely, you say, this sociological case for compassion that you have presented must be a clever way of making the middle class feel good about itself, rather than doing anything that will really benefit the needy. And finally, if I am right, you probably want me to say more clearly just what I have in mind when I talk about making a "case" for compassion.

In response to your question about the definition of compassion, I take it that the problem here is not so much one of arriving at some formal definition as it is one of conceptualizing compassion in such a way that a case can be made for it *specifically*, as opposed to all the other kinds of activities in which one might engage. It is indeed true that I objected to the argument about fulfillment on the grounds that fulfillment can come from almost any activity, and statistical evidence does show that precious little of it actually comes from doing things for people. But now I am arguing that compassion is worthwhile because it contributes to the well-being and wholeness of society. I have even accepted with only a few reservations the view of people who say compassion can include such activities as working on cancer research, taking care of a sick child, or being nice to people at work. Surely one could extend the list until it was pretty much a meaningless aggregation of everything. Why are these activities any different, for example, than sitting home in the evening alone watching television? After all, watching television does link one to the larger society; it even contributes in a small way: you help keep a program's Nielsen ratings up, which makes companies willing to spend money advertising their products on the show, and this keeps advertisers in business and sells products, which creates jobs and keeps our economy growing, which as we all know is the best way to help the poor and needy. Is this not just as much a contribution as spending one's evening teaching some poor teenager how to read—a teenager who still gets hooked on drugs, kills somebody, and spends the rest of his or her life in jail at public expense?

Obviously it is possible to make such arguments. But these are not the arguments most of us would want to make or feel comfortable making. Compassion is, as I have acknowledged, not an absolute but a value we shape according to the culture in which we live. We may be willing to extend its meaning to subsume many kinds of caring, including just trying especially hard to do a job well. But we are not willing to let it subsume all kinds of caring. As we saw in the last chapter, caring and corruption come perilously close to each other; both are kinds of overcommitment. Thus we extol the virtues of heroes who illustrate the kind of caring we admire, and we worry a lot about the dangers of corruption.

The individualism in our culture also tempers our view of compassion in two important ways. We find it much easier to define something as compassion when it is directed toward another individual. Sitting at home watching television is harder to justify, for this reason, than helping a teenager to read. Even more impersonal activities that do not involve helping a specific individual, such as cancer research, are easier for us to defend because our minds can jump readily to some relative or personal acquaintance who might benefit individually. Our individualism also restricts what we are willing to define as compassion because, as we have seen, we recognize many activities as being concerned primarily with gratifying our own needs and, although we consider these legitimate, we do not like to confuse them with compassion. Staying home watching television, we would say, is so obviously a matter of personal gratification that its potential contribution to the society pales by comparison.

This was the way Jack Casey, in fact, defended his decision to show compassion by volunteering for the rescue squad. "Even if every service was provided, people still need an outlet, something to do in their free time. I can think of a lot of things I could do with my free time, like laying around all day watching television or playing computer games. But when I'm here as a volunteer, it adds something back to society. I'm taking my free time that I could be doing nothing with or even something bad with and putting it to good use." In other words, there was a clear distinction in his mind between various ways of spending free time. The important feature of being a volunteer was the contribution he made, not just to himself, but to society.

The question of whether this way of looking at compassion focuses too little on the needy and may in fact be a perspective that fits too easily the reigning assumptions of the middle class is also an important question to consider. Voluntarism is, and has been from its inception, largely a feature of the middle-class. This was well-evidenced in the survey: 72 percent of those with college degrees, for example, had donated time to a volunteer organization at some point in their lives, compared with only 42 percent of those with a high-school diploma.[3] But the argument I have tried to make is not restricted to voluntarism; indeed, it is concerned with the broader question of compassion. As I have suggested, much volunteer work can be devoted to activities, such as the arts or hobbies, that have rather little to do with compassion, and there are many ways other than voluntarism to show compassion. When compassion is defined more broadly, its middle-class location in fact disappears. For example, in the survey more people in the lower educational strata had taken care of people who were very sick and had cared for elderly relatives in their homes than had those in the higher strata.[4] There were also virtually no significant differences across strata in the proportions who had lent money to someone, stopped to help someone having car trouble, tried to get someone to stop drinking or using drugs, or visited someone in the hospital. In other words, compassion is not, and should not be seen as, a middle-class trait.

The case I have made for compassion is an argument that encourages people to recognize the value of transcending class barriers, both in their deeds of caring and in their attitudes. It suggests that compassion creates diffuse connections that bridge the various segmented communities in which we live and reinforces a sense of common membership in the whole society. The stories that people like Jack Casey and Martin Barnes tell, as well as more public narratives such as the story of the Good Samaritan, emphasize the bond that emerges when one human being cares for another human being.

There is, as I observed in the previous chapter, the danger

that compassion in our society is understood so much at the individual level that we lose sight of larger questions about social justice, equality, and reform. For many in the front lines of volunteer or paid service to the needy, these larger questions are very much part of their thinking. They have taken a hard look at some of the traditional promises made by political leaders or by social reformers and concluded that more thinking about solutions is needed. Others, though, do suffer from the delusion that individual caring is all that can be done and all that needs to be done. But this, in my view, is a problem that arises from emphasizing the effectiveness of voluntary caring too much, rather than de-emphasizing it. My argument has been that voluntary caring is generally ineffective—generally only a Band-Aid solution that at most helps some people in need and brings to public consciousness the needs of others— but that there is a great deal more to compassion than just helping the needy. Compassion is a value, a means of expression, a way of behaving, a perspective on society. We hope that it meets real needs, and everything possible should be done to facilitate it in meeting these needs. But whether it actually succeeds at that level or not, compassion still demonstrates our dependence on one another and gives us the hope we need to push ahead individually and as a society. It may help our selves (individually), but it surely is a way of helping ourselves (collectively) as well. As Debbie Carson expressed it, "even the small things provide something for people to look at, something to raise people's values."

Then there is the question of what I mean by a "case" for compassion: I am not seeking to prepare a legal brief or advertising copy for nonprofit organizations soliciting donations and volunteers. In other words, I do not mean to argue that we need a sociological case for compassion because it will mobilize individuals to give more of their time and money to the needy. What I am suggesting is that we all benefit from a better understanding of the social significance of compassion. We benefit as its meaning is amplified. We see that the compassionate person is not merely doing something that contributes to his or her self-esteem as an individual, but that compassion has meaning for us all. It enriches us and ennobles us, even those of us who are neither the care givers nor the recipients, because it holds forth a vision of what a good society can be, provides us with concrete examples of caring that we can emulate, and locates us as members of the diffuse networks of which our society is woven.[5]

· 11 ·

I have maintained throughout that caring is something we understand mainly through stories. To make a case for compassion in abstract theoretical language, therefore, is not likely to carry much weight, unless the same case can be illustrated effectively in stories we can relate to, repeat, and make part of our own experience. Some of the stories I have recited in previous chapters do in fact point to the broader social significance of compassion. Many other such stories are part of American folklore—some, admittedly, that stretch the bounds of credibility by drawing a literal connection between the person helped and the person who returns at some later point to reciprocate the favor. But one story from the folklore of American care giving makes the social case for compassion with exceptional clarity. It was told by a public figure, a man whose writings about helping ourselves were at one time virtually synonymous with American individualism. But this proponent of self-help and individual striving also knew the importance of helping ourselves collectively by caring for others.

The story was of a Swiss girl in her late teens, a girl named Ursula, who had recently come to New York City to live in an American home and learn English in return for doing baby-sitting and other household tasks. Ursula was a rather ordinary young woman, not the kind who gives her life pulling people from a crashed airplane or the kind who starts a great reform movement. Indeed, her act of kindness was extraordinarily trivial. Not having much money herself, but realizing the vast extent of poverty in New York, she decided to buy a dress and give it to some child in the ghetto. At the department store she asked the doorman what part of the city was poorest, got directions from a policeman to Harlem, walked a number of blocks, and eventually found a bell-ringer from the Salvation Army who offered to help her find a little girl in need of a dress. Hailing a taxi, the two traveled on together until they came to a tenement house where the Salvation Army man knew of a poor family with a little girl. Ursula asked the man to take her package to the door, ring the bell, and then leave the anonymous gift. The next day, after some questioning, she hesitantly told the family with whom she was staying about the journey she had made.

It is, as I say, a simple story about an event that seems almost trivial. Amidst the vast squalor of New York's slums one little girl received a dress from an anonymous stranger. The gift is little more than a token, an act that was far more effective in making the young stranger feel good about herself than in eradicating poverty. But it is, after all, a story. And it is the storyteller's own role that enlarges its significance. "How do I happen to know all this?" he writes. "I know it because ours was the home where Ursula lived. . . . To this child from across the sea, we seemed so richly blessed that nothing she could buy would add to the material things we already had. And so she offered something of far greater value: a gift from the heart, an act of kindness."

Like all such stories, this one has a moral, a lesson for the individual, but one that reveals the larger company in which even an individual act of compassion inevitably circulates: "Strange isn't it? A shy Swiss girl, alone in a great impersonal city. You would think that nothing she could do would affect anyone. And yet, by trying to give love away, she influenced many people: herself, the Salvation Army man, the tenement family, the taxi driver, my own family, myself and perhaps, through this retelling of her story, she will influence people all over the world."[6]

Such is the storyteller's hope.

Notes

CHAPTER ONE
AN AMERICAN PARADOX

1. Jane Addams's account of her visit to Tolstoy is found in *Twenty Years at Hull-House* (1910; reprint, New York: New American Library, 1960), 186–99; a brief summary is given in Edmund Wilson, *The American Earthquake* (Garden City, N.Y.: Vintage, 1958), 447–64.

2. These estimates are based on a nationally representative survey of 2,775 adult Americans eighteen years of age or older conducted in March 1988 by the Gallup Organization for Independent Sector, Inc., and reported in *Giving and Volunteering in the United States: Findings from a National Survey* (Washington, D.C.: Independent Sector, 1988), 7.

3. Ibid.

4. Jack Casey was one of one hundred persons interviewed in depth for this study. The interviews were conducted in four regions of the United States. Since a representative national sample of respondents was also surveyed as part of the study, these subjects were selected according to a quota procedure that called for approximately equal numbers of men and women, approximately equal numbers of older people and younger people, a diversity of educational and occupational backgrounds, minority representation approximately equivalent to that in the nation at large, a diversity of religious affiliations, and a diversity of levels and kinds of involvement in volunteer activities. All subjects were currently active in at least some kind of volunteer work. Their ages ranged from sixteen to seventy-eight and their education levels varied from no high school or college training to postgraduate training. I conducted some of the interviews myself; others were conducted by my research associates. All the interviews were transcribed, yielding approximately three thousand pages of transcript. All names are fictional.

5. Independent Sector, Inc., *Giving and Volunteering*, 8.

6. Calculated from table 1.3 ibid., 7.

7. The figures reported in this and the following two paragraphs are from my own survey of a representative adult sample of the United States population age eighteen and over conducted in April and May 1989. A total of 2,110 personal interviews, each lasting approximately thirty minutes, was conducted. The fieldwork was done under subcontract to Princeton University by the Princeton Survey

Research Center, which is an affiliate of the Gallup Organization. Sampling and interview procedures followed standard Gallup Organization guidelines. Unless otherwise indicated, national survey figures reported in this chapter and the following chapters are from this study.

8. Alexis de Tocqueville, *Democracy in America* (1835; reprint, New York: Vintage, 1945), 2:185.

9. John Winthrop, "A Model of Christian Charity," reprinted in *America's Voluntary Spirit*, ed. Brian O'Connell (New York: Foundation Center, 1983), 32.

10. John Witherspoon, *Lectures on Moral Philosophy* (1768; reprint, Newark, Del.: University of Delaware Press, 1982), 109.

11. Tocqueville, *Democracy in America*, 2:185.

12. For a useful overview of the history of voluntarism and philanthropy in the United States, see Robert H. Bremner, *American Philanthropy*, 2d ed. (Chicago: University of Chicago Press, 1988).

13. One valuable survey of voluntary efforts in the United States that also contains a useful bibliography is Jon Van Til, *Mapping the Third Sector* (New York: Foundation Center, 1988).

14. Tocqueville, *Democracy in America*, 2:136.

CHAPTER TWO
CARING AND/FOR OUR SELVES

1. Editorial staff, "They Might Be Heroes," *CV: The College Magazine*, February–March 1989, 38.

2. Calculated from the 1988 Cumulative File of the General Social Survey, a national survey of approximately 1,500 respondents conducted annually by the National Opinion Research Center at the University of Chicago.

3. Independent Sector, Inc., *Giving and Volunteering*, 37.

4. "Giving time through volunteer work to charitable and religious organizations" was correlated + .272 with "Applying your talent, creativity, and energy to the maximum extent possible" and + .111 with "Traveling for pleasure."

5. The percentages of people who gave each response, among those who said being able to do what they wanted was absolutely essential, very important, fairly important, and not very important, respectively, were as follows: helping people in need is absolutely essential, 32, 12, 16, 23; helping people in need is either absolutely essential or very important, 83, 71, 69, 79; involved in charitable or social-service activities, 28, 31, 32, 36; donated time in the past year, 29, 27, 27, 27; cared for someone who was very sick, 27, 22, 25, 30;

stopped to help someone having car trouble, 30, 30, 28, 27; and gave money to a beggar, 25, 23, 20, 29. None of these patterns constituted a statistically significant negative relationship between individualism and caring.

6. The respective percentages were 65 and 55.

7. To both these questions, those who gave individualistic responses were slightly less likely than those who did not to be involved in charitable or social-service activities, but the differences were too small to be statistically significant.

8. I also created an individualism index to see if people involved in caring activities were any less likely to score at the very high end of this scale—any less likely to place high value on all the individualism items consistently. They were not. The scale gave respondents one point each for saying that doing what they wanted, being successful in their work, living a comfortable life, and taking care of themselves were either absolutely essential or very important. In the total sample, 49 percent scored high ("4") on this scale. Among those involved in various kinds of caring, the proportions who scored high on this scale were as follows: among those involved in charitable or social-service activities, 48 percent; among those who had donated time to a volunteer organization in the past year, 50 percent; among those who had stopped to help someone having car trouble in the past year, 51 percent; among those who had cared for someone who was very sick in the past year, 50 percent; among those who said helping people was absolutely essential to them, 58 percent; and among those who said giving time to help people was absolutely essential, 59 percent. In other data, the only negative relationship I was able to discover between indicators of individualism and caring was in a national survey conducted by the Gallup Organization in 1988 as part of a study of religious unbelief. Among those who said they would welcome "more emphasis on self-expression" in the coming years, 25 percent said they were very or fairly active in "civic, social, and other charitable activities in [their] community or neighborhood," as opposed to 29 percent among those who said they would not welcome this change. This difference was only marginally significant. In the same survey I could find no relationships between involvement in charitable activities and other relevant measures of values, such as welcoming or not welcoming "less emphasis on money" or "less emphasis on working hard." These results are from my analysis of data made available to me by the Gallup Organization.

9. Independent Sector, Inc., *Giving and Volunteering*, 9.

10. I shall discuss utilitarianism in relation to caring more extensively in subsequent chapters. My example of the so-called prisoner's

dilemma game here follows the discussion found in Neil Cooper, *The Diversity of Moral Thinking* (Oxford: Clarendon Press, 1981), especially 265–67.

11. Tocqueville, *Democracy in America*, 2:129–35.

CHAPTER THREE
TALKING ABOUT MOTIVES

1. Virginia A. Hodgkinson, *Motivations for Giving and Volunteering* (New York: Foundation Center, 1989). See also Joseph Losco, "Understanding Altruism: A Critique and Proposal for Integrating Various Approaches," *Political Psychology* 7 (1986): 323–48.

2. My perspective on motives follows that of C. Wright Mills, "Situated Actions and Vocabularies of Motive," in *Power, Politics, and People: The Collected Essays of C. Wright Mills*, ed. Irving Louis Horowitz (New York: Oxford University Press, 1963), 439–40. Mills wrote: "To explain behavior by referring it to an inferred and abstract 'motive' is one thing. To analyze the observable lingual mechanisms of motive imputation and avowal, as they function in conduct, is quite another. Rather than fixed elements 'in' an individual, motives are the terms with which interpretation of conduct by social actors proceeds."

3. Independent Sector, Inc., *Giving and Volunteering*, 23, 29–30.

4. These results are from the survey I conducted for this project. See the description given in chap. 1, note 7.

5. Pete Hamill, "Doing Good," *New York*, October 13, 1986, 35.

6. Adam Smith, *The Theory of Moral Sentiments* (1759; reprint, Indianapolis: Liberty Fund, 1976), sec. 1, chap. 1, 47.

7. For overviews, see Maya Pines, "Good Samaritans at Age Two?" *Psychology Today*, June 1979, 66–77; and Daniel Goleman, "Researchers Trace Empathy's Roots to Infancy," *New York Times*, February 15, 1989.

8. Nel Noddings, *Caring: A Feminine Approach to Ethics and Moral Education* (Berkeley: University of California Press, 1984), 83.

9. A careful discussion that not only outlines the major considerations in utilitarian theory but builds on its assumptions is that found in Russell Hardin, *Morality within the Limits of Reason* (Chicago: University of Chicago Press, 1988). Because of its concern with utilitarianism as a feature of popular American culture, the work of Robert Bellah and his collaborators, especially in *Habits of the Heart: Individualism and Commitment in American Life* (Berkeley: University of California Press, 1985), is the most useful reference for the present discussion.

NOTES TO CHAPTER 3

10. Thomas Hobbes, *Leviathan* (1651; reprint, New York: Macmillan, 1962), part 1, sec. 14, 106.

11. Alison France, "Teen-Age Volunteers," *New York Times*, April 9, 1989.

12. Robert G. Hoyt, "An Anthropology for Christmas," *Commonweal*, December 16, 1988, 683.

13. Some of the logic of this kind of account has been captured in Abraham H. Maslow, *Toward a Psychology of Being* (Princeton: Van Nostrand, 1962), in his discussion of being-love as opposed to deficiency-love (39–41), although I do not wish to judge the quality of respondents' accounts in the manner that his discussion implies.

14. Independent Sector, Inc., *Giving and Volunteering*, 29–30.

15. Georgia Harkness, "Jane Addams in Retrospect," *Christian Century*, January 13, 1960, 39.

16. These conclusions are based partly on examining the correlations between all the statements about reasons discussed in this chapter and the statements about values discussed in the previous chapter.

17. This is where my analysis departs from C. Wright Mills's discussion cited earlier. To analyze the vocabulary of motives is not enough; how that vocabulary is organized in speech is the critical issue.

18. Quoted in Italo Calvino, *Six Memos for the Next Millennium* (Cambridge, Mass.: Harvard University Press, 1988), 104.

19. Not counting a couple of statements that I am saving for consideration in later chapters, there were seven statements in all. The figures who selected the following numbers as major reasons were: none (13 percent), only one (14 percent), at least two (73 percent), three or more (57 percent), four or more (42 percent), five or more (25 percent), six or more (18 percent). The figures who selected various numbers as either major or minor reasons were: none (1 percent), only one (2 percent), at least two (97 percent), three or more (93 percent), four or more (85 percent), five or more (71 percent), six or more (53 percent).

20. This conclusion is the result of a multiple regression analysis that, for reasons explained later in the chapter, also included level of education as an independent variable. The measure of reasons given was simply an additive scale that gave respondents one point for each statement they said was a major reason for a person to be kind and caring. The partial betas between this scale and involvement in caring were as follows: charitable and social-service activities (.126), value helping people (.282), value giving time (.233), donating time (.092),

and giving money to a beggar (.071). All relations were significant at or beyond the .05 level of probability.

21. Ram Dass and Paul Gorman, *How Can I Help?* (New York: Knopf, 1987), 10.

22. Paul Ricoeur, "The Critique of Religion," in *The Philosophy of Paul Ricoeur: An Anthology of His Work* (Boston: Beacon, 1978), 214–15.

23. In the survey data it was also interesting that persons with higher levels of education were *less* likely than those with lower levels of education to indicate that the various statements were "major reasons" for caring, and thus were more likely to score somewhat lower on the scale that totaled the number of reasons so selected. Since the better-educated were *more* likely to be involved in most caring activities, and since they often gave multiple reasons for behavior because they interacted in more diverse or cosmopolitan settings, this finding made me think that cynicism about motives (which could be more prevalent among the better-educated) might be the explanation.

24. Noddings, *Caring*, 19.

25. Ibid., 20.

26. On the general problem of activity and passivity in motive language, see Kenneth Burke, *A Grammar of Motives* (Berkeley: University of California Press, 1969), 40–41.

27. The relation between being currently involved in any charitable or social-service activities, for example, and saying that "I want to give of myself" is a major reason for trying to be a caring person, was .202 (Goodman's gamma), whereas the relations between this measure of caring and the various utilitarian reasons (feeling good, expecting others to be kind to me, and getting what I want by being kind) were all statistically insignificant; so was the relation with the statement about just being the sort of person who tries to help; only the statement about religious beliefs was associated with charitable activity at the same level (gamma = .225).

CHAPTER FOUR
FINDING FULFILLMENT

1. Cheryl Simon, "A Care Package," *Psychology Today*, April 1988, 45.

2. Ibid.

3. Gallup Organization, *Survey of Self-Esteem* (Princeton: Gallup Organization, 1982).

4. "Habits of the Hearth: An Interview by Rodney Clapp," *Christianity Today*, February 3, 1989, 20–24.

5. Daniel Bell, "Beyond Modernism, Beyond Self," in *Art, Politics, and Will*, ed. Quentin Anderson, Stephen Donadio, and Steven Marcus (New York: Basic Books, 1977), 213–53.

6. Alvin Gouldner, "The Norm of Reciprocity: A Preliminary Statement," *American Sociological Review* 25 (1960): 161–78; reprinted in *Friends, Followers, and Factions: A Reader in Political Clientelism*, ed. Steffen W. Schmidt, Laura Guasti, Carl H. Lande, and James C. Scott (Berkeley: University of California Press, 1977), 28–42.

7. Respondents were asked to say whether they received a great deal of fulfillment, a fair amount, some, or only a little fulfillment. The figures for those who said they received a great deal from each source were: "your family" (80 percent), "doing things for people" (51 percent), "being good to yourself" (46 percent), "religion or spirituality" (45 percent), "your work or career" (43 percent), and "your leisure activities" (42 percent).

8. These results are from a discriminant analysis that compared the ability of the six sources of fulfillment to predict between respondents who said they were very happy and respondents who said they were fairly happy or not very happy, controlling for respondents' perception of their happiness as children. A sense of the relative strength of the various items can be seen from the correlations between each item and the canonical discriminant function; e.g., happiness as a child (.737), fulfillment from family (.560), fulfillment from leisure activities (.497), fulfillment from doing things for people (.331).

9. Discriminant analyses similar to the one described in the previous note were performed for those respondents (approximately a third of the sample) who were currently involved in charitable or social-service activities and for a smaller group (approximately a quarter of the sample) who were not only involved in charitable activities but also said helping others was very important to them and had been engaged in at least one other kind of helping activity during the past year. In the former, fulfillment from doing things for people ranked last, and in the latter, second to last.

10. These data, from the *Study of Self-Esteem* to which I have already referred, were generously made available to me by the Gallup Organization.

11. These results are from a discriminant analysis that used the twelve paired attributes to predict high, medium, or low levels of self-esteem. Each paired attribute was presented to the respondent along a seven-point scale and the respondent was asked to choose a point that best described himself or herself. In order of importance as predictors of overall self-esteem, they were: confident/fearful, success-

ful/unsuccessful, optimistic/pessimistic, outstanding/ordinary, persistent/give up easily, leader/follower, dependable/undependable, talented/untalented, patient/impatient, generous/selfish, friendly/unfriendly, attractive/unattractive.

12. Discriminant analysis results, in order of importance: your moral standards, your attempts to fulfill your potential as a person, your family, your close friends, your efforts to help others, your status or prestige, your relation to God, your relationships with men and women, your hobbies or leisure activity, your work, your financial well-being.

13. Discriminant analysis results, in order of importance as predictors of self-esteem: your attempts to fulfill your potential as a person, moral standards, status, family, relation to God, relationships with men and women, close friends, work, finances, hobbies, efforts to help others. Work, I should note, comes out lower in all these analyses than it does in other studies because persons with full-time jobs were not separated from persons without jobs.

14. Albert Schweitzer, *Reverence for Life* (New York: Harper and Row, 1969), 124.

15. Mother Teresa of Calcutta, *My Life for the Poor* (San Francisco: Harper and Row, 1985), 104.

16. Seth Mydans, "Sunday on Skid Row: $1 Handshakes," *New York Times*, August 8, 1989, A10.

17. John Stuart Mill, *On Liberty* (1859; reprint, Indianapolis: Bobbs-Merrill, 1956), 76.

CHAPTER FIVE
CONVICTION AND COMMUNITY

1. Among people who say faith is very important to them, the figure for helping people is 78 percent, and for those who say faith is fairly important, 58 percent. A similarly strong relationship exists between the value people place on religious faith and the importance they attach to "giving [their] time to help others": the proportions who say giving time is very important to them are 83 percent among those who say faith is absolutely essential, 68 percent among those who say faith is very important, 42 percent among those who say faith is fairly important, and 39 percent among those who say faith is not very important to them.

2. My analysis of white respondents in a 1988 survey partially sponsored by Independent Sector. Twenty-nine percent of church members involved in small religious groups had done informal vol-

unteer work, compared with 17 percent of members who were not involved; overall, 20 percent of members had done informal volunteer work, compared with 16 percent of nonmembers. Sixteen percent of members involved in small groups had donated time to social-service and welfare organizations, compared with 6 percent of members who were not involved; among all members, 9 percent had, compared with 7 percent of nonmembers.

3. Results from a multiple regression analysis of the 1989 national survey data (betas): church attendance (.204), educational level (.150), age (.071), male (.032), South (.001). The effects for sex and region are not significant at the .05 level of probability. The likelihood of individuals donating time to help the poor, disadvantaged, or needy also increases with frequency of church attendance. This relationship holds when age, sex, region, level of education, and involvement in religious volunteer work are taken into account. Although the effect of church attendance is weakened when these other effects are taken into account, church attendance still bears a stronger relationship to helping the needy than age, sex, or region. Only level of education has a stronger effect. The foregoing are from the 1982 self-esteem survey, based on results of a multiple regression analysis with "donated time to helping poor, disadvantaged, or needy people" as the dependent variable. Standardized regression coefficients for each of the independent variables were: education level (.083), church attendance (.050), South (–.022), male (– .027), age (– .029), and donated time to religious work (.275). The relationships for region, sex, and age are not significant at the .05 level of probability. The relationship for church attendance is marginally significant at the .07 level of probability.

4. The percentages of people who had done each activity within the past twelve months among weekly churchgoers and those who attended less than once a month, respectively, were: beggar (23 percent, 24 percent), car trouble (27 percent, 31 percent), lent money (28 percent, 32 percent), emotional crisis (39 percent, 38 percent), alcohol (29 percent, 27 percent), elderly (10 percent, 10 percent). It is interesting to note that among persons who attend church every week, those who feel they could count on church members to help them if they were in need are significantly more likely to be involved in various kinds of caring activity than those who do not feel they could count on church members for help. For example, 46 percent of the regular churchgoers who said they could depend on church members if they or someone in their family became ill were currently involved in charitable or social-service activities, compared to 30 percent of the regu-

lar churchgoers who did not feel they could depend on church members in such circumstances. The former were also more likely than the latter to say they currently donated time to a volunteer organization, contributed money to charities, and within the past year had helped a friend or relative through a personal crisis. But, again, the relationships between this measure of religious involvement and charitable activities were limited to certain varieties of caring. Persons who felt they could depend on church members were no more likely than persons who did not feel this way to help someone having car trouble, lend money, care for someone who was very sick, give money to a beggar, or visit someone in the hospital.

5. All persons in my survey who were currently employed were asked, "In connection with your work, would you be likely or unlikely to do each of the following?" The proportions of weekly church attendees and less-frequent attendees, respectively, who answered "likely" to each item were as follows: "Visit a fellow worker, employee, or client who was in the hospital" (97 percent, 95 percent); "Bail a fellow worker out of a jam" (77 percent, 80 percent); "Give a birthday present to a fellow worker, employee, or client" (76 percent, 76 percent); and "Discuss a personal problem with a fellow worker" (75 percent, 76 percent). Separate analyses of the responses among men and women showed no differences between churchgoers and less-frequent attendees in either category. Overall, women were considerably more likely than men (90 percent versus 68 percent) to say they would give birthday presents to fellow workers; otherwise, there were no statistically significant differences in the responses of men and women. The only exception to this pattern is that churchgoing women, asked a hypothetical question about meeting a woman on a business trip who asks to discuss a personal problem, are more likely than less-frequent attendees to say they would try to help this person, even if she were a competitor. Faced with the same situation, but asked about a male colleague, men who attend church regularly are no more likely to say they would help than their counterparts who attend church less often. Under a variety of other hypothetical conditions, such as having struggled with the same problem, the person offering to pay for advice, being from the same neighborhood, or believing that the person might be useful to their career, there were no differences between churchgoers and less-frequent church attendees among men or women.

6. Surveys were conducted among more than eight thousand respondents in ten European countries in May 1976. These data, known as the Euro-Barometer 5 Study, are available through the

Inter-University Consortium for Political and Social Research at the University of Michigan. The conclusions reported here are from my analysis of a copy of these data held by the Computer Center at Princeton University. As an indicator of charitable attitudes toward the poor, respondents were asked, "If people like yourself were asked to do something towards reducing poverty, would you be agreeable or not? For example, you could be asked to contribute some money to help." The relationships between responses to this item and frequency of church attendance were statistically significant at or beyond the .05 level of probability, and positive in France (gamma = .198), Belgium (gamma = .332), West Germany (gamma = .135), Italy (gamma = .185), Ireland (gamma = .103), Denmark (gamma = .168), Great Britain (gamma = .103), and Northern Ireland (gamma = .281). In West Germany, Ireland, and Northern Ireland, though, respondents who claimed no affiliation with a church were just as likely to say they were agreeable to giving money to the poor as were respondents who attended church every week. The relationships were not statistically significant in the Netherlands and Luxembourg. Thus, in only five of the societies (France, Belgium, Italy, Denmark, and Great Britain) were there significant and consistent relationships between church attendance and this measure of a charitable orientation. A second question was, "If you were asked to give up some of your time to help those in poverty, would you be agreeable or not agreeable?" On this item, statistically significant relationships appeared in France (gamma = .175), Belgium (gamma = .205), Italy (gamma = .114), Ireland (gamma = .233), Great Britain (gamma = .271), and Northern Ireland (gamma = .190). In Ireland and Northern Ireland those who were religiously unaffiliated were more agreeable than those who attended church every week, and in Italy there were no differences between those who never attended and those who attended weekly. The relationships were not statistically significant in the Netherlands, West Germany, Luxembourg, and Denmark. Using this measure, then, only three countries (France, Belgium, and Great Britain) showed significant and consistently positive relationships. The relationships between respondents' subjective assessment of the strength of their religious attachments and their willingness to give money to the poor were: France (gamma = .173), Belgium (gamma = .246), Italy (gamma = .229), Great Britain (gamma = .130), Northern Ireland (gamma = .384, but the highest group of all were nonaffiliates); Netherlands, West Germany, Luxembourg, Denmark, Ireland, all nonsignificant. The relationships between subjective religiosity and willingness to give time to help the poor were:

France (.164), Belgium (.155, but there were no differences between those who said their religious attachments were of great importance and those who said they were of little importance), Great Britain (.222), and Northern Ireland (.343, but nonaffiliates were highest of all); the Netherlands, West Germany, Italy, Luxembourg, Denmark, and Ireland, not significant. Thus, only France and Great Britain showed consistently positive relationships between the measures of caring and subjective religiosity.

7. The data from which these results and those summarized in the following two paragraphs were derived are described in the following note.

8. Respondents in the self-esteem survey were asked to choose a number between one and seven to express their description of God for each pair of attributes. The gammas for the relationships between valuing helping others and picturing God as caring, loving, watching, and existing were each approximately .280; for all-powerful, .211; for forgiving, .108; and for male, .125. Gammas between donating time to help the needy and these descriptions of God were .273 for caring, .241 for loving, .189 for watching, .260 for existing, .200 for all-powerful, .050 for forgiving, and .040 for male.

9. Among the 1,400 respondents in the study, approximately a fourth had felt afraid of God, two-thirds had felt guilt as a sinner, five-sixths had felt close to God, and about half had felt they were wonderful people. The relationships between the first two and valuing helping others were not statistically significant; the gammas for the latter two were .263 and .233, respectively. The relationships between these items and donating time to help the needy were similar, but not so consistent: with afraid of God, not significant; with guilty as a sinner, significant but weak (gamma = .133); with close to God, significant and moderately strong (gamma = .293); and with feeling you are a wonderful person, not significant.

10. Seventy-three percent of Protestants, compared with 61 percent of Catholics, in my survey said they could depend on church members if they or someone in their family became seriously ill. Although there were only forty-two Mormons in the study, their figures came out highest of all—90 percent said they could depend on fellow church members. The figures for Jews were the lowest (34 percent).

11. There is, however, some evidence that Protestants may be more likely to act on these values than Catholics. By a margin of 35 percent to 26 percent, Protestants are more likely than Catholics to be involved currently in charitable or other social-service activities.

12. These conclusions are drawn from separate discriminant analyses of the values and reasons that discriminate between persons in-

volved in charitable or service activities and persons not involved in these activities among Protestants and among Catholics. Of the nine value statements, faith ranked second as a predictor among Protestants, but fifth among Catholics. Having a comfortable life was a negative predictor in both groups, but ranked eighth among Protestants and second among Catholics. Of the nine reasons analyzed, faith was the strongest predictor among Protestants, but ranked fourth among Catholics; conversely, making the society better was first among Catholics and fourth among Protestants. Helping others being a way to get what one wants in life was ninth among Protestants, but fifth among Catholics. For studies of volunteering and charitable contributions among Protestants, Catholics, Jews, black Christians, and Mormons, see the essays in *Faith and Philanthropy*, ed. Robert Wuthnow and Virginia A. Hodgkinson (San Francisco: Jossey-Bass, 1990).

13. These characteristics and those described in the preceding paragraph are discussed at greater length in my book *The Struggle for America's Soul* (Grand Rapids, Mich.: Eerdmans, 1989).

14. I conclude this from examining several discriminant analyses with liberalism-conservatism as the dependent variable and various combinations of charitable activities as independent variables, with church attendance both included and not included as an independent variable.

15. In comparable discriminant analyses of charitable involvement versus noninvolvement among religious conservatives and among religious liberals, the coefficient for valuing faith was .697 among conservatives and .419 among liberals (respectively, faith ranked first and fourth among nine values as a predictor). The coefficients for religious belief as a reason to be caring were .745 and .077 respectively (ranks one and seven respectively).

16. I draw these conclusions from comparing the absolute discriminant structure coefficients and the relative ranking of these coefficients among religious conservatives and liberals. The desire to give of oneself (.649) ranked second among conservatives in an analysis that included nine reasons, eighth (.068) among liberals. Repaying debts ranked fourth (.254) and ninth (-.008) respectively. Making a lot of money ranked fifth out of nine value statements among conservatives and was negative (-.417); it ranked sixth (-.194) among liberals. Making the world a better place, in contrast, ranked third among liberals (.716) and fourth among conservatives (.433). Taking care of yourself ranked fifth (.243) and ninth (-.007) respectively. In the analysis of reasons, being a stronger person ranked first (.660) among liberals and third among conservatives (.334). Being the kind of person

who cares ranked second (.594) and fifth (.199) respectively. Making society better came in third (.509) and seventh (.128) respectively. And feeling good was fourth (.256) and sixth (.150) respectively.

17. The circumstances of the interview placed Debbie Carson in a position where this kind of double language was particularly appropriate. The interviewer was a member of her church, although the two did not know each other well. But the interview was also being taped for an audience presumed to be outsiders.

18. These figures are from my analysis of the white respondents in a national survey conducted in 1988 by the Gallup Organization. I wish to thank George Gallup, Jr., for making these data available to me.

19. My analysis of these data (whites only) from two 1988 surveys I was able to combine showed a statistically significant relationship of −.256 (gamma) for the first indicator of privatism and −.126 (gamma) for the second. The second relationship was weakened by the fact that virtually everyone agreed with this indicator of privatism (47 percent agreed strongly and 32 percent agreed moderately). Among those who agreed strongly, only 16 percent agreed strongly with the statement about caring for the needy, compared with 32 percent among those who disagreed strongly with the privatism question. When I controlled for church membership, both relationships held among members but were not statistically significant among non-members. This suggests, not surprisingly, that religious privatism is a trend that is likely to have the strongest effects on caring among those who still share religious commitments; among those who no longer value religion at all, privatism is largely a moot question. I also examined the relationships between several indicators of voluntary service and items about moral and religious relativism in the 1988 national survey conducted as part of the General Social Survey. None of these relationships was statistically significant. The questions about service were sufficiently oblique, however, that many other expected relationships did not appear either.

20. Among weekly church attendees, 48 percent of those who experience God's love all the time are involved in charitable activities, compared with 39 percent among those who feel God loves them many times, and only 22 percent among those who feel God loves them only a few times or none of the time (gamma = .243). Among persons who attend church several times a month, the relationship is slightly negative (gamma = −.055), and among persons who attend less than once a month, it becomes statistically insignificant.

21. Churchgoers also differed from less-frequent attendees in the

roles played by several other motives. Wanting to make the society better, for example, was a stronger predictor of charitable behavior among churchgoers than it was among less-frequent attendees. Conversely, doing good because it feels good was a better predictor of charitable behavior among less-frequent attendees than it was among frequent attendees. Motives that focused on the individual, such as becoming stronger through caring or just being a caring person, also played a larger role among the less-frequent attendees than among the regular attendees. Utilitarian reasons played the weakest role among both groups. I emphasize that these results do not pertain to the simple frequency of saying that the various items were major reasons to be caring. They were derived by performing separate discriminant analyses among persons who attended church about once a week or more on the average and among persons who attended less frequently. Each discriminant analysis examined the relative strength of the nine "reason" items to distinguish between persons who were currently involved in charitable and service activities and those who were not. The results ordered the nine items among churchgoers and among less-frequent attendees, respectively, as follows: "My religious beliefs teach me to be kind and caring" (1, 7); "The society is better off when we care for each other" (2, 5); "Helping others makes me a stronger person" (3, 1); "I want to give of myself for the benefit of others" (4, 6); "Helping others is a way of paying my debts for the good things I have received" (5, 3); "I'm just the sort of person who tries to be caring" (6, 2); "It makes me feel good about myself when I care for others" (7, 4); "If I am kind, others will be kind to me" (8, 9); "Being kind and considerate helps me get what I want in life" (9, 8).

22. This value came in third as a predictor among regular churchgoers; fifth among less-frequent attendees. Among church attendees, conversely, being successful at work was a weaker predictor of charitable activity than it was among nonattendees (ranking seventh instead of fourth). Otherwise, the two populations were much the same. Making the world a better place was a positive predictor in each group. Taking other things into account, wanting a comfortable life and a lot of money were negative predictors (but weakly so). And taking care of yourself and being able to do what you want did not discriminate between those involved in charitable activities and those not involved in either case. These results are from discriminant analyses conducted separately for 655 persons in the national survey who attended church every week and 1149 persons who did not. The structure matrix (pooled within-groups correlations) for the two groups, respectively, were: giving time (.823, .728), helping people

(.737, .586), faith (.602, .302), better world (.465, .607), money (−.260, −.188), comfortable life (−.200, −.158), success (.140, .470), what you want (−.077, .131), caring for self (.035, .066).

23. These results are from my analysis of the self-esteem study data that were collected from a national sample in 1982.

CHAPTER SIX
ALONG THE ROAD

1. Luke 10:30–36 (Authorized Version).

2. Will Herberg, *Protestant—Catholic—Jew* (Garden City, N.Y.: Doubleday, 1962).

3. When the joint effects of age and education on knowing the story were examined, education was positively associated with knowing the story among people between thirty and fifty and among people over fifty, but among people in their twenties and thirties, those who had graduated from college were less likely than those who had only some college training to know the story. In other words, education does not seem to increase the likelihood of knowing the story among the young now in the same way that it apparently did for people who are older. Within each level of education, the young were less likely to know the story than the old and the relationship was more strongly negative among those with college degrees than among those with some college or only high-school diplomas.

4. The respective percentages for the two groups of people who had done each thing within the past twelve months were: donated time (36, 18); cared for the sick (29, 20), money to beggar (27, 19), donated money (65, 47), emotional crisis (42, 33). Smaller, but statistically significant, differences were also evident on going door-to-door to raise money, helping someone with alcohol or drug problems, visiting someone in the hospital, and caring for an elderly relative in one's home. On the whole, the effects of knowing the Good Samaritan story, therefore, were as strong as and more consistent than the effects of attending church regularly.

5. The gamma for the first relationship is .333; for the second it is .195, but it is not statistically significant at the .05 level of probability.

6. "Parable of the Good Samaritan," from the *Gospel Book of the Emperor Otto III*, late tenth century (Bayerisches Staatsbibliothek, Munich).

7. Matthew Henry, *Commentary on the Whole Bible: Genesis to Revelation*, ed. Leslie F. Church (1710; reprint, Grand Rapids, Mich.: Zondervan, 1961), 1448.

8. Sue Richard, "To Whom Am I a Neighbor?" *Brethren Life and Thought* 32 (Summer 1987): 180–84.

9. Patrick Tishel, "The Parable of the Good Samaritan," *Epiphany Journal* 6 (Winter 1985): 6–9.

10. Ibid.

11. Ibid.

12. Ibid.

13. For a more complete discussion of the allegorical reading of the Good Samaritan story, see Stephen L. Waites, *Medieval Allegories of Jesus' Parables* (Berkeley: University of California Press, 1987), 209–14.

14. These examples are from a selection of sermons secured from a random sample of clergy listed in *Who's Who in Religion*; those who responded were promised anonymity in return for their cooperation.

15. Kenneth E. Bailey, *Through Peasant Eyes* (Grand Rapids, Mich.: Eerdmans, 1980), 56.

16. This episode is retold in Gordon's book *Miracle on the River Kwai*, a brief portion of which is quoted in J. Steward Miller, "The Neighbor," *Expository Times* 96 (August 1985): 337–38.

17. Raymond F. Paloutzian, "Note on the Attribution and Reinforcement Analysis of Altruism," *Journal of Psychology and Theology* 7 (Summer 1979): 114–17.

18. In addition to the relationship between current church attendance and knowing the story, which I reported earlier, there is also a strong relationship between knowing the story and how frequently one attended religious services as a child. Fifty-six percent of those who attended weekly as a child can still tell the story, compared with 30 percent of those who attended several times a year, and only 26 percent of those who never attended.

19. The relative strength of these two relationships can be seen in the gamma among weekly church attendees (.611), compared with the gamma among infrequent attendees (.313).

20. The possibility of diminishing influence is reinforced by the fact that fewer young people know the story. There are two main reasons they do not know it. One is that they attend religious services less-frequently than do older people. The other is that even those who attend services regularly are not hearing it and learning it. In the survey, the negative relationship between youth and knowing the story was greatly reduced when church attendance was controlled— evidence for my first point. But, as evidence for my second point, the positive relationship between church attendance and knowing the story that was present among people over thirty was only partially reproduced among people under thirty. Specifically, the proportions of people under thirty who knew the story increased from 28 percent

among those who attended less than once a month to 64 percent among those who attended several times a month, but then decreased to 52 percent among those who attended every week.

21. W. H. Auden, "Art and Psychology," in *The Arts Today*, ed. Geoffrey Grigson (London: John Lane, 1935), 18.

CHAPTER SEVEN
BOUNDED LOVE

1. Melody Beattie, *Beyond Codependency* (San Francisco: Harper and Row, 1989), 1–2.

2. Ibid., 2.

3. Ibid., 3–4.

4. Some of this research is summarized in G. F. Solomon, L. Temoshok, A. O'Leary, and J. Zich, "An Intensive Psychoimmunologic Study of Long-Surviving Persons with AIDS," *Annals of the New York Academy of Sciences* 496 (1987): 647–55; and Henry Dreher, "A Conversation with George Solomon," *Advances: Journal of the Institute for the Advancement of Health* 5 (1988): 1–5. For a brief overview, see Bernie S. Siegel, *Peace, Love, and Healing: Bodymind Communication and the Path to Self-Healing: An Exploration* (San Francisco: Harper and Row, 1989), 162–63.

5. Results are from my analysis of the self-esteem survey data described in previous chapters. The relationships reported are all significant at or beyond the .05 level of probability. The relationships for levels of satisfaction also hold when care givers are compared with nongivers, thus ruling out the possibility that satisfaction means doing nothing.

6. These results are also from my analysis of the self-esteem study.

7. Mother Teresa of Calcutta, *Life in the Spirit: Reflections, Meditations, Prayers* (San Francisco: Harper and Row, 1983), 62.

CHAPTER EIGHT
THE TARNISHED IMAGE

1. *The Grapes of Wrath*, produced by Darryl F. Zanuck (Hollywood: Twentieth Century–Fox, 1940).

2. Maria Tatar, *The Hard Facts of the Grimms' Fairy Tales* (Princeton: Princeton University Press, 1987), 89.

3. L. Frank Baum, *American Fairy Tales* (New York: Dover Publications, 1978), 145–64.

4. Ibid., 145.

5. Ibid., 148.

6. *The Confessions of Saint Augustine,* trans. by Rex Warner (A.D. 401; reprint, New York: New American Library, 1963), 119–20.

7. Leo Buscaglia in a lecture for the Public Broadcasting Service, broadcast in Philadelphia on August 14, 1988.

8. Independent Sector, Inc., *Giving and Volunteering,* 61–62.

9. Ibid., 60.

10. These results and those immediately following in the text are from my survey of the American public conducted in 1989.

11. John Steinbeck, *The Grapes of Wrath* (1939; reprint, New York: Penguin, 1976), 542.

12. Ibid., 581.

Chapter Nine
Envisioning a Better Society

1. Margaret Sanger, *An Autobiography* (1938; reprint, New York: Dover, 1971), 60.

2. Ibid., 89.

3. Ibid., 91–92.

4. One of the persons interviewed put the contrast between justice and compassion this way: "Justice can be a very cold process, just deciding for example who owned the cow, or whatever; compassion would focus more on who really needed it."

5. From my survey of a nationally representative sample conducted in 1989. Volunteers—persons currently involved in charitable or social-service activities—were slightly more likely than the public at large to register concern about these issues: 87 percent thought bureaucracies were a serious problem and 71 percent thought government regulations were a serious problem. Not surprisingly, people who expressed concern on one of these items also expressed concern on the other; for example, among those who thought government regulations were an extremely serious problem, 65 percent thought big bureaucracies were an extremely serious problem, but among those who thought government regulations were not a problem, only 17 percent thought bureaucracies were an extremely serious problem.

6. These figures are for white respondents only and are from my analysis of data collected in 1988 and made available by Independent Sector.

7. Among people with grade-school or high-school educations, for instance, 40 percent thought too much emphasis on money was an extremely serious problem, compared to only 27 percent of those with college degrees.

8. My analysis of data collected from a nationally representative

sample in 1988 for Independent Sector shows that 72 percent of the public believe (1) that people should volunteer some of their time to help people, *and* (2) that government has a basic responsibility to take care of people who cannot take care of themselves. In other words, most people believe in a combination of voluntary and government initiatives. In comparison, only 13 percent of the public agree with the statement about government but disagree with the statement about voluntary assistance (i.e., let government shoulder the responsibility alone), and only 10 percent agree with the statement about volunteers but disagree with the statement about government (i.e., think volunteers should do it alone).

9. To cite some specific figures: among people who thought too much emphasis on money is an extremely serious problem in our society, 68 percent said it was absolutely essential to them to give time to help the needy, but this figure dropped to 35 percent among those who thought money was not a problem. Similarly, 67 percent valued helping the needy this much among those who saw government regulation as an extremely serious problem, but only 57 percent did among those who saw it as a small problem (too few thought it was not a problem to calculate reliable percentages).

CHAPTER TEN
THE CASE FOR COMPASSION

1. For those preferring more esoteric examples, the "kula ring" among Melanesian tribesmen is a standard example in the social-science literature; see Bronislaw Malinowski, *Argonauts of the Western Pacific* (London: Routledge, 1922), especially 81–104.

2. Ted Garvey expressed the same idea in these words: "Volunteers are filling the gaps that society is leaving."

3. The proportions of people at each level of education who had ever donated time to a volunteer organization were: grade school, 35 percent; high school, 42 percent; some college, 62 percent; college degree, 72 percent. The percentages for each of the four groups, respectively, of people who were currently involved in any charitable or social-service activities were: 23, 27, 34, and 41.

4. For the two questions, the percentages among those with grade-school educations or only some high school were 68 and 50 respectively, compared to 56 and 31 among those with college degrees.

5. The phrase "enriches and ennobles" is from "Text of Dukakis Speech Accepting the Democratic Presidential Nomination," *New York Times*, July 22, 1988, A10.

6. Norman Vincent Peale, "A Gift from the Heart," *Guideposts*, December 1967, 2–4.

Index